Black Baseball Entrepreneurs, 1860–1901

Sports and Entertainment
Steven A. Riess, *Series Editor*

Other titles in Sports and Entertainment

Black Baseball Entrepreneurs, 1860–1901

Operating by Any Means Necessary

Michael E. Lomax

Syracuse University Press

Permission to reprint textual material from the following sources is gratefully acknowledged:
Michael Lomax, "Black Baseball's First Rivalry: The Cuban Giants Versus the Gorhams of New
York and the Birth of the Colored Championship," *Sports History Review* 28, no. 2 (1997):
134–45, reprinted by permission; and "Black Entrepreneurship in the National Pastime,"
Journal of Sport History 25 (spring 1998): 43–64, reprinted by permission.

All illustrations from the New York Public Library are courtesy of the Manuscript Archives,
and Rare Books Division, Schomburg Center for Research in Black Culture, NYPL,
Astor, Lenox and Tilden Foundations.

The paper used in this publication meets the minimum requirements
of American National Standard for Information Sciences—Permanence
of Paper for Printed Library Materials, ANSI Z39.48–1984.∞™

Library of Congress Cataloging-in-Publication Data

Lomax, Michael E.
Black baseball entrepreneurs, 1860–1901 : operating by any means
necessary / Michael E. Lomax.— 1st ed.
p. cm.—(Sports and entertainment)
Includes bibliographical references and index.
ISBN 0–8156–2970–2 (cl. : alk. paper)—ISBN 0–8156–0786–5 (pbk. :
alk. paper)
1. African American baseball team owners—History—19th century. 2.
Baseball—United States—History—19th century. 3. African American
business enterprises—History—19th century. 4.
Entrepreneurship—United States—History—19th century. I. Title. II. Series.
GV863.A1L65 2003
796.357'64'08996073—dc21
2002154375

Manufactured in the United States of America

❖ ❖ ❖

In memory of Donald F. and Ollie Scott,
my adopted parents,
who were lights of encouragement.

Michael E. Lomax is an assistant professor in the Department of Physical Education and Sport Studies at the University of Georgia. He specializes in the teaching of the history and sociocultural aspects of sports and physical education. He has written numerous articles for such journals as *Society, Journal of Social History, Quest, Afro-Americans in New York Life and History, Journal of African American Men, Journal of Sport History,* and *Sport History Review.*

Contents

Illustrations

Acknowledgments

This study would have never been written without the help and encouragement of many people. But first, I want to give honor to my Lord and Savior, Jesus Christ. Without Christ operating in my life, none of what follows would have been possible.

Steven Riess, Billy Hawkins, and Darren Rhym have been involved, providing their expertise in devising the framework and through a line-by-line edit of the initial manuscript. Melvin Adelman, Marshall Stevenson, Nancy Wardwell, and Paulette Pierce have all reviewed the manuscript at one stage or another and forced me to think through ideas and conclusions in need of refinement. My student and All-American Jonas Jennings shared his experiences as an African American football player playing at a Division I school, and it was very instrumental in shaping my perspective in this study. A special thanks goes to Virginia Feher and the interlibrary loan staff at the University of Georgia, who replied and located numerous sources for this study. Without the encouragement and support of the aforementioned, this book would have never seen the light of day.

Introduction

*R*evising interpretations of the past is essential to the study of history. However, no part of the American experience has, in the past thirty-five years, seen such a broadly accepted point of view as the African American experience in the national pastime: the trials and triumphs of black ballplayers as they confronted racist America, baseball serving as a unifying element to communities in transition, and how the game served to bridge class distinctions. Although these efforts have dramatically expanded our knowledge, the overwhelming emphasis on the experience of players, and the game on the field, limits our comprehension of the structure of black baseball and the multiple meanings the game has had for African Americans. Part and parcel of these deficiencies is the virtual absence of any analysis that intersects the role of local businessmen and communal patterns with black baseball's development. This study examines the forces that led to black baseball becoming a commercialized amusement from 1860 to 1901. Essentially, two themes will serve to guide the narrative: the origins of black baseball's institutional development and the ways in which black baseball entrepreneurs transformed the game into a commercial enterprise replete with internal and external forces that shaped this development.

Tracing the efforts of black baseball entrepreneurs during this period illustrates blacks' overall struggle to compete within the framework of the U.S. economy. Black baseball's institutional development evolved as part of the African American community building in the pre-Civil War era. The game served as a response to the health problems and high mortality rate brought on by the urban pathology affecting U.S. cities. Simultaneously, African Americans utilized baseball to achieve the ultimate goal of integration into mainstream America. The Philadelphia Pythians' attempt to become a member of the National Association of Base Ball Players (NABBP) exemplified the African American effort to assimilate into U.S. society.

Although the Pythians' efforts ended in failure, black baseball's institutional development took root. The black game was transformed into a commercialized amusement by a generation of African Americans who attempted to work within the parameters of a biracial institutional structure. These entrepreneurs operated their segregated enterprises (black baseball clubs) within the fabric of the mainstream economy (professional baseball). Benefiting from white professional and semiprofessional baseball's struggle to place the game on a sound economic footing, several black baseball clubs established a symbiotic business relationship with white teams. At the same time, black baseball entrepreneurs established their own rivalries and constructed an unconventional playing style that made their game uniquely African American. Moreover, black baseball entrepreneurs represented the overall African American effort to create business enterprises to advance their own economic interests.

My intention is to analyze black baseball from a perspective that is closer to business and economic history. I will focus on the black baseball magnates' decision-making processes, the ways in which they marketed and promoted their clubs to their target audiences, and how they endeavored to merge their teams into the developing professional and semiprofessional baseball infrastructure. Naturally, this study must pay close attention to social and cultural developments, particularly how race intersected with black baseball's institutional development and how it shaped the business relationship with white baseball clubs and park managers, and among themselves. This point will be important not only to clarify black baseball's submission to some wider *mentalité*, but also to examine the ways in which these African American magnates may have insulated themselves from the outside forces and thereby either filtered, misread, or distorted the arguments of their constituents. Therefore, it is my contention to examine the choices that confronted black baseball entrepreneurs to show why these early clubs took on their organizational and structural development.[1]

The primary academic histories of baseball give minimal attention to the black experience in the national pastime. Yet the works of Harold Seymour and David Voigt establish the model for the examination of black baseball in the nineteenth century: assessing the plight of black players solely in their relationship to white society. Blacks become passive victims as opposed to active participants in shaping their own experience. Seymour's and Voigt's interpretations of that experience can be summarized as follows. The exclusion of the Philadelphia Pythians from the NABBP established the precedence for drawing the color line in organized baseball. Blacks who played in the minor leagues in the 1880s and 1890s endured racism of the virulent kind. Moreover, blacks did not play a pivotal role in shaping the evolution of organized baseball. Black baseball players then disappear from both narratives, reappearing again in Seymour's and Voigt's third volumes. Seymour chronicles the plight of black teams and players in the late nineteenth century, and Voigt analyzes the reintegration of organized baseball.[2]

Yet Seymour's and Voigt's limited attention reveals a fundamental dilemma in researching black baseball. It is difficult to examine the black experience in baseball because it received sporadic coverage in the black and white press in the late nineteenth century. Instead of systematic research in archives and traditional sources, historians have relied upon more informal ways of obtaining information—primarily, the use of oral history. Although these interviews are valuable in preserving firsthand accounts, they are compromised by the players' magnanimous re-creations, resulting in distortion of the grim realities of racial segregation. In addition, the lack of documentation and the lack of an understanding of African American history generally and baseball history particularly are also symptomatic of much of the writing on black baseball.[3]

By the 1970s, a generation of academics had studied innumerable aspects of African American history; however, they virtually ignored their sporting experience. Therefore, amateur historians have primarily examined the history of black baseball prior to Jackie Robinson crossing the color line. They have basically approached the subject in an uncritical, even celebratory fashion.

The popular study of black baseball in the 1970s began with the works of Robert Peterson and John Holway. In what can best be described as the Peterson model, these efforts provide a broad overview of black baseball in the segregation era, and introduce a host of black stars of the late nineteenth and early twentieth centuries to a new generation. The fundamental underpinning of the Peterson model is that in the era of segregation, the caliber of play in the Negro Leagues was equal, if not superior, to the major leagues.[4]

Sol White's *History of Colored Baseball* was a major influence upon the Peterson model. White was black baseball's first amateur historian of the late nineteenth and early twentieth centuries. He achieved distinction as a player, manager, and promoter of the black game. His book exemplifies the baseball guidebooks of the late nineteenth and early twentieth centuries. Guidebooks were usually published by outsiders, like a restaurant owner or a local merchant, or sporting goods magnates such as Albert Spalding and Albert Reach who were willing to bear the expense of printing to get their advertisements to the public. They also served to widen the scope of the game by enabling fans to keep abreast of the changing rules and teams and to follow, by statistics and articles, the latest deeds of their heroes of the diamond. White chronicled the plight of black players in the late nineteenth century playing in white organized leagues, the origins of the first black professional teams, such as the Cuban Giants, and the establishment of the color line, and he painted a rosy picture for black baseball's future. Although it is an unavoidably sketchy and uneven document, it serves as an adequate overview for the research of future scholars.[5]

The oral histories capture the essence of life of black baseball. They greatly enhance our knowledge, but there are limitations to how they can be used. Human memories tend to gravitate toward exaggeration and romanticism. The reader often receives variations on the same theme with little focus or historical direction, as oral history piles upon oral history. The issue of accuracy is essential in analyzing oral expression of memory in historical research. Memories are limited, and a complete reconstruction of them is virtually impossible. John Bodnar points out that people search for common memories to present needs and refashion the past to please the people with whom they discuss and interpret it. Therefore, questions regarding construction of memory illuminate how individuals, ethnic and racial groups, and cultures establish their own identities and how they connect with larger-scale historical processes. Moreover, as Jules Tygiel points out, oral histories do not speak for themselves; they require commentary to place them into historical perspective.[6]

Researchers use the oral history genre to preserve the black baseball experience. However, their studies have not been contextualized by an understanding of either African American history in general or baseball history in particular. There has been a tendency toward a more emotive than interpretative design in most historical works. This fact has resulted in providing a sense of black baseball that is more experiential than analytical and presenting an abridged view of black history, along with a bias that sets integrated baseball as a universally desired objective and an unqualified good.[7]

The scholarly studies of black baseball began in the mid-1980s and 1990s with the works of Donn Rogosin, Janet Bruce, Rob Ruck, Neil Lanctot, and James Overmyer. Their interpretations may be briefly summarized as follows. Black baseball served as a unifying element of communities in transition, while at the same time bridging the gaps among class distinctions. Teams such as the Kansas City Monarchs and the Homestead Grays were major social institutions in the black community. Rogosin, one of the first academic scholars to examine black baseball, relies heavily on the remembrances of former Negro Leaguers to assess the culture of the black game. He uses black baseball "to open the window of black life during segregation," and shows how the lives of Negro Leaguers reflected the efforts of black society in general and attacked the "porous" barriers of apartheid "ideologically, economically, and emotionally." Bruce, Lanctot, and Overmyer provide an extensive look at the financial and organizational structure of the Monarchs, the Hilldale Athletic Club of Philadelphia, and the Newark Eagles. They also examine their barnstorming excursions and provide insights into these teams' relationships with their respective communities. Moreover, these scholars argue that black baseball developed and prospered after World War I, faltered in the late 1920s, and eventually collapsed in the wake of the Great Depression.[8]

Ruck's examination of sports in black Pittsburgh provides the most comprehensive examination of the linkages between baseball and black community development. Although he explores several sports, baseball is the primary focus of his study. Ruck relates black baseball's accomplishments and failures in Pittsburgh to the socioeconomic realities that were both external and internal to the black community. What is significant about Ruck's work is that he contextualizes baseball with other sports, instead of examining it in isolation. Moreover, he argues that the integration into organized baseball resulted in the black community losing control of its sporting life and served to limit, as opposed to expand, long-overdue opportunities.

Lanctot's examination of the administrative efforts of Hilldale owner Ed Bolden provides the most detailed examination of black baseball's business and economic development. Lanctot explores the Hilldale club's transformation from a sandlot club to a professional enterprise, and illustrates how baseball's historical development in Philadelphia profoundly impacted the origins of this black team. His most important discovery is the remarkably well-preserved financial records of the Hilldale club, housed at the Bill Cash-Lloyd Thompson Collection in the Philadelphia Afro-American and Cultural Museum. The collection is a compilation of financial documents, correspondence, score books, and photographs. His examination of the symbiotic business relationship between black and white semiprofessional teams provides the most in-depth study of professional baseball outside the organized structure. Lanctot points out that Hilldale's success was inextricably linked to its involvement with white semiprofessional teams. Furthermore, Lanctot highlights Hilldale's remarkable success at a time when the majority of Philadelphia's black businesses ended in failure.

Although professional scholars agree that black baseball served as a unifying element within the black community, the claim is more asserted than demonstrated. To validate this position, it is valuable to move beyond the examination of single cities to a comprehensive study of the histories of many communities—carefully studying a range of variables—at different points in time. Historian Kenneth Kusmer states that generalizations drawn from a single community in black urban history have proved problematic, and that many assumptions are more stated than corroborated. He cites Gilbert Osofsky's influential article "The Enduring Ghetto" that stresses the damaging effects of poverty and segregation, resulting in "an unending and tragic sameness about Negro life in the metropolis over two centuries." Osofsky relied primarily upon information from New York and Philadelphia and evidently felt that the two cities could be used interchangeably. Conversely, black baseball scholars have also relied heavily on the generalizations drawn from the communities they studied. The limitation is that often these communities are not representative, and Ruck concludes that the hegemony black Pittsburghers enjoyed in their neighborhood was atypical.[9]

In part, this "limitation" arises from the lack of a scholarly investigation of the evolution of black baseball prior to 1900, but it also reflects a problem that has marked the recent study of black baseball as a whole. Sport historians generally agree that urbanization was the most significant force in shaping America's modern sporting culture. It also facilitated the rise of modern baseball as a commercialized amusement. The demographic shift of the U.S. population from a rural environment to an urban one and the influx of immigrants from Europe led to the emergence of large metropolitan centers. The urban masses sought diversion through whatever means the new urban life provided. Their substantial numbers gave rise to hundreds of clubs and simultaneously supplied audiences for all types of amusements. It also led to the emergence of sports entrepreneurs who attempted to exploit the demand for entertainment by creating the modern business of leisure.[10]

Simultaneously, the impact of urbanization resulted in a complex set of consequences that affected black sports entrepreneurship. Although African Americans established a tradition of black business participation in colonial America, slavery and racism defeated their attempts to develop enterprises to compete on equal terms with businesses that whites developed. As a result, a sequential establishment of small enterprises, including black baseball clubs, represents black American business activity. Black baseball evolved within the framework of a racially repressive society in which blacks had few rights that whites were bound to respect. More important, the North was a more urbanized society, and it provided black baseball with a tremendous advantage to evolve as a profession, despite the fact that 90 percent of the black population resided in the South. Furthermore, blacks that lived in major cities of the North lived in areas where their numbers did not constitute a majority. In other words, although they had their roots in the late nineteenth century, large black enclaves such as Harlem or Chicago's South Side did not emerge until the opening decades of the twentieth century. There were no exclusive black markets in which a prospective entrepreneur could exploit and promote the black game. Furthermore, black clubs, unlike black churches, were not dependent upon the black community for their institutional and operational existence.[11]

In a sense, this book traces the origins of black baseball's institutional development and analyzes the ways African Americans facilitated entrepreneurship in transforming the black game into a commercialized amusement. The book will also discuss the ways in which these black baseball magnates negotiated their business relationships with white club owners and park managers and among themselves. It is my intention to provide a comprehensive modern account of the development of black baseball into a commercial enterprise from 1860 to 1901. This effort addresses a multitude of issues, but two broad themes will serve to guide the narrative. The first is the origins of black baseball's institutional development. The roots of black baseball's organizational structure coincided with the rise of mutual aid societies in the 1840s. Mutual aid societies were essential, in conjunction with the church, in forming the nucleus for the modern black community. Baseball served as a response to the urban pathology affecting U.S. cities, resulting in poor health conditions and a high mortality rate among African Americans. With its origins in the rise of mutual aid societies, baseball assisted blacks in the North in their attempt to wage another more subtle kind of battle. The rise of ball clubs, lyceums, debating societies, and improvement societies exemplified the African American effort to demonstrate their capacity for self-determination, self-improvement, and freedom. The Philadelphia Pythians' attempt to become a member of the Pennsylvania Association of Amateur Base Ball Players represented their effort to assimilate into mainstream America.[12]

Although the Pythians failed to gain entry into this white baseball organization, baseball continued to thrive among African Americans, and the sport's institutional structure took root in terms of its ownership, management, and player force. Rivalries in the form of Colored Championships developed, and the first barnstorming tour and the first interracial contests took place. Furthermore, African Americans that were willing to work within a biracial institutional structure shaped black baseball's commercial origins. In essence, African Americans who reflected the self-help tradition that distinguishes the history of black business activity in the United States formed black baseball clubs into commercial enterprises.

Finally, the ways in which black baseball entrepreneurs transformed the game into a commercial enterprise and the forces, both internal and external, that influenced this development form the second theme of this study. Because of their willingness to work within the parameters of a biracial institutional structure, black baseball magnates recognized that in order for them to conduct business they would have to negotiate with the white power structure, which meant dealing with the new industry that became organized baseball and a host of semiprofessional teams and leagues. Black baseball owners attempted to operate their segregated enterprises (black baseball clubs) within the fabric of a national economy (organized baseball and semiprofessional baseball). Black baseball magnates utilized a business concept known as cooperative enterprises that had its roots in the late eighteenth century. From the outset, early black entrepreneurs recognized that any success in developing black business to some sense of stability could occur only through economic cooperation. Thus, the consolidation of resources became a means to establish business enterprises.

The Cuban Giants emerged as the most successful black baseball club of the late nineteenth century—a direct result of economic cooperation. In the mid-1880s, the Giants evolved from the consolidation of three black clubs into a top-notch independent club. The Cubans established a partnership with a wealthy white businessman and played their home games in Trenton, New Jersey, during the regular season. They developed what could best be described as a local to regional playing schedule. In other words, they played home games in Trenton during the week and barnstormed Connecticut, New Jersey, New York, and Pennsylvania for weekend games. The Giants played games against major and minor league clubs, semiprofessionals, and college baseball teams. During the winter months, the Cubans traveled south, establishing a home base in St. Augustine, Florida. Although the players were hired as waiters, their primary responsibility was to entertain the guests with their skills on the diamond. The Cuban Giants became the model other black clubs attempted to emulate. The Giants' partnership with a white businessman marked the start of white influence in the ownership of black teams, a bitter-sweet legacy.

The Gorhams of New York typified the black club that operated in the late nineteenth century. The Gorhams were formed in Manhattan, at a time when New York's black middle class resided there, and the team's organizers utilized the business strategy of economic cooperation. Because the Gorhams did not establish a home base of operations, they barnstormed the nation for gate receipts, an often precarious existence. The Gorhams made several efforts to establish a home base, many of which turned out to be bad business arrangements. They did, however, establish a rivalry with the Cuban Giants in the form of a Colored Championship series, designed to stimulate interest in the black game. Because there were no substantial black enclaves that could sustain a commercialized amusement, the Cuban Giants and Gorhams marketed their clubs to a white clientele.

The Cubans and Gorhams confronted several obstacles that hindered their efforts to operate in the white baseball world. White player hostility toward blacks made it difficult to maintain any continuity in scheduling games. Organized baseball owners struggling to place the game on a sound economic footing also made it problematic to maintain consistent business relations. This fact was especially true of the minor leagues, whose clubs remained unstable. With the exception of Chicago, most semiprofessional teams and leagues in large metropolitan cities never developed any stability.

Simultaneously, black baseball clubs benefited from white professional and semiprofessional baseball's fledgling existence. Black ball clubs created a demand for themselves once their caliber of play equaled, and at times surpassed, white teams. It made it difficult for white clubs to pass up games with blacks because of the economic benefit. Playing one exhibition game with either the Cuban Giants or the Gorhams could have resulted in a struggling white club meeting its weekly payroll and expenses. Black baseball entrepreneurs had to be more enterprising in marketing and promoting their clubs. Winning games by scores of twenty-one to two or sixteen to one detracted from fan interest. Therefore, the Cubans and Gorhams created an alternative playing style when games became too one-sided. Their clowning antics on the diamond served to entertain the fans in the stands, but when the situation called for it, both clubs could also be fierce competitors.

In 1889, the Cuban Giants and Gorhams of New York played in the Middle States League (MSL), a circuit composed primarily of white clubs from

Pennsylvania. The Cubans' affiliation with this league was in response to the death of their wealthy financial backer, Walter Cook. Joining this league proved ill-advised, because it altered the way the Cubans and Gorhams conducted business. The Cubans' plight was exacerbated by the league officials' unwise move to expand the league structure and schedule, and by several clubs disbanding less than two months into the season. This situation resulted in constant franchise shifting and led to the Gorhams joining the MSL. Because the Gorhams played the majority of their games in Hoboken, New Jersey, and New York, they agreed to move to Pennsylvania to alleviate travel and overhead expenses. The relocation proved unworkable, and the Gorhams pulled out of the MSL in late August. Responding to the low fan turnout and the ineptitude of MSL officials, the Cubans and Gorhams were consolidated into one superclub, with the intent of barnstorming the nation for gate receipts. But the culmination of the Cubans' leadership transition, the MSL's economic instability, and the rise of internal dissension within the Giants' ranks resulted in both clubs dramatically altering the ways they did business in the upcoming years.

Concurrently, organized baseball's maturation process altered the business relationship between black clubs and major and minor league teams. White players' hostility toward blacks had gained wider acceptance, resulting in club owners scheduling fewer games with black teams. This predicament was more symptomatic in the minor leagues, because its white stars threatened to jump to another circuit. Moreover, the players' revolt of 1889 and the subsequent second war with the American Association (AA) resulted in the latter's collapse. This breakdown led to the National League (NL) absorbing the AA's four best clubs, and along with the collapse of several minor leagues, fewer games were scheduled with black clubs.

Yet black baseball clubs continued their symbiotic business relationship with white semiprofessional clubs. Semiprofessional teams emerged in the 1870s. They were called semiprofessionals or semipros to distinguish them from their professional counterparts. Semipros generally belonged to no league but paid their players and charged admission. Semipros often signed their players to one-year contracts that only rarely contained the reserve clause for the following season. At the beginning of each season, players had to make new arrangements. Semipro teams, particularly in Chicago, attempted to form leagues and associations patterned after the National League. Although these leagues and associations were ineffective, they did lead to the creation of rivalries between black and white clubs. Maintaining this business relationship resulted in black baseball entrepreneurs making certain concessions to operate in the white semipro world. Black baseball magnates accommodated racial prejudices by marginalizing the effects of any potential conflict with racist overtones. They had a vested interest in downplaying any possible racial conflicts to sustain their business ties. This assertion is not to suggest that some conflicts that occurred did not have racial implications, but to these late-nineteenth-century black baseball entrepreneurs, such compromises were necessary to advance their economic interests.

The early 1890s were grim years for the Gorhams and the Cuban Giants. The Gorhams never fully recovered from their experience in the MSL, and the team operated as a shell of its former self throughout the rest of the decade. The Cuban Giants operated primarily in the New York area, rarely barnstorming the nation for gate receipts. By the mid-1890s, several players from the original Cuban Giants formed a cooperative enterprise that became the Cuban X Giants. The relationship between the Cuban X Giants and the Cuban Giants was an antagonistic one. However, both clubs played several Colored Championship series for eastern supremacy. By 1900, the Cuban X Giants barnstormed the Cuban islands, marking the start of the symbiotic business relationship between black and Cuban teams.

Simultaneously, two black clubs, the Chicago Unions and the Page Fence Giants, rose to prominence in the West. The Unions became the most successful club that was exclusively black-owned and -operated in the late nineteenth century. They were also formed as a cooperative enterprise, and the Unions' organizers capitalized upon the Windy City's growing population and somewhat stable semiprofessional association. They toured Illinois, Indiana, Michigan, and Wisconsin during the week and played Sunday games in Chicago. The Unions established rivalries with the top white semipros in Chicago and, like the Cuban Giants, developed their own unconventional playing style for games that became too one-sided.

The Page Fence Giants represented an ambitious yet innovative undertaking. The Giants were formed around the familiar concepts of showmanship and top-level baseball, but they also became a source of market promotion for their sponsors. A wire company in Adrian, Michigan, and a bicycle firm in Massachusetts sponsored the Page club at a time when the United States experienced a bicycle craze. The Giants gave bicycle exhibitions before every game and advertised the wire company's product during the contest. The Page club also established the precedence of black clubs traveling on a private railroad car to alleviate any potential racial conflicts, and advertised their sponsors' products. The rise of the Chicago Unions and the Page Fence Giants marked the start of an East-West connection in the form of Colored Championships with the Cuban Giants and the Cuban X Giants. From 1896 to 1900, the eastern black clubs traveled to Chicago to engage in championship series that sometimes included white semipros.

There were several black baseball clubs that emerged after 1860. This study will focus primarily on the Philadelphia Pythians, Cuban Giants, Cuban X Giants, Gorhams of New York, Chicago Unions, and Page Fence Giants—later the Columbia Giants—because these clubs had the most profound impact upon black baseball's development into a business enterprise. In addition, these clubs have more available evidence, essentially newspapers, than any other black clubs of the era. The analysis pursued in this study relies heavily on newspapers and sporting periodicals, because these black baseball magnates left no private papers, diaries, or memoirs to describe the day-to-day operations of black ball clubs. Because their objective was to compete within the mainstream economy, black baseball entrepreneurs published advertisements and articles in the white press. They also made their scheduling arrangements and printed box and line scores in white dailies. Throughout their histories, these clubs did not possess their own playing fields, and it was necessary to examine several newspapers at once to reconstruct events. Moreover, examining several newspapers and sporting periodicals, combined with the oral histories, and contextualized within the framework of African American and baseball history will serve to trace the evolutionary process of black baseball emerging as a business enterprise.

Two issues need to be addressed to help contextualize my analysis of black baseball's general development. The first is the economics of black baseball in this period. This task can be somewhat discouraging, one that historians commonly confront in their examination of sports businesses, owing to the limited evidence. Financial records are nonexistent, but there is a sufficient amount of data to create what can best be described as "inferential economics." Drawing primarily from newspapers, reported attendance figures and ticket prices are used to show a black baseball club's ability to generate revenue. This concept provides only an estimate of a black baseball team's profit potential. Inferential economics also shows a more comprehensive picture of a black club's ability to function in the midst of the racial, economic, and structural barriers they faced. The data certainly confirm that these black baseball teams were excellent gate attractions. The evidence shows how problematic it was for a struggling white club to allow their racial prejudice to override the economic necessity of playing exhibition games with these black clubs. Concurrently, the data reveal how difficult it was for black teams to function outside a large metropolitan center. Finally, the available economic information illustrates how black baseball magnates responded to these economic factors and reveals a clearer picture of the causes and consequences of entrepreneurial decisions.[13]

The second issue deals with the impact that intragroup color dynamics had upon black baseball's institutional development. From the beginning, I argue that mulattoes were in a better position to organize baseball clubs. Although more research is needed in this area, of the wealth owned by African Americans, mulattoes controlled a sum vastly disproportionate to their members in the African American community. However, I am not suggesting that mulattoes were the only African Americans who played baseball in the late nineteenth century. The desire to win ball games transcended social stratification and intragroup dynamics. Because of this paradox, I struggled with deciding whether to use the contemporary term *African American* to describe the magnates and players in this narrative. As John Mencke points out, unlike Latin America there has never been a widely used word to specify people of mixed ancestry.[14] The word *mulatto* technically refers to the offspring of one white parent and one black parent. I use the term in a more general sense to include all people of mixed black and white ancestry, but particularly the ones who show marked physical signs of white blood, especially skin color. I use the word *black* to include all people of African ancestry, particularly ones possessing a dark skin tone, and as an inclusive term, I used the term *Afro-American* to designate all those persons of African ancestry, whether mixed or not. I trust the variations on these three usages will be evident by the nature of the text.

There has not been a clear chronological definition in examining black baseball. The general pattern has been to summarize the black experience in the late nineteenth century, highlight the rise of the Negro Leagues, lead up to Jackie Robinson crossing the color line in 1947, and briefly sketch the decline of the Negro Leagues in the 1950s and 1960s. I chose 1860 to begin this study to highlight the emergence of black baseball's institutional development from the rise of mutual aid societies. Furthermore, I also sought to illustrate how the transformation of black baseball from mutual aid societies to a commercialized amusement was dramatically impacted by the forces, both internal and external, that shaped the black experience after emancipation. I chose 1901 to close this account because the arrival of a Cuban All-Star team to America in 1899, the Cuban X Giants' barnstorming of the Cuban islands the following year, the collapse of several of Chicago's elite white semipros, and the breakup of the

Chicago Unions marked a definitive turning point in the evolution of black baseball clubs. White semiprofessional clubs in New York and Chicago formed into leagues and associations and sought to establish a governance structure to sustain them. Black baseball entered a brief period of cutthroat competition, as Afro-American entrepreneurs attempted to capitalize upon the baseball craze. Like their white counterparts, black baseball entrepreneurs made several efforts to form leagues and associations. Likewise, the rise of black migration from the South to the North, leading to the emergence of large black enclaves such as Harlem and Chicago's South Side, and the spatial patterns that migration created in these metropolitan centers resulted in a significant transformation of black baseball in the early twentieth century. I provide an epilogue in the final chapter to analyze the business practices that emerged in the day-to-day operations of black clubs, and examine why whites became involved in the ownership of black teams. I also discuss the reasons white clubs played black teams in the first place, and why whites patronized games between two black clubs.

More than a century ago, black baseball entrepreneurs saw an opportunity to seize upon the baseball craze that swept the United States. Stanislaus Kostka (S. K.) Govern, Ambrose Davis, William Peters, and to a lesser degree Bud Fowler, Frank Leland, Benjamin Butler, Julius Avendorph, and Clarence Williams operated by any means necessary to advance their economic interests in the national pastime. These black baseball entrepreneurs were not merely passive participants responding to forces that impacted them. They sought to form black baseball as a business enterprise in their own image.

Black Baseball Entrepreneurs, 1860–1901

1

Entrepreneurship and the Rise of Black Baseball

On January 18, 1860, the *Weekly Anglo-African*, a New York-based Afro-American newspaper, reported a "grand festival" given by Robert and Joseph Henson of the Henson Base Ball Club of Jamaica, Long Island. The festivity commemorated the Henson Club's victory over the "Unknowns" of Weeksville, Long Island. The Hensons also received a beautiful prize ball. At first, the Hensons were denied the use of a banquet hall because "the prejudice is so strong here at present against colored people." But after securing the hall, Jamaica's Afro-Americans availed themselves of some music, dancing, and eating.[1]

During the post-Civil War years, several newspapers reported contests among all-black teams. Clubs emerged from as far east as Newark, New Jersey, to as far west as Rockford, Illinois. The presence of these Afro-American clubs reflected a remarkable feat among blacks in their pursuit for both freedom and self-determination. These clubs emerged at a time when urban society underwent a dramatic transformation. The forces that shaped modern America—industrialization, urbanization, and immigration—operated in Afro-American communities within a framework of institutional racism and structural inequality. Although these forces manifested themselves in diverse ways in most cities, Afro-Americans could not compete on equal terms with either native-born Americans or the thousands of newly arrived immigrants.

Despite numerous obstacles, the mere presence of Afro-American baseball clubs illustrated their enjoyment in participating in ball games, particularly as it was the new "national pastime." During slavery, special occasions and seasonal celebrations enabled blacks to engage in ball games as part of their leisure activities. Recreational activities were an integral part of leisure celebrations, and as northern states began passing acts of gradual emancipation, ball games gave way to baseball, which became an essential part of emancipation celebrations. Additionally, the internal forces that impacted black baseball—middle-class formation, entrepreneurial and economic activities, and the rise of mutual aid societies—began to take root in antebellum America. Both middle-class formation and the rise of mutual aid societies were instrumental in the development of black baseball into an organized sport.

With the possible exception of South Africa, the United States, more than any other modern country in the world, developed from the beginning a unique socioeconomic and political structure. It was a structure that was simultaneously racist, stubbornly capitalist, and committed to a limited form of bourgeois democracy. In electoral politics, free blacks from the eighteenth century onward found it difficult to exercise their right to vote. For example, North Carolina permitted some blacks to vote in 1667 but repealed the measure in 1715. When George Washington was elected in 1789, no southern state permitted blacks to vote. In the North, the institution of slavery existed until the opening decades of the nineteenth century. Moved primarily by the rights of man, state legislators in Pennsylvania in 1780 and New York in 1799 passed acts of gradual emancipation. Thus, being born on New York or Pennsylvania soil guaranteed freedom, and slaves from other states sought asylum there.

When slavery ended in the North by 1830, some 150,000 persons of African descent lived there. Chattel slavery was not replaced with freedom, justice, and equality for Afro-Americans, though. The demise of slavery exposed the enduring corruption that permeated northern society: self-righteous white racism, economic greed, and a deep-seated irrational fear of blackness. Although slavery no longer served its purposes, a society so fully committed to those terrible aforementioned afflictions needed an alternative system to keep blacks in their proper place. Therefore, new legal and extralegal barriers to black equality had to be constructed. As a result, the strange career of Jim Crow had already begun in the antebellum North by the time the most recent Afro-Americans from the South had arrived.[2]

Legally, Afro-Americans were second-class citizens, their plight often determined by the whims and prejudices of federal, state, and local officials. They secured no rights that the masses of white people were bound by law to respect. Under the various land-grant bills, Afro-Americans were denied access to public land, thus limiting important economic opportunities. For example, in 1846, German settlers of Mercer County, Ohio, passed a resolution that exemplified this denied access to public space. The legislation stated that "blacks of this county be, and they are hereby respectfully requested to leave the county . . . on or before the first day of March 1847." If blacks refused "to comply with this request, we pledge ourselves to remove them, peacefully if we can, forcibly if we must." The German settlers passed another resolution: "That we who are here assembled, pledge ourselves not to employ or trade with any black or mulatto person, in any manner whatever, or permit them to have any grinding done at our mills after the first day of January next." Beyond threats and economic strangulation, the final pledge made the immigrants' position clear: "We will resist the settlement of blacks and mulattos in this county to the full extent of our means, the bayonet not excepted." As historian Vincent Harding states, "Ohio's German settlers had discovered a typical white freedom in America and fully exercised it."[3]

At the same time, growth, economic transformation, and the structural development of northern cities affected blacks adversely. The result of the new industrial order and the emergence of the factory system occurred within a context of widening occupational opportunities, particularly for whites. In 1847, less than one-half of 1 percent of the black male workforce was employed in factories. It should be noted that this situation occurred when thousands of Irish immigrants were engaged in factory work. The manufacturing sector had traditionally provided the first step up the occupational ladder to new arrivals to the city. Between 1850 and 1880, the number and proportion of skilled positions increased significantly with the economy's expansion. This increase benefited immigrants and especially their American-born children in terms of upward mobility. Further development of the new industrial order led to the professionalization of police and fire departments and the expansion of the public school system.[4]

A more profound effect upon the antebellum populace, in conjunction with industrialization, was the railroads. By 1865, a railroad network extended some thirty-five thousand miles, and increased to fifty-three thousand miles five years later. This mode of transportation increased market size, destroyed local economies, and placed individuals in an intensely competitive economy. The enlarged market created opportunities for many, while at the same time producing drastic change and bitter disappointment for others. For example, in the decade of canal supremacy, high shipping costs enabled small businessmen to establish modest manufacturing firms throughout the state of Pennsylvania to supply local needs. The railroads reduced shipping costs drastically; they enabled enterprises in Philadelphia and Pittsburgh to ship their wares into the hinterland, thereby damaging, if not destroying, smaller businesses.

Improved transportation did aid some counties; from 1840 to 1860, Schuylkill, Cambria, and Luzerne Counties, noted for their iron and coal, rose to prominence. However, many firms in Pennsylvania's interior failed, drastically reducing the number of employees in the manufacturing sector. A fundamental result of the transportation revolution was the concentration of manufacturing activities in fewer locations. Ironworks, coal mines, and textile plants declined in other parts of the state.[5]

Economic transformation in the antebellum period resulted in an internal reshuffling of both resources and business activities. Some individuals managed to successfully compete in the new market system and continued business as usual. Others switched to endeavors that promised better rewards. Afro-Americans were hurt by these changes. From the outset, blacks were not only excluded from the new and well-paying positions in the expanding factory system, but also driven out of traditionally unskilled jobs, denied apprenticeships for their sons, and prevented from practicing skills they already possessed. The 1847 census identified 5 percent of the black male workforce in the relatively well-paying hod carrier and stevedore occupations. A letter, written by one "P. O.," attested to this job displacement: "That there may be, and undoubtedly is, a direct competition between them (the blacks and Irish) as to labor we all know. The wharves and new buildings attest this fact, in the person of our stevedores and hod-carriers as does all places of labor: and when a few years ago we saw none but blacks, we now see nothing but Irish." "P. O's" letter proved perceptive. According to the 1850 census, the percentage of black hod carriers and stevedores in the male workforce declined in three years from 5 percent to 1 percent. Moreover, the 1850 census reported occupations for the entire country and included 30 percent more black male occupations than the 1847 census. The number of black hod carriers fell sharply from ninety-eight to twenty-eight and stevedores from fifty-eight to twenty-seven.[6]

Afro-Americans did not reap the benefits of increased opportunities in skilled positions brought on by economic expansion. Frederick Douglass appealed to antislavery bosses to give young blacks employment as blacksmiths, apprentices, cabinetmakers, and joiners, but the majority of abolitionists focused upon the plight of the slaves rather than their Afro-American neighbors. In regards to the few blacks already in a trade, they "either have too little capital or too little enterprise to bring up and employ apprentices and journeymen."[7]

Despite the various political obstacles, racial oppression, and economic reshuffling, Afro-Americans would make concerted efforts to carve a niche in business. Being pressed into menial jobs, such as domestic service, considered a badge of inferiority, did not hinder Afro-American efforts for both freedom and self-determination. It was within the context of these menial jobs that Afro-Americans would make attempts to facilitate entrepreneurship.

During the pre-Civil War era, a significant group of free blacks had already existed. At the time of the first decennial census in 1790, there were 59,000 free blacks in the United States, and thirty years later the number had climbed to 488,000, of whom 44 percent lived in the South Atlantic states and 46 percent in the North. The remaining 10 percent were located in the south-central states and the West. Blacks trained as skilled artisans, domestic servants for wealthy white families, or entrepreneurs catering to the needs of a white clientele would, in the decades following the Civil War, become the nucleus of the black middle class in northern cities such as Boston; Baltimore; Washington, D.C.; Philadelphia; and New York.[8]

In addition to occupational status, a long history of free ancestry was treasured, especially if one's forebears included distinguished white people. Some free blacks not only belonged to old families, but also restricted themselves to marrying within the group, socializing only with other members, and striving to maintain similar lifestyles. Distinguishing characteristics of status groups lies in the criteria used to determine membership eligibility. In addition to family background, membership in social clubs and churches and skin color are just some of the most common traits that status groups use to establish boundaries. Some members emerge as acknowledged leaders, as either well or less respected, and eventually an informal hierarchy of most members from lowest to highest occurs based on the criteria unique to the group. At this level, it may be athletic ability or hosting lavish parties that determines who holds the position at the top. In the larger society, those individuals with the most desirable characteristics in a community rank highest, and if substantial enough they may form a group.[9]

Throughout the antebellum period, a system of color caste emerged among Afro-Americans. There was, however, little or no distinction among northern whites in recognizing color differences. Some whites may have preferred hiring mulattoes, essentially the offspring of slave women and white masters, to blacks, but generally speaking, Afro-Americans were viewed as a single inferior group. Historian Leon Litwack argues that although a light complexion did not guarantee a black's place in the socioeconomic hierarchy, "it often afforded him greater economic opportunities, which, in turn, assured him of a high rank in Negro society." Because they believed mulattoes to be more intelligent and physically attractive than pure blacks, some whites were more inclined to hire mixed-bloods. As Litwack points out, such preferences invariably led some mulattoes to develop a sense of superiority to blacks. However, mulattoes were still excluded from white society. Suffering the same legal proscriptions imposed on blacks, most mulattoes accepted their positions among the elite in the Afro-American community. In many instances, they also provided much of the Afro-American community's militant leadership.[10]

Free blacks in the North were not employed in the skilled trades to the same extent that they were in the South, but they excelled in business endeavors. Around 1840, free blacks in New York City published a newspaper, the *Colored American;* operated two first-class restaurants in the downtown financial district; and ran six boardinghouses, two dry goods stores, a hairdressing establishment, two coal yards, a confectionery, and a fruit store. River shipping afforded free blacks excellent moneymaking opportunities. Those blacks who became boat stewards made large sums for themselves by placing contracts for supplies and pocketing the discounts. Furthermore, when traveling from place to place along the river route, they had frequent opportunities to trade on their own account.[11]

Free blacks created entrepreneurial opportunities for themselves in personal service enterprises, owing to the fact that whites tended to avoid such ventures. Because of their servile status, free blacks had an advantage here. As a result, personal service occupations were available to black entrepreneurs and constituted a source of considerable income. Such enterprises required a small amount of capital at the beginning. One of the most profitable personal service enterprises among blacks was barbering. In the North and South, barbering enterprises, catering to a wealthy white clientele, emerged as one of the most prosperous businesses for Afro-Americans, placing them among the occupationally elite in antebellum black America. Antebellum black barbers were also leaders in promoting the institutional development of the black community. Through their contacts with leading citizens, they had the opportunity to learn the ways and habits of the white aristocracy and make friends with influential whites. Ruben West, a free black barber of Richmond, Virginia, earned several thousand dollars at the trade. He ran four chairs in his shop and employed a free mulatto and two slave assistants. John Good of Berne, North Carolina, using the revenues of his barbering business, comfortably supported the daughters of his deceased master until they were married. John B. Vashon, one of Pittsburgh's Afro-American elite, was originally from Virginia. Contemporaries pointed out that Vashon could pass for white, but he took pride in his African heritage. In conjunction with his barbershop, Vashon opened the first public city bathhouse west of the Alleghenies in 1820. He was also a member of the National Negro Convention.[12]

Successful black entrepreneurs often extended their services beyond their own communities. In several cities, black restaurateurs, caterers, boot makers, tailors, and barbers acquired a fashionable white clientele. Yet maintaining a good reputation among whites required black businessmen to show proper respect and not to tamper with deep-rooted prejudices. Black restaurateurs and barbers frequently had to bar members of their own race. A New York restaurateur called a friend from the dining room and offered to serve him behind a screen or in the kitchen. He explained that "his customers *now* were not as those in William Street, where he formerly kept." Members at an Ohio Negro convention condemned such practices. Any "colored man who refuses to shave a colored man because he is colored" is "much worse than a white man who refuses to eat, drink, ride, walk, or be educated with a colored man." An Afro-American businessman engaging in such behavior was "a party *de facto* to riveting chains around his own neck of his much injured race."[13] Inasmuch as the same convention called upon blacks to equal whites in terms of wealth and enterprise, this assertion must have presented somewhat of a dilemma to many successful black entrepreneurs.

Afro-Americans established a variety of enterprises in the nation's preindustrial economy that paralleled mainstream American business. Blacks owned transportation enterprises, participated in extractive industries, and were also inventors and manufacturers. Furthermore, free blacks were also informal bankers and investors in internal improvements, municipal and government bonds, and bank stock; real estate speculators; brokers; developers; commissioned brokers; and owners of large slave plantations.[14]

Yet the small number of black businesses exemplified a lack of opportunity. It occurred not because of a lack of efficiency, but largely owing to a half-free status carrying numerous social and economic hardships that white merchants never had to face. In addition, there were only a few blacks in the North, and their small numbers in a particular city were not sufficient to support local businesses. In other words, no exclusive black market existed prior to the Civil War that a prospective black entrepreneur could exploit. Furthermore, businesses in the North were better developed, requiring more efficiency and capital than in smaller southern urban communities, and blacks had fewer opportunities to figure in the business world. By the mid-nineteenth century, moreover, German and Irish immigrants drove blacks out of menial service in many northern cities. The unprecedented industrial development of the North and West tended to leave the small black businessman behind. The black enterprises that did exist illustrated the courage of black businessmen who risked their resources that might be damaged or destroyed in a race riot.

Segregation, exclusion, poverty, and the lack of business opportunities did not completely define the black experience in the early and mid-nineteenth century. Newcomers to New York and Philadelphia, for example, were also likely to see the emerging institutions in the black community. The church was recognized as the key institution. It helped the black community's identity in terms of race and class, was both an expense and a source of professional employment, and served as a forum for discussion and the focus of much social, intellectual, and recreational life. Emerging institutions exemplified a philosophy that became popular in the late nineteenth century, the doctrine of self-help. These institutions were black-operated and were almost always affiliated with the church.

The culmination of mob violence; the need for food, shelter, clothing, and public advocacy; and their precarious financial condition led free blacks to organize for mutual assistance. However, mutual aid established on a sound insurance basis required a kind of training and experience they lacked; inefficient organization was their greatest handicap. In an effort to increase the membership of mutual aid societies, blacks found that they might serve as centers of religious worship and of secular and fraternal interest, as well as be a source of financial aid. As a result, these societies tended to take on a religious character and ritualistic ceremony. Sometimes they were fundamentally religious or social at the outset. Later, the insurance feature was added as a means of gaining additional members.[15]

In 1780, the African Union Society was the first free mutual aid society on record. Newport Gardner, a black musician and businessman, established it in Newport, Rhode Island. Founded essentially for the purpose of providing benefits to widows and children, the African Union Society also made loans to debt-encumbered members, provided apprenticeships for youths, and encouraged thrift. Members were also encouraged to use their savings to purchase property and develop real estate.[16]

The Free African Society of Philadelphia was the most historically significant socioreligious and economic society. Founded by Richard Allen and Absalom Jones in 1787, the formation of this society was in response to Allen and other comrades being excluded from a white church where they had worshiped for years. The Free African Society carried on a number of activities, notably responding to the city's need for willing nurses and workers during the great yellow fever epidemic of 1792.

The formation of both the African Union Society and the Free African Society marked the start of a proliferation of mutual aid societies, as well as other types of associations. In 1813, there were 11 benevolent societies in Philadelphia; twenty-five years later, that number increased to 100, with a membership of 7,448. In 1838, these societies had taken in $18,851 and had expended $14,172. Ten years later, there were 106 of these societies, with a membership of 8,000. According to Dorothy Porter, between 1828 and 1841, 9 literary societies were also founded in the Quaker City. In New Haven, Connecticut, Amos G. Beman, a moderate black minister, organized "circles of improvement," a benevolent society, and temperance societies around his church. According to one student, Beman's objective was to evolve "a social fabric in his congregation and people." Between 1828 and 1841, New York City had 6 literary societies; by 1845, it had 50 benefit societies.[17]

Without question, these organizations met a pressing need. Afro-American populations in the North remained relatively stable and small throughout most of the nineteenth century, primarily because of an exceedingly high death rate. Historian Carter G. Woodson states that in some communities, as many as 25 to 40 percent of Afro-Americans died, leading some to think that the "race would soon become extinct." Between 1800 and 1865, the number of Afro-Americans in Manhattan wavered between 9,000 and 15,000, about 1 percent of the city's population. In each decade preceding the Civil War, the Afro-American population actually declined. In fact, by 1865 there were fewer blacks in Manhattan (9,943) than there had been in 1820 (10,368). Whereas adding an insurance feature may have served to increase membership in mutual aid societies, groups also collected dues to defray the expenses of members in the black community who had lost loved ones. Many of these organizations collected dues for both sick benefits and death payments.[18]

The funds generated from mutual aid societies were also used to stimulate black business development. Historian Juliet E. K. Walker argues that the constitutions of several mutual aid societies stipulated that once a certain amount of money was accumulated by an organization, members could borrow funds in rotation to be used as venture capital to establish businesses. The African Benevolent Society of Wilmington, Delaware, and the Brown Fellowship Society in Charleston, South Carolina, provided in their bylaws that members could borrow money for business activities. Pooling money deposited by members to pay for funeral and burial expenses established the foundation for the institutional development of black insurance companies. Concurrently, business-loan capabilities of mutual aid societies provided the foundation for early Afro-American banking activities.[19]

The rise of mutual aid societies also assisted blacks in the North in their efforts to wage another more subtle kind of battle. Through a plethora of clubs, lyceums, debating societies, and improvement societies, Afro-Americans attempted to prove to the white world (and no doubt to their doubting brothers and sisters) that they were worthy of all the things they fought for. As Harding points out, blacks sought to "bind up the wounds of their own community, to improve the quality of its life, to serve its needy, to demonstrate their capacity for self-determination, self-improvement, and freedom."[20] More important, they built the black community from within, preparing it for the continuing stages of its struggle toward a new humanity.

Even more significant, the rise of mutual aid societies marked the beginning of the development of black baseball as an organized entity. These societies provided the opportunity to develop the essential skill—organization—needed to run both a business and a social operation. The organization of baseball clubs within the black community could possibly have served to combat the health problems brought on by urbanization. As we shall see later, the rise of mutual aid societies coincided with the efforts of white reformers formulating a sports creed, an ideology designed to make certain sports respectable to stimulate white middle-class participation. But first, it is necessary to briefly examine the leisure patterns that facilitated the ball-playing tradition among blacks during slavery.

The ability to pursue leisure activities was contingent upon time off on the weekends, special occasions, and the planting and harvesting cycles. Saturdays and Sundays were normally set aside for rest and relaxation on plantations. A few celebrations were staged when there was a plantation visitor, or when a member of the master's family had a birthday or got married. The most extensive slave holidays were seasonal celebrations observed annually when the most critical plantation chores, planting and harvesting, had been completed.[21]

Although some plantations celebrated Thanksgiving and Easter, Christmas was the biggest slave holiday between the slack period of fall harvesting and spring planting. As early as the eighteenth century, upstate New York slaves observed Pinkster, a slave Easter celebration of parading, dancing, drinking, and eating. Christmas was the longest and most universally observed slave holiday during this or any other period in the slaves' calendar year. Frederick Douglass cited ball playing as one of the most popular leisure activities of a slave's Christmas holiday. He indicated that "by far the larger part [of the slave population] engaged in such sports and merriments as playing ball, wrestling, running footraces, fiddling, dancing, and drinking whiskey." In regards to playing ball, Douglass was probably referring to some variations of "rounders" or "town-ball," two of the most popular ball games on slave plantations.[22]

Spirited athletic contests were an integral part of slave holiday customs. As northern states began the process of emancipating slaves, these contests were borrowed from the slave custom as the foundation of emancipation celebrations. Ball games gave way to baseball as it began to grow in popularity, and it remained the most popular emancipation celebration event.

By the 1860s, a plethora of newspapers reported contests among black baseball clubs. In 1863, the *Brooklyn Eagle* reported a local game between the Unknowns and the Monitors with the headline: "A New Sensation in Baseball Circles—Sambo as a Ballplayer and Dinah as an Emulator." The *Newark Daily Advertiser* stated "considerable excitement was created among the colored 'boys' of this city . . . by a base ball match between the Hamilton Club of this city and Henson Club of Jamaica, L.I. both composed of the descendants of Ham." All-black nines swept through black communities of many U.S. cities and towns during the 1860s. They appeared in Newark, Camden, and New Brunswick, New Jersey; Boston; Chicago and Rockford, Illinois; Ripley, Ohio; Washington, D.C.; Pittsburgh, Philadelphia, and Carlisle, Pennsylvania; Brooklyn, New York City, Utica, Buffalo, Niagara Falls, Albany, Rochester, Johnstown, and Lockport, New York; Baltimore; and New Orleans, among other places.[23]

Numerous factors contributed to the emergence of several all-black teams in the 1860s. By 1860, free blacks were concentrated in six areas that included cities such as Baltimore, New York, Boston, and Philadelphia. Free blacks were inclined to reside in urban areas. There were 25,600 Afro-Americans in Baltimore, 22,000 in Philadelphia, 12,500 in New York, 10,600 in New Orleans, and 3,200 in Charleston. The greater opportunities, both economic and social, no doubt accounted for their tendency to concentrate in cities.[24]

The concentration of free blacks in urban areas coincided with the efforts of Afro-American leaders advancing an ideology of self-improvement and moral reform. Black leaders held middle-class occupations and outlooks. Joseph Gusfield has argued that the U.S. temperance movement as a whole was closely connected with questions of social status. During the 1830s and

1840s, "[a]bstinence was becoming a symbol of middle-class membership. . . . [I]t was one of the ways society could distinguish the industrious from the ne'er-do-well; the steady worker from the unreliable drifter."[25] Temperance was emblematic of the gulf between the respectable middle class and the degraded lower class. Black leaders sought to cast their lot with the middle class. Should the black race be classified as a race of drunkards, even sober blacks would be infected by this racial stereotype. The entire race must make itself respectable.

The quest for racial respectability occurred almost simultaneously with the efforts of white middle-class reformers developing a positive sports creed. The sports creed was one of several responses to the urban pathology that accompanied the growth of cities. Some observers, such as Walt Whitman, were enthusiastic about the pace and excitement of urban life, whereas others were appalled by the materialism, loss of pastoral values, and dangers. They feared that overcrowded, impoverished industrial cities like Manchester would develop, threatening traditional moral values and the national character.[26]

The promotion of sport as a remedy for urban pathology was an integral part of the public health movement of the 1840s. Congestion and sanitation were major problems in U.S. cities, resulting in physical and moral degeneracy and even death. The single biggest concern was epidemics, particularly cholera, of which there were severe outbreaks in 1832–1833 and 1849. Philadelphia's coroner attributed the high mortality rate in black districts to intemperance, exposure, and malnutrition. After conducting an inspection in 1848, the coroner reported that many Afro-Americans had been "found dead in cold and exposed rooms and garrets, board shanties five and six feet high, and as many feet square, erected and rented for lodging purposes, mostly without any comforts, save the bare floor, with the cold penetrating between the boards, and through the holes and crevices on all sides." According to the report of the city inspector of New York City in 1857, a tuberculosis epidemic resulted in a mortality rate that was twice as fatal among blacks as compared to whites. To prevent further catastrophes, physicians recommended that cities improve their water supplies, instruct residents in sound dietary habits, provide greater access to fresh air, and encourage moderate daily exercise to build up resistance.[27]

Baseball served as an antidote to the pressing health problems of free blacks in the nineteenth century. There is no evidence to suggest that national black leaders such as Frederick Douglass, Henry Highland Garnett, or Martin Delany advocated the need for recreation to alleviate health concerns. But the presence of these black clubs in the 1860s illustrates that local black leaders at the grassroots level saw baseball as a possible solution to the health problems within their respective communities. Moreover, the sport was targeted as a vehicle to promote and instill values championed by the white middle class. At a time when black leaders stressed the need for self-improvement and moral respectability, and attempted to establish an elite social status for themselves within the black community, the new national pastime served to advance high moral character and promote good health habits among the Afro-American populace. In other words, baseball would be a catalyst to "elevate the race."

Finally, both the inexpensiveness of the game and the abundance of vacant lots made it easy for the average person to participate. Baseball also benefited from the fact that most adults knew the game because they had played it as children. Their familiarity with and nostalgia for it combined to make them good spectators. As we shall see later, although blacks at times found it problematic to find a field to play on—a direct result of racial hostilities that occurred from time to time—this obstacle did not dampen their enthusiasm.[28]

The origin of black middle-class formation, entrepreneurial and economic activities, and the rise of mutual aid societies combined to facilitate the rise of black baseball clubs in the 1860s. Baseball had been established as a social institution within the black community. Moreover, despite the uneven playing field in which black baseball clubs evolved, their formation illustrated the Afro-American pursuit for both freedom and self-determination.

2

From Social Organization to Commercial Enterprise

The Philadelphia Pythians emerged as one of the most prominent Afro-American baseball clubs in the 1860s. The club was composed of notable mulattoes who were members of Philadelphia's black citizenry and who became the foundation of the city's black middle class in the late nineteenth century. Baseball became an event through which the mulatto elite could socialize with other members of their "distinguished" group and maintain a similar lifestyle by staging weeklong galas that generated enthusiasm in the black community. Although the ball club's organizational structure, social life, and match play mirrored contemporary white baseball clubs, the Pythians symbolized black Philadelphia's pursuit of self-determination and race elevation.

From 1867 to 1871, internal and external forces impacted black amateur baseball and shaped the direction of the black game for the next seventy-five years. The Philadelphia Pythians' exclusion from the Pennsylvania Association of Amateur Base Ball Players (PAABBP), and the formal ban of all black clubs from the National Association of Base Ball Players, embodied America's racial attitudes. This setback marred the Pythians' aspirations of achieving a symbolic victory in race relations and establishing a true championship between black and white clubs. Although the evidence is limited, black clubs appear to have been evolving along the same lines as their white counterparts toward commercialization. They charged admission for games, established their own championship series, and, despite their exclusion from the NABBP, competed occasionally against white clubs.

By the mid-1870s, much of the history of black baseball was lost, owing to a decline in white press coverage. Black baseball clubs' transformation into commercial enterprises marked the start of their separation from black community development. In other words, black baseball clubs were no longer reliant upon the black community for their institutional or operational existence. However, the forces that influenced the development of modern white baseball—the political economy, industrialization, and urbanization—created a complex anomaly for Afro-Americans who sought to capitalize upon the baseball craze. This chapter analyzes the forces that led to black baseball evolving into a commercial enterprise. It is divided into three parts. Part 1 examines the rise of the Philadelphia Pythians and their attempt to join the PAABBP, leading to the drawing of the color line by the NABBP. Part 2 discusses the forces that led to black baseball evolving along the same lines as white baseball clubs toward commercialization. Finally, part 3 examines how these forces shaped the complexities that Afro-American baseball entrepreneurs faced in transforming the game into a commercial enterprise and briefly summarizes the ways in which they responded to them.

Legally, socially, and economically, black Philadelphians lived in a world of varying degrees of discrimination, replete with unpleasant surprises and dead ends. The end of slavery raised high hopes, but for most blacks it did not bring any real material gain. Social discrimination was inescapable for urban blacks everywhere in the nineteenth century because virtually all were in constant contact with the far larger white city. As late as 1900, Philadelphia had the largest black population of any city in the North, with 62,613 Afro-American residents, just ahead of New York's 60,666.

Philadelphia did not support a "ghetto," as its black housing was never completely segregated. The largest concentration was located in the Seventh Ward, bounded east and west by Seventh and Twenty-fifth Streets and north and south by Spruce and South Streets, with somewhat smaller numbers in the Eighth Ward to the north, the Fourth Ward to the south, and the Fifth Ward to the east. The social center of the population was at the corner of Seventh and Lombard Streets. Such social landmarks as Gil Ball's saloon, the James B. Forten School, the political meetinghouse at Liberty Hall, and the College Settlement were all located within a block of this corner. Other landmarks such as the Institute for Colored Youth and the Church of the Crucifixion were not much farther away, but this district was shared with other ethnic groups, both immigrant and native born. No ward in the city had a black majority, and conversely no ward was completely white.[1]

Philadelphia's Afro-American population was scattered throughout the city. A fundamental reason for these dispersed residential patterns, an irregular central cluster with a smaller number of scatters, was essentially economic.

Among Philadelphians, generally the most important determinant of residence was the location of work. For blacks, this factor meant assembling in the often unmapped alleys and streets behind the elegant town houses of Spruce and Locust Streets, and in a number of less concentrated areas. White hostility kept blacks out of some neighborhoods, except as live-in servants, but as Afro-Americans increased in numbers, they tended to move west along a relatively narrow strip bounded by Locust Street on one side and Bainbridge on the other.[2]

Blacks lived in this quasi-segregated society that was full of contradiction and uncertainty. There were no signs to show which hotels, restaurants, and saloons tolerated Afro-American patronage. The only test was experience. Moreover, even though the treatment of blacks varied by class, age, and institution, there was no identifiable elite or working class, Catholic or Quaker, child or adult who could be counted on to behave consistently.

Within this world of contradiction and uncertainty, baseball emerged as the premier leisure activity among black Philadelphians. In 1866, two clubs emerged among the Quaker City's black citizenry: the Excelsiors and the Pythians. Little is known about the Excelsiors' players or organizers. According to Harry Silcox, a rivalry developed between these clubs that prompted some families and friends to be at "loggerheads with one another." By 1867, the Pythians rose to prominence as the Quaker City's top black club.[3]

The Pythians' rise to notability was primarily through the efforts of two men: Octavius Catto and Jacob White. Octavius Valentine Catto was born in Charleston, South Carolina, on February 22, 1839. His father, William T. Catto, was a Presbyterian minister, and his mother, Sarah Isabella Cain, was a descendent of one of the most distinguished mulatto families of Charleston, the De Reefs. When Octavius was five years old, the Presbyterian church called his father to Philadelphia. The elder Catto's intellectual curiosity and emphasis on scholarly pursuits provided a model for Octavius to pursue later in life. Furthermore, his father's belief in individual responsibility and a life anchored by deep religious convictions formed the core values by which the younger Catto would live. Every individual had a responsibility to contribute to the progress of humanity, never to be nullified by the will of the masses. Individual responsibility as advocated by the elder Catto included a life based on Christian morality and virtuous behavior. These family values motivated the younger Catto to strive for an education, struggle to improve the plight of mankind, and adopt a Christian way of life. In addition to the Pythians, Catto was the corresponding secretary of the Pennsylvania State Equal Rights

League, and was the spark behind the efforts to end streetcar segregation in 1867. Despite his stocky size, Catto was an agile baseball player, and while a student at the Institute for Colored Youth, he learned to play cricket in games played against the Lombard School. He also met Jacob White there.[4]

Jacob C. White Jr. was born in 1837, and grew up among the most prominent Afro-Americans in Philadelphia. White possessed a shrewd business mind, and his father, a renowned barber by trade, invested his earnings in land and became a wealthy man. The family's prosperity allowed the younger White the privilege of access to the inner circle of Philadelphia's elite Negroes. White was the club's entrepreneur who worked behind the scenes. He was also secretary and manager of the Lebanon Cemetery, which ranked with or next to Olive Cemetery as the biggest single enterprise run by blacks in Philadelphia. He later became principal of the Robert Vaux Consolidated School and was also asked by W. E. B. DuBois to edit his classic work, *The Philadelphia Negro*. As the secretary of the Pythians organization, White took on the task of scheduling matches, soliciting patronage from black community residents, and organizing the galas at the end of each game.[5]

The Pythians organization consisted of four clubs, and it amounted to a kind of roll call of future black politicians, educators, and lawyers of the next thirty years. Yet the majority of players, as in contemporary white baseball clubs, were artisans, petty proprietors, and clerks. The Pythians were native-born Americans and were slightly older, an average of twenty-eight, than their white counterparts, and nearly 70 percent of them were mulattoes (versus only one-quarter of the total black population). Many were also active in other black social and civic organizations. Approximately two-fifths belonged to the Banneker Institute, a literary and debating society that shared a room with the baseball club. One-third of the Pythians were affiliated with civil rights organizations, such as the Pennsylvania State Equal Rights League and the Social, Civil, and Statistical Association of the Colored People of Pennsylvania.[6]

The Pythians' organizational structure exemplified the mutual aid societies that emerged in the 1840s and 1850s. It was governed by a constitution, bylaws, and elected officers. In addition to White (the secretary) and Catto (the team captain), the Pythians elected Colonel Jacob Purnell, an Underground Railroad and Civil War hero, as club president. Members paid dues and met regularly in a second-floor room at Liberty Hall.

Much like the contemporary white clubs, scheduling games with black clubs was quite formal. To arrange a match, a club first issued a written challenge to the club it wished to play. The challenger had the option to accept or reject the invitation. Matches could consist of a single game, but clubs usually challenged one another to a "home-and-home" series. The captains of both clubs would agree on a mutually acceptable umpire, and notify the press of the upcoming match. The prize in most matches was either a game ball or silk U.S. flags. At the end of the game, a spokesman from the losing club would present the prize to the winners with a short speech, and a representative of the winning club would respond in kind.[7]

Presentation of the prize did not end the affair. Baseball provided black Philadelphians with a social event that, in some cases, lasted an entire week. The players were showered with picnics, dances, and lunches. Women planned social activities that caused great excitement within the community. In September 1867, the Bachelors from Albany were the first black team to visit Philadelphia. Later that same month, the Mutual and Alert baseball clubs of Washington, D.C., visited the city. The Mutual club had on its roster two prominent young Afro-Americans: Charles R. Douglass, son of Frederick Douglass, and Hugh M. Brown, the future principal of the Cheyney Training School. The Pythians compiled a nine-and-one record that year.[8]

The game and the social events that followed were relatively expensive undertakings. To secure revenue, the Pythians charged dues of five dollars for active members and one dollar for inactive ones, the latter serving as the club's fan base. The players themselves sought patronage from members of the black community. In addition to the entertainment, the dues were needed to buy equipment and to ensure that the Pythians remained essentially an elite organization. Despite the expense, the Pythians paid their bills on time. In 1867, the Pythians amassed revenue in the amount of $789.32; after paying their expenses of $786.50, the club retained a balance of $2.82. Moreover, Jacob White's elite status and his ties with black Philadelphia's "distinguished citizenry" were also instrumental in securing the club's high standing, and no doubt contributed to the club's ability to meet its financial obligations.[9]

The Pythians organization also endured the conflicts that arose among black Philadelphia's elite citizenry. William Still, the abolitionist of Underground Railroad fame and a rival of White, canceled his Pythians membership. His paternalistic attitude toward White and his differing views over "race progress" were at the root of the dispute. Their conflict was further intensified over the tactics used to end streetcar segregation in the Quaker City. Instead of celebrating victory, Still chose to go back over tactical differences with the younger and more militant agitators, first by defending himself and lecturing them. In any event, Still felt his patronage would better serve his newly emancipated brethren in the South. He indicated, "Our kin in the south famish for knowledge, have claims so great and pressing that I feel bound to give of my means in this direction to the extent of my abilities in preference to giving for *frivolous amusement.*" White replied that his resignation was moot because the older man had yet to pay his dues; beyond that point, he stated, "neither the acquisition nor the disposition of your means is of interest to us as an organization." [10]

A more pressing obstacle for the Pythians than the White-Still debate was finding a field to play on. South Philadelphia provided several green pastures available as possible sites. The threat of hostile Irish Americans forced the club to cross the Delaware into Camden or the Schuykill into Fairmont Park. One solution to this obstacle was an arrangement made with the all-white Philadelphia Athletics. The Pythians shared the Athletics' facilities, and Harry Hayhurst, the A's captain, umpired the all-black nines' important games. At that time, relations were good and had a chance of getting better. In 1868, Jacob White congratulated the Athletics after a "brilliant victory" that upheld "the pride of Philadelphia on the base-ball field." Athletics president Philadore S. Bell thanked White for these "manifestations of confidence from our brethren in the city, that have met us on all sides." [11]

While White and Bell expressed mutual respect for each other, Octavius Catto had his own more militant agenda. According to Catto, the skill of the Pythians was attracting "considerable interest," and a little anxiety among the white fraternity. A "true championship," especially for supremacy in Philadelphia, would match both blacks and whites together. Considering their mutual relations with the Athletics, not to mention the eternal optimism that blacks felt at the end of the Civil War, the possibility of such a contest seemed plausible.

Catto sought to integrate his Pythians within the framework of the championship system that had emerged between white clubs in the early 1860s. The accepted practice was that the championship club retained its crown until a challenger beat them twice in the same year, in a best-of-two-out-of-three series. Historian Melvin Adelman points out that between 1861 and 1865, sportswriters did not comment on the inequities of this system, possibly because it was still in its infancy, but it appears that the series proved adequate during the Civil War years. Only a few clubs challenged for the title, and the championship series was confined to the New York metropolitan area, the winners from 1863 to 1865 having undefeated seasons. [12]

By the end of the Civil War, the championship system, in conjunction with commercialism, sparked the movement toward professionalizing the white game. Prior to the war, white teams rarely scheduled more than a dozen games a year. By 1867, several clubs in New York City and Brooklyn were playing twenty games a year. Three years later, all three professional clubs—the Atlantics, Eckfords, and Mutuals—were playing more than fifty games annually. There is no evidence that black clubs played twenty or more games a year. Yet there are indications that by 1867 blacks were billing their contests as "championship series." The *Newark Daily Advertiser* reported a match between the Excelsiors of Philadelphia and the Unique Club of Brooklyn for the "championship of the United States." The *New York Clipper* reported a match between the Monrovia Club of Harrisburg and the Shaw Club of Carlisle, Pennsylvania, for the "[s]tate championship of the colored clubs."[13] It appears that black clubs were also headed down the road toward commercialization. More important, a "true championship" between black and white clubs would also serve to "elevate the race," win or lose.

The effort to arrange a championship series with the Athletics illustrates the attempts of the mulatto elite to gain acceptance into mainstream America. Given the mania surrounding baseball at this time, the game became a way in which the status group could try to pattern their lives after middle-class whites. A great deal of emphasis was placed on white values and the imitation of affluent whites, an attitude that inclined the black elite to separate themselves from the rank and file of black society. As Roger Lane points out, Philadelphia's black elite was a tightly closed group, a society hard to penetrate by outsiders. The Pythians sought to create an acceptable moral image that emulated white middle-class values. Club members were prohibited from drinking liquor, playing cards, and gambling. They would also not tolerate "unbecoming language or conduct" that would bring disrepute on the club or the Banneker Institute. The *Philadelphia Sunday Mercury* reported that the Pythians were a well-behaved, "gentlemanly set of young fellows . . . [who] are rapidly winning distinction in the use of the bat."[14]

Gaining acceptance into mainstream America, however, does not adequately explain the Pythians' significance to Philadelphia's black community. In the post–Civil War era, the fortunes of Catto's Pythians reflected what was happening to the race as a whole. The ball club's formation coincided with the Equal Rights League beginning to assert its local leadership. It was within the ranks of the mulatto elite that the most aggressive agitators for civil rights emerged. In addition, baseball provided the Pythians with a vehicle to establish a network with blacks from other sections of the country. Games with black clubs from Chicago, Brooklyn, Albany, and Washington, D.C., permitted social intercourse and discussion of the major political and social issues of the day. Communications between various black communities of the North had been enhanced, and Catto's leadership among blacks was becoming more evident. Even in his leisure time, Catto became a central figure in efforts to remove discriminatory barriers facing blacks. As we shall see later, his aggressive nature and quest for equality had exceeded the role that whites expected of blacks. In this case, he offended the lower-class baseball fans. But in the case of Afro-Americans, Catto's efforts illustrated the subtle warfare used as a means of gaining assimilation into mainstream American society.[15]

The Philadelphia Pythians exemplified the quest for self-determination among Afro-Americans in the post-Civil War era. Baseball became a vehicle to assimilate within the fabric of mainstream America and simultaneously elevate the status of Afro-Americans. Regardless of whether a black team won or lost, a championship between blacks and whites would serve to eliminate racial barriers and establish a sense of equality in the minds of blacks. Gaining acceptance in the white baseball club's national body—the National Association of Base Ball Players—would illustrate a symbolic victory in the struggle for racial equality. The Pythians' optimism, however, would be thwarted when the white baseball world erected another barrier.

Exclusion from the National Body

In 1858, New York's four oldest clubs—the Knickerbockers, Gothams, Eagles, and Empires—formed the National Association of Base Ball Players. The formation of the NABBP was pivotal in the history of the sport, "marking the close of one baseball era and the beginning of another, in which players and their representatives would meet annually in convention to revise rules, settle disputes, and control their own game." Although it was often weak and ineffective, the NABBP was baseball's first centralized organization, governing the sport for the next thirteen years. By the eve of the Civil War, membership in the association had increased to more than sixty clubs, the majority from New York and the surrounding vicinity.[16]

To join the association, clubs needed a minimum of eighteen members; they were also required to submit an application thirty days before the annual convention, so that a club's character and standing could be investigated in time to be voted on. A two-thirds vote was required for admission. Each member club was allowed two delegates and two votes. At first, dues were five dollars, but over the years they were reduced to fifty cents.[17]

As baseball enthusiasts, journalists, and clubs spread the gospel of the national pastime across the United States after the Civil War, national, state, and local sports organizations attempted to guide the game's growth. The NABBP acted in many ways to recognize and encourage regional and national expansion. It voted to rotate the annual meeting site among several cities, including Philadelphia (1867), Washington, D.C. (1868), Boston (1869), and New York (1870), making its conventions accessible to more players and clubs. In a conscious effort to broaden representation, the association elected officials from a variety of cities. In 1866, the *New York Clipper* encouraged the selection of Senator Arthur P. Gorman of the Washington Nationals as the new NABBP president. In view of the ongoing Reconstruction debate, the paper added, "the [baseball] fraternity should prove to the world that sectionalism is unknown in our national game." Because the South would enter the convention for the first time, "the election of the president of the 'Champion Club of the South' would go far to prove the absence of any narrow sectional ideas in the National Association." The convention chose Gorman and warmly greeted southern delegates from Virginia, Kentucky, and Tennessee. The following year in Philadelphia, the convention selected a president from Cincinnati and the remaining officers from Madison, Wisconsin; Jersey City; Rockford, Illinois; Brooklyn; and Lowell, Massachusetts.[18]

In another move toward regional and national expansion, the NABBP shifted its system of representation from individual clubs to state associations. One delegate was assigned for every ten clubs in a state body. The *New York Clipper* stated that the welfare of baseball was contingent upon bringing in state and regional organizations as branches of the parent organization. In this way, the new system would "bring under the influence and control of the playing rules of the National Association . . . hundreds of clubs in distant towns and cities who would otherwise be 'out in the cold.' "[19] In 1868, the NABBP formally adopted this format of state representation, although it did permit a few individual clubs to send delegates if their states lacked a formal association.

At the regional and state levels, clubs joined together to standardize rules, regulate competition, sanction championships, debate issues, and instruct delegates to the national meetings. Proponents of the formation of state associations argued that they served many needs of ballplayers and clubs, particularly in arranging matches and settling disputes. These associations, such as the

Pennsylvania Association of Amateur Base Ball Players, formed in 1866, struggled to establish themselves as thriving bodies. In addition, most of these aggregations enrolled only a small fraction of the baseball clubs in their jurisdictions. Apathy plagued their organizational efforts. Moreover, their annual meetings were marred by interclub disputes and dissatisfaction over professionalism, commercialism, and corruption.[20]

It was within this context that the Philadelphia Pythians attempted to become a member of the PAABBP. Raymond Burr served as the Pythians' delegate at the state convention held in Harrisburg on October 16, 1867. While the Committee on Credentials prepared its report, other delegates formed in small groups to discuss what action should be taken regarding the admission of the Pythians' delegate. The convention secretary, D. D. Domer, informed Burr that a brief survey of the delegates revealed that the majority opposed seating him. Domer advised the Pythians' delegate "to withdraw [rather] than to have it on record that [the Pythians] were blackballed." Burr declined, preferring to wait for the credentials committee's report.[21]

The committee reported favorably on all credentials except for the ones presented by the Pythians, which they intentionally neglected. A resolution to accept their report was "hastily passed," and another delegate moved that the committee be discharged. Burr was about to object when a Mr. Rogers of the Chester Club indicated that the committee had not reported on the Pythians, a "colored" organization from Philadelphia. Harry Hayhurst of the Athletics and a delegate representing the Batchelor Club of Philadelphia intervened and asked that the matter be deferred until the evening session. They argued it was unfair that approximately twenty-two men present should have the responsibility of rejecting a delegate when perhaps "a greater portion of those present in the evening would be in favor of his acceptance." The convention agreed and turned to other business.[22]

After the adjournment of this first session, members of the convention gathered around Burr. Although they "all expressed sympathy for our club," only about five were willing to vote for its admission. The others told him that they would "in justice to the opinion of the clubs they represented be compelled, against their personal feelings, to vote against [the Pythians'] admission." Furthermore, most of the delegates, including Domer and Hayhurst, tried for a second time to persuade Burr to withdraw his application. Again he refused, but this time he telegraphed home for instructions. Catto told Burr "to fight if there was a chance."[23]

When the evening session convened, roughly the same number of delegates were present as in the morning. Burr, facing the prospect of being black-balled, withdrew the Pythians' application. He said that all the delegates "seemed disposed to show their sympathy and respect for our club by showing every possible courtesy and kindness and Secretary Domer even gave him a pass home over the Philadelphia Central Railroad."[24]

In December 1867, the issue of black membership reached the full national association. The NABBP upheld the Pennsylvania state association's exclusion of black membership and adopted a formal ban on the inclusion of black players and clubs. An organization spokesman claimed: "It is not presumed by your committee that any club who have applied are composed of persons of color, or any portion of them; and the recommendations of your committee in this report are based upon this view, and they unanimously report against the admission of any club which may be composed of one or more colored persons." The spokesman added that the purpose of excluding black clubs was to "keep out of the convention the discussion of any subject having a political bearing, as this undoubtedly had."[25]

Melvin Adelman asserts that the press's reaction toward the exclusion of black clubs followed traditional political lines. The Democratic *Brooklyn Eagle* opposed the inclusion of black players and clubs, arguing along the same lines as the NABBP. The Republican *New York Times* argued that sober-minded delegates should have thoroughly condemned this prohibition as inconsistent with the events of the past decade. The nonpartisan *Wilkes Spirit of the Times* pointed out that only in the United States did color bar players from participating in sports. The paper added that it was not "a lessening of dignity nor in the least disparaging" for white men to compete with blacks. The *New York Daily Tribune* took a different approach, sarcastically labeling the NABBP's actions as "cowardly."[26]

Historians have analyzed the NABBP's formal ban in different ways. Harold Seymour states that the committee's reaction was an "ingenious bit of casuistry and evasion." Adelman argues that if the national pastime was the symbol of the American way, it was just as clearly the embodiment of America's racial attitudes. Warren Goldstein finds it interesting that even in so politically insignificant a gathering as a convention of baseball players, one presumed price of "national" (or organizational) unity was the exclusion of black players from membership. Robert Burk compares the decision to the post-Civil War political landscape. He points out that the representatives of machine-based, more ethnically diverse clubs in both the Northeast and the Midwest used their political clout to adopt a policy of racial exclusion to suit their own social prejudices.[27]

These historians' interpretations of the NABBP's policy of racial exclusion are valid. The exclusion of black players and clubs was an embodiment of northern racial attitudes. As the treatment of free blacks prior to the Civil War clearly demonstrated, Americans in the free states were not at all eager to see large numbers of free blacks in their midst. Even most "radical" northerners had no intention of allowing blacks to become citizens on an equal plane with white Americans. But it does not explain adequately why excluding black players and clubs was justified on "political" grounds.[28]

Several factors contributed to this obvious evasive tactic used by the NABBP bureaucracy. The first was the homogenous makeup of black amateur clubs in the post-Civil War era. Economically, mulattoes were in a better position to organize baseball clubs. Although more research is needed in this area, Theodore Hershberg and Henry Williams provide some compelling evidence in their study of blacks and mulattoes in Philadelphia. For example, of the wealth owned by Afro-Americans, mulattoes controlled a sum vastly disproportionate to their members in the Afro-American population. Eighteen percent of the population in 1850 owned 43 percent of the real property; in 1860, 31 percent of the population owned 53 percent of the real property; by 1870, they owned 57 percent of the real property and 58 percent of the total wealth.[29]

A second factor was the Pythians' status as an elite organization. Their exclusivity suggests that the clubs the Pythians played were also members of the mulatto elite. However, this statement is not to suggest that mulattoes were the only Afro-Americans who played baseball during this period. They were not. The desire to win baseball games transcended social stratification and intragroup dynamics. What is important here is the influence of the ideology of the men who formed these early black clubs.

For the mulatto elite, baseball served as a means to elevate the race from its political, economic, and social plight. The sport was, and continues to be, promoted among Afro-Americans as a tool to eliminate racial barriers. A somewhat idyllic picture of blacks and whites engaging in a friendly game of baseball would, theoretically, work for the good of the race and the nation. Yet at the same time, mulattoes agitated for full participation in the "body politic" of U.S. society. The national pastime served as a means to that end. In essence, men who sought to achieve their ultimate goal of integration into mainstream American society formed these early black baseball clubs.

The Pythians' attempt to join the PAABBP coincided with Afro-American efforts to fight for their civil rights. In several states, Afro-Americans took the initiative in fighting oppressive legislation. Simultaneously, changes in white sentiment connected with the Civil War made it possible for Afro-Americans to achieve their successes. However, it appears that black men had to battle every step of the way for the recognition of their rights of citizenship. For example, in 1865 and 1866, Illinois and Indiana repealed their anti-Negro testimony and anti-Negro immigration legislation, more widely known as "Black Laws." In Illinois, the agitation was conducted by the Repeal Association, organized by Chicago black men under the leadership of John Jones, a prosperous merchant-tailor. Under the leadership of noted caterer and protest leader George Thomas Downing of New York, blacks fought against segregated schools in Rhode Island. In a campaign that began in 1857, they finally achieved victory in 1866. In Washington, D.C., incidents occurred when streetcars refused to pick up black people. Afro-Americans protested, and Senator Charles Sumner obtained a law prohibiting such discrimination in 1865. The practice, however, continued. It was not until Sojourner Truth secured the arrest and dismissal of a streetcar conductor who had assaulted her that the matter was settled.[30]

If members of black amateur clubs participated in such militant activities, then it was no doubt this behavior that disturbed whites who attended the conventions in Harrisburg and Philadelphia. It should be noted that Catto was a frontline agitator in the battle to end streetcar segregation in Philadelphia. The Pythians' efforts to join the PAABBP occurred simultaneously with this desegregation effort. Thus, the Pythians were more than just ballplayers; they were an expression of the mulatto elite's desire to assimilate into the mainstream of American society. Acceptance into both the PAABBP and the NABBP would exemplify that a state of racial equality existed, at least on the ball field.

Afro-Americans were not behaving the way whites expected them to because of their militant agitation for civil rights. Octavius Catto always contended that the black man was equal to the white man in all respects—including the baseball diamond.[31] No doubt such sentiments and arrogance, in conjunction with the mulattoes' agitation for civil rights and the bigotry of white players and officials, provided the ideological justification for excluding black clubs on "political grounds."

The Pythians' exclusion from the PAABBP combined with the formal ban by the NABBP represented a minor setback in race relations in the baseball world. Because most white clubs opposed the Pythians' admission, the ban also thwarted Catto's aspiration of a true championship between black and white clubs. But the ban was somewhat insignificant, owing to the internal problems the NABBP confronted that resulted in the association splitting into two factions, amateurs and professionals. As spectators gravitated toward professionals, their demand for the best players and teams helped intensify competition. Smart individuals seized the opportunity to capitalize on the situation, and promoters converted the sport into an amusement business. Others attached themselves to baseball, legitimately or otherwise, and established auxiliary organizations ranging from sporting goods to gambling. The Cincinnati Red Stockings' sensational success as a professional club in 1869 resulted in other cities, such as Chicago, being envious of the club's fame and the instantaneous visibility they brought to the Queen City. That same year, the professionals were in virtual control of the convention, while the amateurs correspondingly lost influence. In other words, the Pythians' efforts to join the state association occurred simultaneously with the professionals gaining control of the amateur association and leading it down the road toward professionalization and commercialization. What the ban meant for black clubs was that instead of growth and commercial development occurring within the mainstream of the baseball world, they would evolve on its outskirts.[32]

Creeping Toward Commercialization

Although the evidence is limited, by 1869 black amateur baseball clubs appear to have been traveling down the same road as their white counterparts toward commercialization. Black clubs continued their version of the championship series. Despite the ban on black clubs imposed by the NABBP, the press reported several interracial contests taking place for the first time. There were also indications of black games being played for gate receipts, with no extracurricular activities taking place after the contest.

The early Colored Championships were essentially local affairs. They were primarily billed as matches for the "colored" championship of a particular state. One club, the Unique Club of Williamsburgh, Pennsylvania, reportedly claimed the "colored championship of the United States." According to the *Wilkes Spirit of the Times*, the team had not lost two games with any club since 1865, their first year as an organized club. However, by 1869 their streak ended when the Lone Stars of Philadelphia defeated them, "much to the [Unique Club's] surprise and disgust," as reported in the *New York Clipper*.[33]

In October 1870, the *New York Clipper* reported a Colored Championship series in Illinois between the Blue Stockings of Chicago and the Rockfords of Rockford. They played a "home-and-home" series, the latter game played at the fairgrounds in Rockford. The Blue Stockings, composed primarily of employees from various hotels and restaurants, defeated the Rockfords, twenty-eight to eighteen, in the final game of the series and claimed the Colored Championship of Illinois.[34]

The press also reported the first known barnstorming tour by a black club. The Mutual Club of Washington, D.C., played a series of games in upstate New York against Lockport, Niagara Falls, Buffalo, Rochester, Utica, Canajoharie, and Troy. They won seven games and, according to the *Clipper*, declined several challenges owing to "want of time." The Mutuals spoke "in the highest terms of their treatment on the tour."[35]

Although there is no evidence to indicate that they played in a Colored Championship series, the Philadelphia Pythians also began traveling down the road toward commercialization. In 1868, as a means of strengthening their club, the Pythians recruited both John Cannon and George Brown. Cannon was "considered by white [players to be] a baseball wonder," whereas Brown was one of "the best amateur [pitchers] of his day." The following year, the Pythians added four of the best players from the Excelsiors: Frank J. R. Jones, Andrew Glasgow, Franklin H. Jones, and Pliny Locke. Losing their best players resulted in the Excelsiors disbanding. It also marked the start of the Pythians looking for players outside their "exclusive group" to maintain their competitiveness. Sustaining this competitive edge forced weaker players, such as Daniel Adger Jr., the son of a prominent store owner and later a postal worker, into resignation.[36]

Although there was still resistance from the white fraternity, the Pythians played in the first reported interracial contest. In September 1869, Colonel Thomas Fitzgerald, a former president of the Athletics and editor of a local newspaper, the *Philadelphia City Item*, arranged a contest between the A's and the Pythians. The Athletics refused Fitzgerald's overtures, but the *Item*'s editor did arrange a match between the Olympics and the Pythians. The Olympics defeated the Pythians, forty-four to twenty-three, in front of a large crowd attracted by the novelty of the match. The *Wilkes Spirit of the Times* praised the experiment, stating that "old-time prejudices are melting away in this country." The paper was optimistic that "now the prejudice has been broken through here, it will be entirely swept away." Two weeks later, the Pythians played and defeated Fitzgerald's white *City Item* ball club, twenty-seven to seventeen.[37]

Two other interracial contests were reported in the press. In October 1869, the Alerts of Washington, D.C., challenged the Olympic club, a charter member of the NABBP. According to the *New York Clipper*, the game was played "in the presence of a large assembly of both sexes and colors, and quite a number of prominent government officials." Despite the large crowd, the Alerts were no match for the Olympics, as the former was drubbed, fifty-six to four.[38]

The most interesting contest took place in Boston the following year. Both clubs called themselves the Resolutes, and to resolve the conflict, a match was scheduled in which the victors remained the Resolutes and the losers changed their name. The black Resolutes won the game and retained their name.[39]

The emergence of interracial contests was significant to the history of black baseball. It marked the beginning of what would later be described as a symbiotic business relationship between black and white clubs. This relationship would be vital to the success of black baseball clubs. As black clubs improved, entrepreneurs capitalized upon whites' fascination with Afro-American clubs playing on the same level as white clubs on the diamond. White baseball club owners found it to be good business to schedule games with black clubs who proved to be good gate attractions.[40]

Further evidence of commercialism emerged. Colleges, such as Howard and Lincoln Universities, offered direct challenges to the Pythians with no social events following the game. In 1869, the Mutual Club of Washington, D.C., arranged a game, promising only "a suitable boarding house" and to "share with you the proceeds of the gate and assume no other responsibility." Mutual secretary Charles R. Douglass added, "I understand now that such is the rule with all clubs." The Mutuals expected to draw a good gate. Later that same year, the Uniques of Chicago came to Philadelphia. An enclosed ground was available, and "thousands" paid to see the game. Next came the Monrovia Club of Harrisburg. All these games ended in Pythians victories, and they finished the year undefeated.[41]

By 1871, the Pythians had reached their peak in popularity and success; however, it was short-lived. On October 10, Octavius Catto was on his way to vote when he was drawn into an argument with a white man and shot to death. Blacks considered this act a case of premeditated murder. Catto had long been a target of white hostility, owing to his leadership role in the black community and his militant stance in advocating civil rights for Afro-Americans. He was also becoming more of a national figure, aiding in the administration of the freedman schools. Catto's Republican friends praised him for his prominence "in politics [and] being looked up to and confided in by his people as a man of earnest conviction and judgments beyond his years." The violence that had occurred on election day resulted in a riot in which at least two other blacks were killed and many other blacks and whites wounded before the melee subsided. On October 21, a mass meeting of both black and white citizens passed resolutions deploring the bloodshed and censuring city officials for not maintaining order. Investigations of the riot revealed more police abuses than mob violence.[42]

By 1872, the Philadelphia Pythians disbanded. It is evident that Octavius Catto's death contributed to the club's demise. He had been its driving force. The team's exclusion from the PAABBP, however, and the emphasis placed on seeking the best players to maintain the club's competitive edge may also have been causes for the club folding. As historian Eric Foner points out, free blacks welcomed the end of slavery. However, many resented the elimination of their unique status and feared being submerged in a sea of freedmen. Inclusion of players such as George Brown and John Cannon served to diminish the Pythians' unique status and the team's sense of exclusivity. Moreover, on the national level, the NABBP's formal ban excluding black players and clubs was a minor setback in the Afro-American quest for self-determination and race elevation.[43]

However, baseball continued to grow in popularity among Afro-Americans. Although the evidence is limited, the black game continued to travel down the road toward commercialization. Throughout the 1870s, however, the white press's coverage of black games declined, and much of black baseball's historical development was lost. Yet the various obstacles that prohibited black baseball from developing into a commercial enterprise were already present.

The Enduring Legacy

By the early 1870s, prospective black baseball entrepreneurs confronted an enduring legacy that permeated the history of black baseball. The forces that shaped the development of modern white baseball—the political economy, industrialization, and urbanization—created a complex set of consequences for black baseball entrepreneurs. Despite these circumstances, black baseball entrepreneurs exploited their most valuable assets, the players, to capitalize upon the game's popularity. But first, it is necessary to illustrate briefly how the aforementioned forces influenced the development of modern white baseball.

Historian Roger Ransom argues that one of the most far-reaching changes in antebellum America was the development of an industrialized system. It required the creation of both an economic system and a wage labor force, geared to an urban rather than a rural environment. By the end of the 1840s, Americans were leaving their farms and moving into the cities, taking up jobs in a vast array of industrial and related occupations. Moving to the city involved profound changes in a family's lifestyle. They left a world in which the family was fairly isolated from its neighbors and largely self-reliant for its needs. The rural dwellers entered a world where contact with neighbors on a daily basis was inevitable, and where one also depended on others for a plethora of basic needs.[44]

The economic and social interdependence that came with urban life carried over into the political arena. To the city dweller of mid-nineteenth-century America, political parties served very important social roles. They offered a vehicle for people to deal collectively with an environment that was constantly changing and at times seemed very threatening. Joel Silbey describes what he terms "an intricate web of interactive institutions" working within the community and functioning "in a most partisan fashion." He further explains that parties had several means to keep in touch with their constituencies, including newspapers and pamphlets, social organizations—like baseball clubs—and volunteer fire companies.[45]

The social organization of these cities also contributed significantly to the rise of modern baseball. Metropolitan centers, such as New York, Newark, Boston, and Philadelphia, grew more diverse in race, religion, and ethnicity. Many urbanites sought a sense of identity and fellowship in voluntary associations for political, religious, cultural, or sporting purposes. Consequently, baseball players followed this practice. The complex social structure of these cities resulted in men grouping themselves by neighborhood, vocation, wealth, or membership in some common social or religious association. As historian George Kirsch points out, sportsmen who banded together were also trying to preserve and strengthen their social identities in an increasingly impersonal environment.[46]

Both the increase in population and the pattern of pluralism in U.S. cities contributed to the commercialization of baseball. The urban masses were essentially cut off from most of their former modes of recreation. As a result, they sought diversion through whatever means the new urban life provided. Their substantial numbers led to the development of hundreds of clubs while at the same time supplying audiences for all types of amusements. Urbanization also gave rise to the emergence of sports entrepreneurs, who satisfied the growing demand for entertainment by creating the modern business of leisure. For example, in 1862, William H. Cammeyer opened the Union Grounds in Brooklyn, providing a playing field rent free to three ball clubs. In exchange, the ball clubs permitted Cammeyer to charge a ten-cent admission fee to their contests. Cammeyer's venture illustrates that the introduction of business into baseball did not rest upon the distinction between private clubs and private ownership. Instead, it was a willingness of the public to pay the price. Cammeyer's successful venture spurred others to follow suit. In 1864, Thurlow Weed, a famed Whig political operative, also converted his skating grounds into a ball field.[47]

The culmination of the political economy, industrialization, and urbanization gave rise to the formation of baseball clubs and the emergence of both spectatorship and the sports entrepreneur. However, these same forces created a complex set of consequences that affected black entrepreneurship generally and black sports entrepreneurship specifically. On the one hand, they facilitated a racist society that made both black entrepreneurship and black business development illusions. Simultaneously, the need to protect private property, which had safeguarded and promoted the institution of slavery before the Civil War, also provided the basis for black entrepreneurial expression.

The political economy also gave rise to the proscriptive legislation that severely limited any enterprise undertaken by free blacks. It fostered a racially repressive society in which blacks had few rights that whites were bound to respect. Three decades of Jim Crow segregation in the North prior to the Civil War dramatically retarded the growth and expansion of black business development. In the 1850s, new challenges tested the perseverance of the North's 200,000 Afro-Americans. They were legally barred from settling in some states, and confined to a diminishing number of inferior jobs. They looked on with dismay at the passage of more repressive state and federal legislation, a Supreme Court decision that stripped them of citizenship, a revived colonization movement, and a new antislavery political party, which demonstrated little regard for the plight of northern blacks.[48]

Both the impact of the political economy and urbanization dramatically influenced the demographic makeup of the northern Afro-American population. In 1870, less than 10 percent (317,545) of the total Afro-American population (4,880,009) resided in the North. Ten years later, 426,180 out of a total population of 6,580,773 lived north of the Mason-Dixon line.[49] In northern cities such as New York and Philadelphia, blacks did not live in areas where their numbers constituted a majority. Thus, prior to the early twentieth century, it was virtually impossible to market a business enterprise, not to mention a commercialized amusement, exclusively to a black consumer market.

A final factor was the complex anomaly that the protection of private property created. As historian Juliet E. K. Walker states, the most distinctive feature of the U.S. free enterprise system—access to and protection of private property—was also an important factor that allowed blacks to participate in the antebellum economy as entrepreneurs. Black property ownership was established in seventeenth-century colonial America. In the eighteenth century, free blacks confronted the erosion of their civil rights and political liberties, and efforts that were made to deny them the right to own property. However, the founding fathers did not move to suppress black property ownership, although, as Milton Freedman emphasizes, "The failure to impose such barriers clearly did not reflect any special concern to avoid restrictions on Negroes." Moreover, Freedman also states that the concern "reflected rather a basic belief in private property which was so strong that it overrode the desire to discriminate against Negroes."[50] In spite of racism, access to the ownership of private property provided an opportunity for free blacks to establish business enterprises prior to the Civil War.

However, at the same time, the fact that so few blacks were entrepreneurs, and their limited success, also indicates that in the pre-Civil War era, laws, customs, and traditions worked together to minimize black access to the acquisition and development of private property. There were no William Cammeyers among black people who transformed their private property to capitalize upon the baseball craze. Yet, as Adelman suggests, it was the public's willingness to pay rather than private ownership that contributed to the rise of modern baseball. One cannot deny that white sports entrepreneurs had a considerable advantage over blacks in capitalizing upon the baseball craze because the opportunity favored them in gaining access to property. This fact, more than anything else, resulted in black baseball entrepreneurs becoming reliant upon whites to use their ballparks to play games. Throughout history, only a handful of Afro-Americans owned their own ballparks.[51]

Despite these consequences, black baseball entrepreneurs continued to make efforts to capitalize upon the game's popularity. In the decades after Reconstruction, Afro-American entrepreneurs in baseball reflected the continu-

ation and expansion of entrepreneurship within the tradition of self-help activities that had distinguished black economic endeavors. This continuation
marked the transition of black baseball from a social organization designed to
elevate the race from its political, economic, and social plight to a commercialized enterprise seeking to tap into the new market economy that would become professional baseball.

The successful black baseball entrepreneur attempted to operate a segregated enterprise (black baseball) within the fabric of the national economy
(professional white baseball). In this way, black baseball entrepreneurs showed
a willingness to work within the framework of a biracial institutional structure,
emphasizing self-reliance and racial cooperation rather than protesting
against mounting injustices. To accomplish this feat, black baseball entrepreneurs secured leasing agreements with white park owners, primarily in and
around large metropolitan centers such as New York and Chicago. They
sought to make business arrangements to schedule games with the newly
emerging major and minor leagues, semiprofessional clubs, and college baseball teams.[52]

None of them would have been successful without black baseball entrepreneurs exploiting their most valuable assets, the players. Afro-American
baseball entrepreneurs had to locate black players and develop their skills to a
level that would match, and at times surpass, white players in the major and
minor, semiprofessional, and college ranks. Moreover, they also had to keep
their player rosters intact, as a means of operating over a period of time. Black
entrepreneurship in the national pastime exemplified Arthur H. Cole's assertion that "entrepreneurial endeavors will rise through crevices in societies
made rigid by tradition or force."[53]

3

The Birth of a Commercial Enterprise

*T*he emergence of black baseball as a commercial enterprise exemplified the continuation and expansion of entrepreneurship, within the tradition of self-help activities that had distinguished black economic endeavors in antebellum America and the post–Civil War era. The rise of black professional teams coincided with the transformation of white organized baseball into a commercial enterprise, the changing attitude business had toward baseball, and the rise of the mulatto elite after emancipation. In 1876, the National League was formed by a group of clubs that sought to place the game on a sound economic footing. Certain collusive practices emerged to stabilize markets and limit unrestrained competition for players. Although the systemic dimension of organized baseball began in 1876, the maturation of its institutional structure did not emerge until the late 1880s. It was within this time frame that a window of opportunity for Afro-American teams opened up, primarily in the minor leagues, only to close by the early 1890s.

Simultaneously, the changing attitude of U.S. businessmen toward baseball resulted in the appearance of company-sponsored teams, who became a source of company pride. Their success led to transforming the prior ambivalent attitude on the part of businessmen to one of full-fledged acceptance. This change, combined with the rise of the black middle class, enabled blacks to shape the dimensions of black baseball's future. Early Afro-American entrepreneurs would either seek out white investors to obtain capital to operate a ball club or attempt to become a representative of a particular city in order to attract the best ball clubs to that city or to compete in a minor league. These decisions resulted in some white power brokers gaining control over the principal assets that constituted a professional ball club. Although their business relationship was a paternalistic one, blacks still established the business practices that sustained an independent club.

To understand the transformation of black baseball clubs into commercial enterprises, it is necessary to examine the forces that led to the emergence of organized baseball. In 1870, baseball entered a new period. The conflict that had marked the relationship between the NABBP's amateur and professional factions was at an impasse. The association's fall meeting was marred with bitter words between the two groups and resulted in the amateurs walking out of the convention. The incident provided the commercial clubs with an opportunity to branch out on their own. On March 17, 1871, ten representatives met in New York City and formed the National Association of Professional Base Ball Players (NAPBBP).[1]

The NAPBBP operated for five years. The association was beset by what baseball historian Harold Seymour refers to as "the cancerous evils" of gambling, hippodroming—the fixing and throwing of games—and revolving.[2] Gambling and hippodroming had plagued baseball since the 1860s. Gamblers, no longer satisfied to gamble, wanted a sure thing, so they arranged the outcome of the game in advance by bribing the players. Revolving, the process of changing teams from season to season, occurred because of the free labor market that existed in baseball. Players made arrangements with clubs and even accepted compensation in advance, only to move elsewhere in response to a better offer. As revolving, hippodroming, and gambling became more flagrant, spectators began to stay away from the games, resulting in a call for reform.

The league's most pressing problem was probably the one-sided competition. In 1875, the Boston Red Sox won the pennant by winning seventy-one games and losing eight; the Red Sox had also won the previous four pennants. Their closet rival, the Athletics, won fifty-three games and lost twenty. The Atlantics, who finished last, might just as well not have been in the league, losing forty-two of forty-four games. The gap between the pennant winner and the rest of the league was even greater in other years. Spectators lost interest owing to the disparity in playing strength. As long as these unstable conditions remained, investors would not risk losing money in a baseball venture.

In 1876, the National League was formed by a group of clubs that sought to bring greater financial stability to the game. In response to the low fan turnout in small cities and high player salaries—a direct result of revolving— certain collusive practices emerged to relieve those pressures. The league attempted to stabilize markets by granting exclusive territorial rights to franchises and establishing a minimum size for a city as one condition for league entry. Player salaries constituted a large percentage of team costs. Concerned with the financial consequences of unrestrained competition for players, the league secretly introduced a player reservation rule to gain control of labor costs. These practices eventually led to placing the game on a sound economic footing.

The National League began with no sanction against revolving during the off-season. The free market for players led to bidding wars and even higher player salaries as teams tried to increase their chances of winning a pennant. The owners recognized that some action had to be taken if player salaries were to come down or even remain at a reasonable level.

Whereas labor relations are of prime importance in any business, they are especially significant in baseball, a particularly unique enterprise. Like any other businessmen, baseball owners are interested in turning a profit. Owners must market their product successfully, and their teams must approximate each other in skill to accomplish this outcome. Contests have to be sufficiently interesting in order to attract fans. People would hardly pay to see a champion Anaheim Angels team play a high school team. This circumstance is why no single owner can sell the product by himself. He must market in cooperation with his fellow owners. Major league owners are not only competitors but also partners who must cooperate with each other to a much greater degree than in more conventional enterprises.[3]

No one recognized the need for cooperation among fellow owners more than William A. Hulbert. On February 2, 1876, he assembled interested parties from St. Louis, Louisville, New York, Philadelphia, Boston, and Hartford and founded the National League of Professional Base Ball Clubs. The formation of the National League was significant in the structure and conduct of the sport. Up to this point, baseball organizations, amateur or professional, were primarily player associations. The formation of an organized league transferred power from players to owners. Restrictive measures were enacted in an effort to bind players more tightly to clubs. In essence, Hulbert sought to bring order to professional baseball by "reducing the game to a business system such as never heretofore obtained." Another element to this system was the establishment of a league bureaucracy composed of club owners, a league president, a secretary, and a board of directors, with the authority to enforce rules and supervise league operations.[4]

The prospective owners drew up a league constitution and formulated business practices that constituted organized baseball. Generally speaking, the league had two broad objectives. Club owners sought to elevate baseball and make ball playing "respectable and honorable" by enacting "proper rules" for the conduct of the game. They also had a desire to protect and promote the "natural interests" of clubs and players and to establish and regulate the baseball championship of the United States. Restrictive measures in the form of controlling consumer markets were introduced to improve baseball's business operations. Commonly referred to as territorial rights, each league club was given exclusive control of its own city and surrounding area within a five-mile radius. No league club could play an outside team in another league city, even if the local league club consented; the constitution allowed but one club to a city. Theoretically, other clubs could join the circuit, but in reality they had little chance of doing so. The owners had no intention of having more than eight clubs in the league. A member club had to leave before a new one could enter.[5]

The nature of the National League's collusive agreements enabled baseball to establish a moral agenda. This lofty moral image, shrouded in the rhetoric of Christian propriety, forbade any club from scheduling games on Sunday and selling alcoholic beverages on its grounds. This agenda also outlawed betting or pool selling, banned players from fraternizing with the fans, and empowered umpires to eject rowdy fans. Severe penalties were enacted against players who engaged in unacceptable behavior. The notion of an acceptable moral image was vital to the success of a commercialized amusement.[6]

In an effort to maximize profits, the league owners instituted population requirements for league admission and developed a balanced schedule. To ensure gate receipts, a new club had to represent a city of not less than seventy-five thousand, unless given special exemption by unanimous vote of the incumbent members. Two blackballs were enough to block admission of a new club. Members were required to pay annual dues of one hundred dollars. Each club played ten games with every other club between March 15 and November 15. Five of the ten games might be played on the club's home grounds.[7]

The National League devised business practices that were pivotal to professional baseball's development. It provided a wellspring uniquely designed to nourish the formation of a monopoly and of competition. Under NL auspices, member clubs competed with each other for prestige and receipts, but only within the parameters of the proposed structure. In the following years, the league brought stability to professional baseball, the disruption of bitter trade wars, and even racism. The National League provided a high caliber of play on the field and trouble with ballplayers. It built up public confidence in the national pastime, and, at times, created public discontent.[8]

Yet the origins of organized baseball's business practices were not enough to maintain its financial stability. Economist Paul Gregory argues that the adoption of the first reservation rule on September 30, 1879, was due largely to the numerous player desertions that had occurred in the previous four seasons. Under this collusive agreement, each club could reserve five ballplayers for the 1880 season. Other teams were permitted to sign any other player from a club's rosters. The aim was to hold player salaries down as teams reserved their five best players, but the rule was contingent upon the cooperation of club owners not tampering with each other's reserve players.[9]

The creation of the reservation rule enabled owners to stop revolving altogether and provided them with tremendous operational autonomy. It was also instrumental in the creation of the first uniform contract. Before 1887, player contracts contained no reserve clause, but the reserve rule enabled clubs to enforce regulations against players found guilty of being drunk or otherwise engaging in conduct reprehensible to baseball. Players guilty of such transgressions could be suspended and become ineligible to play for any other club in the league.

The founders of the National League did not always follow their objective of limiting professional baseball to large cities. Before the close of the 1876 season, both the Philadelphia Athletics and the New York Mutuals refused to go west for their final scheduled games. Both clubs stated that they had lost money and did not want to go deeper in debt. As this act was a direct challenge to league authority, attention was focused upon the league's directors. After gaining the presidency, William Hulbert, at the league's winter meeting, moved to expel both clubs. This stand was a bold move on behalf of the league's new authority, but it cost the league its two largest cities. The NL named no replacements and despite the potential profit losses operated with six clubs the following year.[10]

The expulsion of Philadelphia and New York exemplified the league director's willingness to forego profits, based on the supposition that the public must first be convinced that major league baseball was honest. Perhaps after a few years of humility and sacrifice, the public would reward them by coming to the games in droves. David Voigt has found that from 1876 to 1880, that National League owners lost on average $2,220.84 per season. A strategy of emphasizing respectability over profits appears naïve from a modern view, but it should be noted that the United States was in the midst of a financial depression during these years. The American public did not enjoy the luxury of spending money for frills like baseball. Therefore, the league's policy of staying the course and focusing on its public image seemed plausible.[11]

Yet the directors' persistent moral boycott of New York and Philadelphia left the league vulnerable to an outside challenge. One newspaper writer urged clubs from excluded cities such as Pittsburgh, Washington, and Baltimore to form a real major league. His point of view was valid because the National League of 1880 was indeed a small-town circuit. They had taken in towns such as Milwaukee and Indianapolis, only to replace them with Troy and Syracuse. In 1879, the addition of Cleveland and Buffalo would once again make the National League an eight-club circuit.[12]

In 1882, the National League faced its first challenge to its operational autonomy. The American Association was financed by wealthy brew masters and saloon keepers and had franchises in Baltimore, Cincinnati, Louisville, Philadelphia, Pittsburgh, and St. Louis. The following year, the AA expanded to eight clubs, adding New York and Columbus. Because the American Association was financed by wealthy brew masters and had franchises in larger cities, the National League sought a compromise with their rivals. Their compromise resulted in the creation of the National Agreement, which became the constitution of organized baseball.

On February 17, 1884, three organizations—the National League, the American Association, and the Northwestern League—met in a "harmony" conference to formulate the National Agreement, also known as the Tripartite Pact. League officials first addressed the disposition of players. The reserve clause was extended to cover eleven players on each club; eventually, it would be extended to cover the entire roster. Men reserved by the league and the association were guaranteed a minimum salary of $1,000; men reserved by the Northwestern League would receive at least $750. All contracts were for seven months, and no club was to negotiate with players for the following season until October 10. A twenty-day waiting period was required for clubs to bargain with released players. The leagues agreed to acknowledge each other's suspensions and expulsions of players by refusing to sign or play a club that had utilized them. Finally, an arbitration committee was formed, composed of three representatives from each circuit, and league classifications were established. The National League and the American Association were classified as "major leagues," whereas the Northwestern League was a "high minor league."[13]

The National Agreement marked the beginning of organized baseball. It was the first formula that regulated competition among leagues for players and territories. The agreement was also the first official document to include the reserve provision—a major source of controversy for organized baseball in the following decades. It served to tighten the reserve clause's effect and curtailed the bidding wars for players among clubs and leagues. In terms of territorial rights, the National Agreement contributed immensely to the permanence and value of the club franchises.

The National Agreement also impacted organized baseball's race relations. Organized baseball's business practices would be reshaped significantly in 1884 by the threat of an outside rival league, contributing to the drawing of the color line in its player force. Moreover, the war's aftermath would influence the business ties that black independent clubs attempted to negotiate with whites.

Organized Baseball's Race Relations

The process of systematic exclusion, known as the color line, was a culmination of white hostility toward black players, the continued maturation process of organized baseball's structure, and the major league owners' response to these forces that shaped their discriminatory and exclusionary behavior. Theoretically, the National Agreement was to exemplify a network of clubs and associations working in agreement with some general plan of enforcing contracts and barring players deemed detrimental to the game. League officials, however, did not envision the emerging power struggle within the organizational structure. Both the National League and the American Association scheduled exhibition games with minor league teams under agreement protection and with the top independent clubs. These games would be a valuable source of revenue for the struggling minor league clubs, particularly games with the era's most prominent team, the Chicago White Stockings, the modern-day Cubs. But the combination of the major league magnates' refusal to sign black players and the white players' opposition to playing clubs with blacks marked the beginning of drawing the color line in organized baseball. It began with the most influential owner and club in major league baseball, Albert Spalding and his White Stockings, even though in the 1880s, not all major or minor league clubs fully embraced Spalding's rationale for exclusion.

Moses Fleetwood Walker was the first Afro-American to play in the major leagues. Walker was born on October 7, 1857, in Mount Pleasant, Ohio, a Quaker settlement and a safe station on the route of the Underground Railroad. He was raised in nearby Stuebenville where his father was a minister. The son of Dr. Moses W. Walker and Catharine O'Hara Walker, Fleet grew up with two brothers, William and Weldy, and two sisters, Sarah and Mary. In

1881, Walker began his baseball career as a catcher for Oberlin College's varsity baseball team. The following school year, Fleet left Oberlin and attended the University of Michigan, becoming its catcher. After a brief stay there, Walker moved to Pennsylvania, and during the summer of 1882, he signed with an independent team in New Castle that played in various small towns throughout western Pennsylvania and eastern Ohio. Walker's talent on the diamond attracted the attention of William Voltz, former sports editor for the *Cleveland Plain Dealer.* Voltz worked for a group of businessmen who were forming a professional baseball team in Toledo. He signed Harlan F. Burkett, a curveball pitcher at Oberlin, who recommended Walker to him. Voltz signed Walker as the second player on the Toledo Blue Stockings, which entered the Northwestern League in 1883.[14]

The Northwestern League, formed in 1879, was the first organized league in the western part of the country. The league originated in four cities: Davenport and Dubuque, Iowa; Omaha, Nebraska; and Rockford, Illinois, but collapsed after only one season. The league re-formed in the autumn of 1882, and two years later became the first minor league to seek protection under the National Agreement. It operated in eight cities: Bay City, Grand Rapids, and East Saginaw, Michigan; Fort Wayne, Indiana; Springfield, Peoria, and Quincy, Illinois; and Toledo, Ohio.[15]

Walker found playing baseball in small midwestern towns a racially uncomplicated experience. He spent his first year with a winning team, playing in a relatively favorable environment that probably fulfilled his desire for excitement and financial gain. Local newspapers in Ohio and throughout the Northwestern League praised Walker as a "man of fine education and a perfect gentleman."[16]

On August 10, 1883, Walker experienced his first encounter with racial prejudice in professional baseball. It was the first of four such encounters with the era's most prominent star, Adrian C. "Cap" Anson. The White Stockings' manager and first baseman batted over .300, including two seasons over .400, for twenty-one of his twenty-five years. He was the first player to accumulate more than three thousand hits in his career. As a manager, Anson was a stern disciplinarian, known for punishing beer drinkers with fines of one hundred dollars and conducting bed checks with a legendary thoroughness. Sensitive players detested Anson's domineering attitude. Anson also had an innovative side in terms of game strategy. He had fielders back each other up on fielding plays, used offensive and defensive signals, and experimented with pitching rotations. In 1883, Anson's legendary persona was still in its infancy, and he was renowned as the large, loud, and intimidating manager of the Chicago White Stockings.[17]

When Anson brought his White Stockings to Toledo, he announced his team would not play if Walker played. This position stunned the *Toledo Blade*, which indicated that when the National League club had arrived at the Union depot, they were mistaken for Haverly's Mastadons or Callendar's Consolidated, two black teams. Evidently, the Chicagoans' sunburned faces left it "a matter of doubt as to their being tainted with black blood." Toledo club officials informed Anson that Walker had a sore hand and was not scheduled to play. Anson was not content with this declaration and indicated that the White Stockings would not play ball "with no nigger." In response to this obvious threat, the Toledo management instructed the White Stockings manager that "he could play his team or go just as he blanked pleased." Fearing the possible loss of their share of the gate receipts, and no doubt providing a plausible explanation for his actions to Albert Spalding, Anson backed down. Walker was put in right field and played the entire game.[18]

This episode was significant because of the *Blade*'s high esteem of Walker and its admonishment of Anson. The newspaper praised the black catcher's genteel manner and scholarly demeanor. On the other hand, the *Blade* blasted Anson, charging him and his club with containing "a greater proportion of the 'bum' element than any ball club in America." Furthermore, the newspaper added that Toledo had played exhibition games with American Association clubs, such as New York, Columbus, and St. Louis, without incident. In the case of the National League, however, "the Chicago club was of more delicate fiber, more susceptible to deleterious influences and hence could not play, with a colored catcher against them."[19] Clearly, Walker was both a media and a fan favorite in Toledo.

In 1884, Walker became the victim of a conspiracy. Toledo became a member of the AA when the association expanded to twelve clubs. Organized baseball was experiencing its first outside threat from a rival league, the Union Association. Under the direction of the National League, war was directed against these outsiders through threats of player raids or direct competition within a particular territorial region. During the war, an event occurred that at first seemed unrelated to Walker's plight. Initially, the reservation system was designed to protect a team's roster, but there was no method by which a player could be transferred between clubs. The St. Louis Browns wanted to transfer the contract of pitcher Tony Mullane to Toledo. However, a business practice was not established whereby Mullane could be released without giving clubs other than Toledo the right to sign him. A. G. Mills, then the National League president, ruled that a qualified release was not possible under the National Agreement. Mills, however, suggested that a letter be circulated among the clubs stating the Browns' intention and asking clubs not to negotiate with Mullane. This crude waiver rule established the precedent known as the "gentlemen's agreement." [20]

In April 1884, Toledo manager Charlie Morton had agreed to another exhibition game with Chicago, contingent upon the assurances that Walker would not play. Jonathon Brown, Spalding's secretary, assured Morton that although "the management of the Chicago Ball Club have no personal feeling about the matter . . . the players do most decisively object and to preserve the harmony in the club it is necessary that I have your assurance in writing." The White Stockings secretary also warned Toledo that if it went back on its word after Chicago arrived, the ball club would not take the field and nonetheless claim a guarantee of one hundred dollars for their troubles.[21] On game day, Fleet Walker was held out of Toledo's lineup.

Why did the Blue Stockings give in to Spalding's demands, when a year earlier they had defended their right to play Walker? Several factors led to Toledo's capitulation. First, the AA's expansion move failed to recognize its new members' financial status, personnel, or facilities. The move illuminates baseball historian David Voigt's thesis regarding the ability of National League officials to cleverly persuade the association to expand, in an effort to weaken their organization, which resulted in a culmination of factors that included increased travel expenses, weakening the American Association's competitive balance, and decreased revenues owing to these new teams being poor gate attractions at home games.[22]

Second, the plight of the Toledo club clearly exemplifies the ill-advised move to expand. Toledo found itself in a new, faster level of competition. As a member of the Northwestern League, it had competed in a circuit whose teams never traveled more than a couple hundred miles from home. In the American Association, Toledo played as far east as Brooklyn and as far west as St. Louis, with ten other stops between those terminals. Toledo suffered as a gate attraction when scheduling exhibition games. Top independents and minor league clubs would much rather schedule exhibition games with Anson's White Stockings or the St. Louis Browns, with their star player-manager Charles Comiskey, than a Toledo club whose previous notoriety extended within a radius of only two hundred miles. Even more destructive was that the Northwestern League had to replace Toledo with another franchise in

Stillwater, Minnesota, which expanded its closely knit tristate format, resulting in increased travel expenses. In other words, the trade war over players and the constant franchise shifting marred the major league owners' attempt to bring stability to their fledgling new industry, resulting in five minor leagues collapsing during the Union Association war.[23]

Throughout the Union war and the subsequent 1885 season, National League officials positioned themselves to set the agenda for organized baseball. When the American Association was found in violation of the ten-day waiver rule in a Brooklyn-Cleveland player deal, Spalding demanded that the association either expel Brooklyn or allow Henry V. Lucas's Union Association St. Louis club to gain entry into the senior circuit. This adjustment permitted the National League to operate a franchise in that territorial market. The American Association's position was further weakened when John B. Day, owner of the New York clubs in both circuits, weakened the Metropolitans by creating more favorable situations for the National League Giants. For example, Day compelled the Mets to start games earlier when both his teams played on the same day. To add insult to injury, the Mets were relegated to the less desirable diamond on the old Polo Grounds. Despite stiff opposition by the American Association, its officials yielded to the demands of National League magnates. Albert Spalding emerged as the dominant owner in organized baseball. This situation placed him in an advantageous position to influence organized baseball policy—which included the exclusion of black players at the major league level.[24]

The gentlemen's agreement between Toledo manager Charlie Morton and Albert Spalding established the precedence for drawing the color line in organized baseball. Both the Union Association war and Anson's opposition to playing clubs with black players were influential in Spalding sanctioning his manager's racist behavior. Given the constant presence of racism, the elimination of blacks from organized baseball is not simply attributed to the onset of Jim Crowism or to men such as Cap Anson. Organized baseball was engaged in a trade war that it was not sure it could win. It should be noted that the expansion of the American Association, which enabled Toledo to become a member, and not an attempt by the owners to sign black players landed Walker and his brother Weldy in the major leagues. Moreover, throughout the late nineteenth century, not one National League club had a black player on its roster. The Union war had a dramatic impact upon organized baseball's restrictive business practices, enabling the owners to gain tighter control over their labor force. These practices also impacted organized baseball's race relations. While the owners fought wars over the services of white players, they appeared more than willing to utilize their collusive behavior to exclude black players from the major leagues. Such action was consistent with northern racial attitudes, which had no intention of allowing blacks to compete on an equal playing field with whites.

However, in the beginning, major league owners did not fully embrace the color line. Instead, the owners established a double standard. On the one hand, the owners colluded together by not recruiting, or encouraging the signing of, black players. This fact is evident owing to the fact that no black player played in the major leagues after 1884 until Jackie Robinson crossed the color line in 1947. In essence, the founding fathers of organized baseball had passed this exclusionary behavior pattern on to the next generation of owners. On the other hand, major league owners, particularly in the American Association, had no problem scheduling games with the top black independents. In the upcoming years, John B. Day's Metropolitans and Chris Von der Ahe's St. Louis Browns would consistently schedule games with black independents, but as white player hostility toward blacks increased, club owners scheduled fewer games with black clubs.

Organized baseball's race relations evolved around the owners' second broad objective: to promote the "natural interests" of clubs and players and to establish and regulate the baseball championship of the United States. Black players became a casualty of organized baseball's maturation process because the owners deemed them "detrimental to the game." No doubt the owners' behavior toward black players was also influenced by Fleet Walker's treatment in Louisville in 1884. Press reports, however, reveal a confusing picture. The *Sporting Life* indicated that Walker, "who was several years ago forbidden to play on Louisville grounds on account of his color, was frequently applauded in that city last week for his fine catching." On the other hand, the *Toledo Blade* reported that Walker was hissed and insulted because of his color. When Louisville appeared in Toledo, the *Blade* reported that the club was so roundly booed that the paper had to remind them that the players were "gentlemanly and honorable" and were not responsible for the conduct of their fans in Kentucky. This inconsistent fan behavior could lead to even more negative consequences. Such an incident served only to rationalize on business grounds the owners' exclusionary behavior. While organized baseball was undergoing its maturation process, and the genesis for the color line emerged, a baseball subculture was also going through its infancy.[25]

Independent Ball

The emergence of organized baseball coincided with the rise of the mulatto elite after the Civil War and semiprofessional teams. Both the distinction of white ancestry among a subordinate group and the opportunities to exploit this characteristic for economic and social gain led to the emergence of a small mulatto elite in urban communities in the North and South. Feeling privilege over the unmixed blacks around them, they distanced themselves and developed their own social and community life. Their lifestyles were often patterned after the habits of whites whom they were able to observe closely because of their frequent contacts in service capacities. This clearly defined status group of mulattoes that had appeared by the Civil War ascended to the top of the social ladder; they would continue to grow during the fifty years after emancipation.[26]

With their roots in white society, the mulatto elite evolved primarily through a paternalistic relationship with upper-class whites. In the larger cities of the North as well as the South, craftsmen, barbers, headwaiters, and other small businessmen serving the needs of a wealthy white upper class played a prominent role in the local black elite. Although this situation was a continuation of the roles some free blacks had assumed before the Civil War, for others these occupations offered the only opportunity to rise above the common condition of the black masses. Historian David Katzman calls barbering the "single most important black business of the era."[27]

It was from within the ranks of the mulatto elite that aspiring entrepreneurs sought to capitalize on the baseball craze by creating a business enterprise. The mulattoes' relationship with the wealthy upper class placed them in contact with power brokers who could finance such a venture. More important, these black baseball teams would cater to a white clientele, and would reflect an effort on the part of the mulatto elite to gain acceptance in U.S. society by assimilating to American middle-class ways.

The rise of the mulatto elite after emancipation occurred almost simultaneously with the emergence of semiprofessional, or semipro, teams. In the 1870s, semipro teams could be classified into three categories: local teams or "stay-at-homes," traveling teams, and touring teams. Local teams usually played games within close proximity of their home base. These teams developed a close-knit network with other semipro teams, perhaps within a hundred-mile radius, to decrease travel and overhead expenses. Traveling teams had no home base and barnstormed the nation for gate receipts. Touring teams fell under both classifications and were the elite of the semipro teams. The culmination of possessing their own grounds and possessing a reputation as a "crack" team enabled these clubs to expand their travel itinerary and establish rivalries with teams in more lucrative markets, like New York City. Independents generally did not belong to a league but paid their players and charged admission. They commonly discharged their players in the winter, unless they toured the South. Independents often signed their players to one-year contracts, only rarely containing the newly created reserve clause for the following season. At the beginning of each season, players had to make new arrangements. During the season, independents paid their players either a weekly salary or on a "co-op" plan, a method in which a team's share of the gate receipts was divided among the players and owners.[28]

Semiprofessional teams utilized the same business practices as organized baseball in terms of generating and distributing revenues. A home team would share a percentage of the gate receipts (normally 40 percent) or pay a guarantee (a fixed amount usually set at $250, commonly referred to as a "heavy guarantee") to the visiting team. This guarantee was essential to attract the top clubs to their home grounds.[29]

The emergence of independent teams into professional enterprises was the direct result of the changing attitude that business had toward baseball. At first, the business community was ambivalent toward the game. Large numbers of young blue- and white-collar workers and some employers played amateur baseball. However, there was little formal support and occasional outright opposition from many businessmen. There were several businessmen in Chicago who were willing to structure their workers' leisure-time play within the context of company activities. By 1870, Chicago featured more than fifty company clubs. Two years later, as many as thirty company teams played ball in a single afternoon. The principal groups of companies engaged in regular play were wholesale dry goods firms, printers, metalworkers, and several manufacturing concerns. Yet by the early 1880s, some resistance on the part of businessmen toward baseball remained. In 1882, the *New York Metropolitan* reported that "a few years ago a certain shortsighted class of American employers engaged in quite a crusade against the national game of baseball on the absurd plea that the game prevented their employees from attending to their business." But, the paper added, "The fallacy of this opinion was soon made plain to them . . . and since then they have changed their idea on the subject, and now commercial nines, encouraged by sensible employers, form the ma-

jority of the amateur class of the metropolitan baseball fraternity." Company-
sponsored teams appeared, and their success led to transforming the prior ambivalent and antagonistic attitude on the part of businessmen to one of
full-fledged acceptance. Employers began to recognize that baseball was com-
patible with business, a central reason the game was popular among urban
workers in the first place.[30]

By the early 1880s, the rise of the mulatto elite, the transition of amateur
teams into semiprofessionals, the changing attitude of business toward baseball, and the continuation and expansion of entrepreneurship within the self-
help tradition led to a movement that created several all-Negro teams.
Aspiring entrepreneurs seized an opportunity to capitalize on the novelty of an
all-black team playing baseball on a "major league" level. These clubs were
race-based in terms of the players on the field (the labor force) and the day-to-
day management of the enterprise. Simultaneously, the business arrangements
established by these entrepreneurs exemplified the paternalistic business relationship the mulatto elite had with affluent whites. Of the three principal assets that constituted a professional baseball club, black entrepreneurs
controlled the franchise and players under salary, whereas whites overwhelm-
ingly controlled the playing facilities.

From 1881 to 1885, the press reported the emergence of several all-black
teams. The *New York Clipper* suggested in 1881 that the Colored Championship of St. Louis be waged by its local black clubs: the Reds, Browns, and the
Black Stockings. According to the *Cleveland Leader*, the Black Stockings enjoyed the pick of the best colored players in the country. In 1882, the *Cincinnati
Enquirer* noted, "Philadelphia has a nine of colored professionals." This team
could have possibly been the Orions, one of the strongest teams in Philadelphia at that time. The *Sporting Life* reported in August 1884 that the Athletics
beat the Mutuals, thirty to five, at Baltimore, then the Mutuals "failed to pay
their unfortunate brothers from Philadelphia their share of the receipts, and
the latter had to walk home." In 1885, the *Sporting Life* also reported that the
Falls City Club of Louisville could justify its claim as the Colored Champions
of Kentucky, after winning twenty-two of twenty-three games. That same
year, although it provided no box scores, the *New York Sun* announced the Colored Championship series between the Remsen and Alpine Clubs, two local
black nines in the Gotham area.[31]

The Cuban Giants were the most prominent Afro-American club of the
era. They emerged from the consolidation of three black teams into a top-
notch independent club. A wealthy capitalist sponsored the Giants during the

Cuban Giants manager and co-owner S. K. Govern. *Courtesy of the New York Public Library.*

regular season. The Giants developed a "stay-at-home" travel schedule, playing games in New York, Connecticut, New Jersey, and Pennsylvania from April to October. They also scheduled exhibition games with National League, American Association, and Eastern League (EL) clubs, circuits that constituted organized baseball. They exemplified the independent team employed to represent a city.

Although the evidence is limited, the Cuban Giants' origins were the result of the entrepreneurial efforts of two men: Frank Thompson and S. K. Govern. Frank Thompson was born in Charleston, West Virginia, in 1855. According to the *New York Age*, Thompson became one of the best-known headwaiters in the country. In 1871, he began his career in the hotel industry as a waiter at the Ocean House in Cape May, New Jersey. By 1878, he was promoted to headwaiter. Stanislaus Kostka Govern was born on October 16, 1854, on St. Croix, in the Virgin Islands. He emigrated to the United States at age thirteen, serving as a cabin boy aboard the training ship the *Monongahela*. Like Thompson, Govern worked in the hotel industry, serving as a headwaiter at the Rittenhouse Hotel, as well as the Columbia and Scarborough Hotels in Atlantic City, New Jersey. He also served as a contributing editor to the *Philadelphia Tribune* during the newspaper's early days. Although not much evidence is available, Govern evidently had a brief acting career. According to the *People's Advocate*, Govern performed in the Shakespearean play *Pizarro* as a member of the Ira Aldridge Dramatic Company. From 1881 to 1884, Govern managed the Manhattans of Washington, D.C., a black semipro club.[32]

In October 1884, Govern's and Thompson's paths crossed when the former organized the Hotel Brotherhood U.S.A. Govern's effort to organize hotel employees into a union was in response to salary inequities among black and white waiters and bellhops. Supposedly, white waiters and bellhops received higher wages than their black counterparts. A special committee, which included Govern and Thompson, was formed to draft resolutions denouncing this discrimination in wages "and other harmful statements as published by the hotel proprietors."³³ The formation of the Hotel Brotherhood marked the start of a business relationship between these two men that would have a dramatic upon the development of black professional baseball.

In 1885, the Cuban Giants were formed. As the headwaiter of the Argyle Hotel, Thompson hired waiters known more for their baseball skills than their ability to wait tables. The *New York Age* reported:

> Mr. F. P. Thompson, formerly of Philadelphia, but now of the Hotel Vendome [in Boston], organized in May 1885, the Philadelphia, Keystone Athletics. On July 1, they transferred to Babylon L.I. During the month of August a consolidation of the Keystone Athletics, the Manhattans of Washington, D.C., and the Orions of Philadelphia, took place, under the name of the Cuban Giants. The proprietors were Messrs. F. P. Thompson, L. [*sic*] K. Govern and C. S. Massey.³⁴

The Cuban Giants' formation coincided with leisure activities becoming an integral part of the resort hotels in the Gilded Age. The involvement in sport, whether as a participant or as a spectator, was advocated as a vehicle for alleviating some of the problems inherent in the transformation of the United States into a modern industrial country. In terms of the resort hotel industry, sport provided its clientele with leisure activities designed as an outlet from the rigors of their career pursuits, as well as a means of flaunting their "elite" social status.³⁵ The emerging leisure component also enabled aspiring entrepreneurs, such as Frank Thompson and S. K. Govern, to seize an opportunity to establish a commercial enterprise.

The caliber of play by the club led Thompson to transform it into a professional ball club. According to Sol White, the Athletics played against the strongest teams of New York City and Long Island, winning six, losing two, and tying one. Thompson needed a wealthy financial backer and a road manager who was a good booking agent and knew the game of baseball. To attract a wealthy investor, a strong black independent club with talent on the same level as the top white independent teams, if not clubs in organized baseball, would have to be assembled. Evidently, the consolidation of Govern's Manhattans and Thompson's Athletics was attractive enough for John F. Lang, a white entrepreneur from Philadelphia, to finance them.[36]

Finally, the signing of the Philadelphia Orions' three top players completed the evolutionary development of the Cuban Giants. White argued that Lang was behind this obvious player raid of the Orions. He added that the "move was one of the most important and valuable acts in the history of colored baseball." It made the Cuban Giants one of the strongest independent teams in the East. However, the evidence suggests that it was Govern who was the catalyst for this move. Of the three men who made up the Giants' management team, Govern had the most experience in running a ball club. Even White conceded that Govern was a "smart fellow and a shrewd baseball man."[37] Although the signing of Shep Trusty, a pitcher; George Williams, a second baseman; and shortstop Abe Harrison made the Giants a strong independent, it also marked the beginning of a legacy that would plague black baseball throughout its history. Raiding semipro clubs of their top players would cripple many of the great black teams and drive many of their entrepreneurs out of the game.

When the Argyle closed on October 1, 1885, the Cuban Giants embarked on their first road trip. The weekly newspaper the *Babylon South Side Signal* indicated on October 10 that the Giants had played several games since leaving the Argyle and were victorious in every one. The club had even managed to schedule a game with the New York Metropolitans of the American Association, although they lost eleven to three. A few days later, the Afro-American club met the association's Philadelphia Athletics, losing that game thirteen to seven, but a *Sporting Life* correspondent stated that the A's needed help from the umpire to ensure victory.[38] The victory over the Bridgeport, Connecticut, team, champions of the Eastern League, was the high-water mark of the Giants' inaugural season, and it established their reputation as a top independent team.

The formation of the Cuban Giants typified the black entrepreneurs who embraced a business concept known as the cooperative enterprise.[39] Cooperative enterprises had their roots in the black community in the late eighteenth century. Early black entrepreneurs recognized that if they were to attain any success in developing black business to an appreciable level in the black community, it would come only through economic cooperation. It was evident to them that no concrete help in obtaining capital and credit could be expected from white America. S. K. Govern and Frank Thompson, however, were willing to operate within the framework of this evolving biracial institutional structure. They would make attempts to establish business connections with major and minor league clubs, semiprofessional teams, and college baseball teams. A partnership with a white businessman, particularly one with political and economic resources, provided the Cubans with a considerable advantage in their day-to-day operations. Moreover, with its victory over the Bridgeport club, the Cuban Giants captured the attention of a New Jersey "capitalist" who saw them as a "valuable asset."

Finding a Place to Call Home

In 1886, the Cuban Giants established a home base in Trenton, New Jersey. Financing by white businessmen and securing a playing facility enabled the Giants to establish business practices that ensured economic stability. A home base provided the Cubans an opportunity to develop a profitable market in which to operate. They established good press relations, scheduled games with the top clubs of the era, and created the "respectable" image needed to ensure white middle-class patronage. Concurrently, the Giants' inaugural season illustrated the primary obstacles that plagued independent teams. Playing facilities with poor access and games scheduled with weak teams adversely impacted attendance. Moreover, because the Giants were not affiliated with an organized league, they were vulnerable to player raids.

In the late nineteenth century, Trenton, New Jersey, could best be described as a city trapped by its "honorable past." Its image was formed primarily by the events of the colonial and American Revolution era. In colonial days, Trenton was an important link between north and south, a kind of halfway house between New York and Philadelphia. Trenton was also renowned for George Washington and his Continental army's surprise attack and victory over Hessian troops in the American Revolution. In the business world, Trenton was known for its manufacturing of American pottery, wire making, and bridge building.[40]

Trenton's image as a baseball town was precarious. In 1884, Trenton was a charter member of the newly formed Eastern League, a loop that had clubs in Allentown, Baltimore, Harrisburg, Newark, Reading, Richmond, and Wilmington, Delaware. From the outset, the Trentons developed a reputation as a rowdy and "undisciplined" club. Players fighting among themselves and refusing to play did not win the club any favor with Trenton fans. The Eastern League was adversely impacted by the war for players between organized baseball and the Union Association. By August, the Reading club had disbanded, Richmond had joined the American Association, and Wilmington had defected to the Union Association. The league finished the season with five clubs. Trenton won the Eastern League pennant with a record of fifty wins and forty losses. In 1885, the club relocated to Jersey City, leaving Trenton with no representative in the organized baseball world.[41]

It was within this context that the Cuban Giants became Trenton, New Jersey's representative in the baseball world. Evidently, John Lang was not willing to finance the Giants for the 1886 season. On April 30, the *Trenton True American* reported that Harry Simpson of the Trenton Browns had signed several of the "Cuban Giants" for the local club. In an effort to revive interest in professional baseball in Trenton, Simpson sought to organize a strong independent club and simultaneously capitalize on the novelty of a black team playing at a high caliber. Apparently, his efforts paid dividends. On May 4, the *True American* reported that the "prospects for base ball in Trenton this season are looking up." The Browns had defeated the Jersey Blues of Hoboken, New Jersey, eight to seven.[42] Signing the Cuban Giants players along with the enthusiasm of the press captured the attention of a "capitalist" who would seize an opportunity to invest in a commercial enterprise with promising potential.

Walter I. Cook was a descendent of one of the wealthiest and oldest families on the eastern shore. He was the youngest of three sons born to Elizabeth and William Grant Cook. His father was the director of the Trenton Banking Company, the Trenton Savings Fund, the Camden and Amboy Railroad Company, and the New York Division of the Pennsylvania Railroad Company. Walter, in association with his brothers, Edward and Henry, established the Cook Brothers real estate and insurance business. In May 1886, Walter Cook, along with his partner, John M. Bright, assumed control of the Cuban Giants and secured the services of S. K. Govern to manage the club. It was unclear how Bright and Cook assumed ownership of the club. Jerry Malloy argues that Simpson sold the team to Cook. However, no evidence was uncovered to indicate that this transaction took place. Given Govern's shrewdness as an entrepreneur, it is likely that the Cubans' manager negotiated a deal with Cook, once the latter expressed interest.[43]

Although white investors financed the Cuban Giants, Afro-Americans ran the day-to-day operations. In many ways, the Giants' management team was ahead of its time. It exemplified the modern corporation with its separation of management from ownership. In addition to Govern, the Giants also had a club secretary, George Van Sickle, but the former was the driving force. Much

like the modern-day general manager, he signed players to one-year
contracts, utilized the press to schedule games, and was even responsible
for selling season tickets. Player
salaries were determined by position:
pitchers and catchers were paid
$18.00 per week plus expenses, in-
fielders $15.00 per week plus ex-
penses, and outfielders $12.00 per
week plus expenses.[44]

The Giants established a method
of scheduling games that became the
model for black clubs to emulate—
the booking system. The successful
manager utilizing this system had an
uncanny ability to attract the best
clubs on a consistent basis. To attract
major league clubs, like the St. Louis
Browns, Govern would offer either
40 percent of the gate receipts or a
"heavy" guarantee, usually $250. Be-
cause the Cubans were a full-time enterprise, Govern booked minor

John M. Bright, co-owner of the
Cuban Giants. In the 1890s, he
became the sole proprietor of the
Genuine Cuban Giants. *Courtesy of
the New York Public Library.*

league clubs, local clubs, or college teams to round out the schedule. A flat
guarantee, normally $150, was offered to these clubs. In this way, Govern op-
erated his segregated club within the framework of the major and minor
leagues, college teams, and semiprofessional baseball.

The Giants were composed of players who hailed primarily from Pennsyl-
vania or Virginia and had previously played on black semiprofessional teams.
Ben Holmes, Arthur Thomas, Benjamin Boyd, Clarence Williams, Shepard
Trusty, William White, Richmond Robinson, and Harry Johnson formed the
nucleus that made the Cuban Giants the elite among black clubs in the East.
Ben Holmes began his playing career as a third baseman for the Douglas Club
of Washington, D.C., in 1876, and also played with the Hartfords, Nationals,
Mets, and Athletics. Arthur Thomas began as a catcher for the Manhattan
Base Ball Club of Washington, and was described as a "good general . . . a
good batsman, [and a] fair base runner." Benjamin Boyd played third base for

From 1884 to 1901, Clarence Williams served as catcher, first baseman, and manager of the Cuban Giants and Cuban X Giants. *Courtesy of the New York Public Library.*

the Manhattans in 1874 and the Mutuals in 1875, and played shortstop for the Cuban Giants in 1884 and 1885. Clarence Williams began his career as a left fielder for the Harrisburg club in 1882 and caught for the Middleton Base Ball Club of Pennsylvania the following year.[45] Together these men provided Trenton with some excellent baseball at the semiprofessional level.

The Cuban Giants were a race-based enterprise designed to cater to a white clientele. Early promoters of professional baseball sought to create a lofty moral image, shrouded in Christian propriety, as a means of selling their enterprise to the middle-class spectator. The notion of an acceptable moral image was vital to the success of a commercialized amusement. It had to possess and advocate values that appealed to a "respectable" class of citizens who judged this product not only on merit but also on the perceived quality of those individuals who endorsed it. To accomplish this task, a vocabulary was constructed that championed the values of this "respectable" class: temperance, sobriety, and moral respectability. Moreover, the most valuable commodity of this industry, the players, would represent this image formed by the owners. In essence, the lofty moral image was a marketing campaign to sell professional baseball to the middle-class spectator.[46]

Black baseball players were also expected to embody the values advocated by the white middle-class spectator. The *Trenton True American* praised the Cuban Giants for being "thoroughly disciplined," a behavior that did not describe clubs from previous years. In addition, the Giants were lauded for being gentlemen both on and off the field. The *Trenton Times* not only acknowledged the Giants' fine fielding and batting, but also gave them generous applause for their conduct. Such praise served to aid the Giants in winning favor with Trenton fans.[47]

Despite the concerted efforts of the Cuban Giants' management team, the club's opening season illustrated the obstacles that independent teams confronted. Because they were not affiliated with a league, the Cubans could not rely upon a fixed schedule of league games. This situation placed them in an uncertain position of scheduling contests with semipro clubs and college teams that were no match for this talented black club. Consistently winning games by scores of twenty-one to four or sixteen to one hardly made games interesting enough for fans to patronize. This predicament resulted in the club scheduling a large number of road games, particularly in the New York area. In addition, if the Giants desired to attract either a major or a minor league club to their home base, they had to ensure a substantial guarantee. The sporadic home attendance made doing so a difficult and often uncertain undertaking.[48]

Trenton fans patronized the Giants when major league clubs came to town. On May 27, 1886, the St. Louis Browns of the American Association invaded Chambersburg grounds. It marked the first time the Cuban Giants packed the ballpark. The *True American* reported that by the time the game started, "there was not an unoccupied seat anywhere." Hundreds of "kranks" stood along the right field area, and "[e]verybody who is anybody was on hand. From bank officials down to everyday sports [fans], the fever had apparently 'caught on,' and the [result] was a good natured, wildly enthusiastic assemblage of over two thousand people." Although the Giants lost nine to three, St. Louis, according to the *Trenton True American*, was so satisfied with the turnout that they indicated they would return later in the year.[49]

The fever pitch brought on by the St. Louis Browns' visit was short-lived. The Giants could rely on only a limited number of home games with big league clubs. Western clubs, such as Cincinnati or Kansas City, could be counted on only when they made their eastern swing against league clubs. Furthermore, because the Cubans were not affiliated with a league, they were subjected to player raids.

Minor league teams in the 1880s had no problem taking a black player if it would help their ball club. George Washington Stovey, considered the first great Afro-American pitcher of the late nineteenth century, played primarily on white teams. In June 1886, Govern signed this "southpaw" to a contract that ran through October 15. It is evident that Stovey had a great reputation up to that time. His signing attracted the attention of Patrick Powers, manager of the Jersey City Blues of the Eastern League. On June 24, 1886, the *Trenton Times* reported that Powers had made efforts to lure Stovey to his club. The Jersey City manager offered Stovey two hundred dollars a month; the left-hander refused. Two days later, Powers went to Trenton with a notification from George M. Ballard, president of the Eastern League, ordering Stovey to report to Jersey City the following day. Evidently, Stovey had signed a contract with the club a few days earlier. In what could be considered blackmail, Powers made the Cuban Giants an offer they could not refuse. If the Giants enforced their contract with Stovey, Eastern League clubs would refuse to schedule games with them. The Giants capitulated, although it was a "hard deal" for them. Powers admitted that the contract the Giants had with Stovey was binding and made a cash offer for him.[50]

The Stovey signing exemplified the vulnerable existence of an independent club. Exhibition games between league clubs and top independent clubs were a means of economic survival in the early years of organized baseball. However, independent clubs, regardless of whether they were well managed and financed, were also vulnerable without some semblance of protection. Legally, the Cuban Giants had a right to go to court and prevent Stovey from playing with Jersey City. From a business standpoint, however, it was not in the Cuban Giants' best interests to pursue the matter if it meant the loss of lucrative exhibition games. Therefore, a compromise was inevitable. League affiliation appeared to be the solution to the Cubans' attendance problem and susceptibility to player raids.

In mid-July 1886, it appeared that the Giants had the opportunity to join a minor league. The Meriden club of the Eastern League disbanded. Rumors circulated that the Giants would take their place. According to Govern, Eastern League president George M. Ballard assured the Giants' management that the Cubans would take the Connecticut club's place. The only drawback appeared to be whether the Giants would assume Meriden's schedule along with its poor record or start "fresh on their own account." However, on July 20, the Eastern League rejected the Cuban Giants' application and decided to play out the season with five clubs.[51]

The press cited racial discrimination as the driving force that governed the EL's decision. The *Newark News* stated, "While the dusky team is classed among the first class clubs . . . there is little prospect of it being admitted, as the color line will be drawn tight." The *Meriden Journal* added, "[T]he dread of being beaten by the Africans had something to do with the rejection of the application of the Cuban Giants." Meriden, the paper added, "is glad that it is out of a League in which race prejudice is so strong that a first class club is refused admission simply because its players are black."[52]

Race was an issue that influenced the league officials' decision to reject the Cuban Giants' application. Such a move went against the protocol established by the NABBP that dictated excluding black clubs from league entry. However, there were some EL clubs that had black players on their rosters. Before Meriden folded, Frank Grant played second base and was the club's superstar. Jersey City had the flame-throwing George Stovey, while Fleet Walker played for Joe Simmons's Waterbury club.

A more significant factor was the precarious existence of the Eastern League itself. The EL began the season with franchises in Bridgeport, Hartford, Jersey City, Long Island, Meriden, Newark, Providence, and Waterbury. According to *Spalding's Guide*, bad management and a lack of harmony among the league clubs led to its catastrophic existence. Prior to Meriden disbanding, Providence and Long Island had also dropped out of the loop, leading to some efforts by the league officials to replace the lost franchises. Moreover, because of their sporadic home attendance, the Cuban Giants played their weekend games in New York City and Hoboken, New Jersey. Games scheduled at both the Polo Grounds and the Elysian Fields were lucrative contests that the Cubans were reluctant to lose. Because the EL was a member of the National Agreement, it adopted the National League's policy forbidding league clubs from scheduling games on Sunday. The Cubans' reluctance to give up Sunday games was influential in EL officials rejecting their application. Moreover, it was just not in the Giants' best economic interests to join this fledgling league.[53]

On September 13, 1886, Walter Cook announced that the Cuban Giants would not play any more home games. He indicated that the biggest drawback to the club's attendance was the "inferior" location of Chambersburg Grounds, making it virtually inaccessible for fans. For example, the Cubans had an average attendance of 870 fans in their opening season. With ticket prices at $0.25, the average revenue the Giants accrued was $217.50, which meant the club operated at a loss. To recover some of this lost expenditure, the Giants scheduled exhibition games on, for example, Long Island, New York. In three games reported in the *True American*, the Giants' average attendance was 3,000 fans, netting a profit of $450 a game. One game in New York met the club's weekly payroll, plus expenses of $300.[54]

Despite these obstacles, it appears that black baseball was making inroads in the commercialized baseball world. The Cuban Giants' reputation as a first-class club inspired other black baseball entrepreneurs to develop ball clubs that could compete at both the major and the minor league levels. The Giants' marginal success would lead a black entrepreneur in Pittsburgh to call for a "colored baseball league," patterned after the National League.

These efforts exemplified the continuation and expansion of entrepreneurship, within the tradition of self-help that had distinguished black economic endeavors in antebellum America. Despite the sporadic evidence, nothing illustrates this trend more than the continuation of the Colored Championship series of the late 1860s. Furthermore, the efforts to schedule games with major and minor league teams, semipros, and college baseball clubs illustrate how the mulatto elite who became involved in baseball attempted to assimilate into white society. Their efforts were predicated on a strategy that would later be attributed to Booker T. Washington, the doctrine of self-help. Black baseball entrepreneurs focused solely on creating an enterprise that could compete in the white organized baseball world. Their strategy reinforced Juliet E. K. Walker's assertion that black entrepreneurs created enterprises to serve their own economic interests.[55] In essence, to make black baseball a viable commercial enterprise, they would have to go where the money was. This fact meant making the effort to penetrate the newly created enterprise that became organized baseball. At the beginning of the 1887 season, optimism in black baseball circles ran high, but by the end of the season, the window of opportunity began to close.

4

Windows of Opportunity and Mounting Obstacles, 1887

*W*hile the Cuban Giants addressed the obstacles impacting their profitability, several black entrepreneurs attempted to form a black professional league. The marginal success of the Cuban Giants in 1886 led several investors to attempt to establish a Negro league patterned after the National League, limiting membership to clubs in leading cities. The league represented an overtly ambitious undertaking, as black clubs would travel as far east as Boston and as far west as St. Louis. Long trips meant increased travel and overhead expenses, leading many of the prospective entrepreneurs not to make a full commitment to this venture. The unwillingness of the Cuban Giants to join the circuit doomed it to failure, but the rise of the National League of Colored Base Ball Players, more commonly known as the National Colored League (NCL), did further illustrate black entrepreneurs' efforts to advance their economic interests in baseball. It also exemplified the continued effort among black baseball entrepreneurs to operate their segregated enterprises within the fabric of organized baseball.

Simultaneously, the Cuban Giants' management team made a series of moves to increase their profitability. They took initial steps to solve their home attendance problems while at the same time securing leasing agreements at several parks in New York and New Jersey for weekend games. The Cubans sought to schedule more games with major and minor league clubs. A rivalry emerged between the Cuban Giants and the Gorhams of New York, a black club from Manhattan. For the first time, the Cuban Giants' unconventional

According to Sol White, in 1887 the Cuban Giants were the "happiest set of men in the world." *Courtesy of the National Baseball Hall of Fame Library, Cooperstown, N.Y.*

playing style on the diamond became more evident. By the end of the season, the Cubans would be the first known black independent to make an extended barnstorming tour through the West and the South. Moreover, securing leasing agreements in New York and New Jersey, combined with the extended barnstorming tour in the South and West, transformed the Cuban Giants from the ranks of a local club into an elite touring team.

By the end of the 1887 season, as independent black clubs made some dramatic progress, race relations between black and white players declined. Increased racial hostility by whites toward black players led International League (IL) officials to establish a formal ban against signing the latter. The plight of the IL reinforced the owners' fears, particularly in the major leagues, that integrating their rosters would lead to player unrest. Black players were victimized simultaneously by organized baseball's maturation process, as the early minor leagues struggled to achieve economic stability. The threat of white players leaving their leagues, because of the presence of black players, and constant franchise shifting made it difficult for the minor leagues to establish a sound economic footing. The Cuban Giants also felt the sting of racial hostility, as the St. Louis Browns boycotted a contest between the two teams scheduled in upstate New York. Furthermore, white hostility toward blacks—which dramatically influenced owner behavior—and the economic instability of the minor leagues made business arrangements between organized baseball clubs and black independents problematic. Concurrently, black clubs benefited from the instability of the white clubs. As the Cuban Giants and Gorhams exhibited their ability to draw large crowds, one exhibition game with these clubs could possibly meet the weekly payroll and expenses of these struggling white teams. In spite of this precarious existence, black baseball entrepreneurs continued to advance their economic interests in the national pastime.

The National League of Colored Base Ball Players

The National League of Colored Base Ball Players represented the only time a segregated league attempted to operate within the structure of organized baseball. By the late 1880s, several black independent teams were operating adequately. They had developed stay-at-home schedules, operating within a hundred-mile radius of their home base or point of origin. Although the NCL ended in failure, it represented the first time black baseball received national attention in the professional baseball world.

On November 17, 1886, the *Sporting Life* reported that Walter S. Brown, a black Pittsburgh newsstand manager, had announced that six clubs were committed to organizing a black professional league. Brown sought to form an eight-team league, with aspirations that the Cuban Giants would join the circuit and give the league some credibility. However, on November 29, the Cubans indicated they would not join the league, citing long traveling distances between cities as their major concern. Cubans manager S. K. Govern, however, remained involved in the league in an "unofficial" capacity. Despite the Giants' rejection, Brown remained firmly committed to the prospective black league.[1]

On December 9, the National League of Colored Base Ball Players held their first convention at Eureka Hall in Pittsburgh. Delegates from Philadelphia, Cincinnati, Baltimore, Washington, Louisville, and Pittsburgh laid the foundation for the upcoming season. The league adopted the use of the Spalding baseball, and after a lively debate sought protection under the National Agreement. John "Bud" Fowler headed the Cincinnati delegation, and he was also selected to serve on the constitution committee. Fowler would play a pivotal role as a black baseball promoter and entrepreneur. Born in Fort Plain, New York, on March 16, 1858, Fowler spent his childhood in Cooperstown, New York, where he learned to play ball on the Cooperstown Seminary campus. In addition to his baseball skills, Fowler was also a barber. In 1877, he was a member of the Maple Leafs of Guelph, Ontario, Canada, in the International Association. For the next twenty-five years, Fowler drifted around the country, from Massachusetts to Colorado, playing wherever Afro-American players were permitted. He played on crossroads farm teams, in mining camps, in pioneer settlements of the West, and in cities in the East. In 1884, Fowler was a member of the Stillwater club of the Northwestern League, and he and Moses Fleetwood Walker became the first Afro-Americans to play in organized baseball. In 1885 and 1886, Fowler continued to play in the minor leagues, appearing with Keokuk in the Western League (1885), Pueblo in the Colorado League (1885), and Topeka in the Western League (1886).[2]

Philadelphia's delegation was made up of a consortium of entrepreneurs that appeared to have little in common, outside of making baseball a paying proposition. The Pythian Base Ball Association elected the following officers: Gilbert A. Ball, president; Herman Close, corresponding secretary; and Albert J. Reach, treasurer. Robert G. Still was elected, along with Ball, as a delegate to the convention. Gil Ball was born in 1850, and he came to Philadelphia from Virginia at a young age. He was an anomaly among people raised in the Quaker City because of his lack of schooling. Historian Roger Lane argues that Ball found ways of capitalizing upon his youth and strength at the voting booth back home. Politics always had room for "a tough young man who could be counted on to show up at the polls with twenty others who would do what he told them." Ball's connections with the Republican Party enabled him to open a successful saloon in 1877. The saloon was a significant route to power in Philadelphia, where a man could be useful to the police and politicians on the one hand and to his people on the other. In this case, Ball could help "his people" by creating an opportunity for talented Afro-Americans to play professional baseball.[3]

Herman Close and Robert Still also contributed to the Pythians' organizational efforts. Little is known about Close's early background. The corresponding secretary's affiliation with Ball and Still would suggest that he was a member of black Philadelphia's elite citizenry. Robert Still was the son of that disgruntled Pythian supporter William Still. Unlike Ball and the elder Still, who were members of the GOP, the younger Still was an avowed member of the Democratic Party. A graduate of the Institute for Colored Youth and Lincoln University, Still was a reformer, a newspaper editor, and the head of the "Afro-American" section of the Democratic Party. In addition to being a delegate to the convention, Still would also serve as the Pythians' field manager.[4]

Ball and his two associates' business relationship with Albert Reach exemplifies the kinds of business ties blacks made with whites in the baseball business. It also illustrates how black entrepreneurs utilized the cooperative enterprise strategy to advance their economic interests. Reach was a star infielder for the Philadelphia Athletics during baseball's amateur era. One of the first known ballplayers to be paid for his skills on the diamond, Reach turned down an attractive offer from the Baltimore Marylands because his connection with the Athletics allowed him to commute to Philadelphia from his home in Brooklyn. By 1869, he opened a retail outlet in the Quaker City, selling cigars and other goods, including baseball equipment. One of his early and valued customers was Octavius Catto's Philadelphia Pythians. By 1874, Reach's stock reached an estimated value of three thousand to four thousand dollars, and by the next decade he expanded his line of sporting goods, making his emporium in Philadelphia the leading sporting goods manufacturer at that time. He accomplished this feat by farming out products to be manufactured to companies such as the Shibe Brothers, who made baseballs on the side. By the late 1880s, Reach had integrated into manufacturing and had agents around the country selling his brand. However, Reach and another sporting goods firm, Wright and Ditson, found themselves dwarfed, and then devoured, by Albert Spalding's dynamic enterprise. In any event, Reach's association with the new league gave the circuit some semblance of credibility.[5]

On February 3, 1887, the Boston Resolutes and the Gorhams of New York became the seventh and eighth members of the NCL. Little is known about the backgrounds of the organizers of these clubs. The *Sporting Life* reported that Marshall Thompson managed the Resolutes. The Gorhams were formed in 1886 and were headquartered in Manhattan, at a time when many of New York's black middle class resided there. The management team consisted of club owners Ambrose Davis and Phillip Snipper, and field manager Benjamin Butler. According to the *New York Age*, Butler was affiliated with the theatrical profession, managing a "first class concert company." The organizational makeup of the Gorhams' management team suggests that they, like the Pythians, utilized the business strategy of economic cooperation to run their ball club. The Gorhams were a traveling team, barnstorming the nation for gate receipts. Throughout their brief history, the club leased playing facilities as far south as Easton, Pennsylvania, and as far north as Newburgh, New York.

They had developed a stay-at-home schedule, playing white semipro teams in New York, New Jersey, and Connecticut. They secured leasing agreements with park owners to schedule games.[6]

At the same time, Brown made allegations that some members of the older associations were tampering with his players and trying to cripple the league. Under the terms of the National Agreement, a league placing a franchise in major league territory would have to seek permission to operate there. Evidently, neither the National League nor the American Association viewed the NCL as a serious threat and granted them permission to operate in their territory. In addition, the *Sporting Life* questioned whether the Colored League needed protection. In an editorial titled "Do They Need Protection?" it was argued that:

> The progress of the Colored League will be watched with considerable interest. There have been prominent colored base ball clubs throughout the country for many years past, but this is their initiative year in launching forth on a league scale by forming a league . . . representing . . . leading cities in the country. The League will attempt to secure the protection of the National Agreement. This can only be done with the consent of all the National Agreement clubs in whose territories the colored clubs are located. This consent should be obtainable, as these clubs can in no sense be considered rivals to the white clubs nor are likely to hurt the latter in the least financially. Still the league can get along without protection. The value of the latter to the white clubs lies in that it guarantees a club undisturbed possession of its players. There is not likely to be much of a scramble for colored players. Only two such players are now employed on professional white clubs, and the number is not likely to be ever materially increased owing to the high standard of play required and to the popular prejudice against any considerable mixture of races.[7]

Although white clubs may not have scrambled for black players, Brown's allegation of tampering was warranted. There was one man who had a vested interest in seeing the NCL fail: Albert Goodwill Spalding. According to David Voigt, it appeared that Reach "might become the octopus of the [sporting goods] industry." His business relationship with Catto's Pythians illustrates that the Philadelphia magnate had a history of supplying black clubs with equipment. This association with the prospective black league showed that a potential lucrative market existed. This fact could explain Govern's "unofficial" involvement in the league—obtaining baseball equipment for the Cuban

Giants at discount prices. In essence, Reach attempted to corner the market among black independent clubs, revealing how the mulatto elite's business connections with affluent whites placed them in a vulnerable position. Their business venture with Reach occurred at a time when Spalding was making his move to monopolize the sporting goods industry. Furthermore, one sure way to cripple this black league was for Spalding to encourage his fellow owners not to schedule exhibition games with Colored League clubs.[8]

Brown had other internal problems to deal with in his organization. On December 7, 1886, two days before the NCL's first convention, the *Binghamton Daily Leader* announced that Bud Fowler had signed with the Binghamton Bingos of the International League. It is evident that race was an obstacle for Fowler in his efforts to play in white leagues, resulting in his constant movement from club to club. However, Fowler also had a reputation for being an itinerant, leaving clubs for unknown reasons. In addition to his playing ability, Fowler had an uncanny ability to spot black talent, a valuable asset for the NCL. Fowler's signing, however, posed the question of how committed these black clubs were to the league.[9]

Several factors led to a lack of commitment by these black clubs. First, as the Northwestern League can attest, early minor leagues evolved from a regional format. For example, an aggregate of clubs within a hundred-mile radius of each other developed a close-knit circuit. In addition to scheduling league games, contests with top independent teams were arranged on a regular basis. This plan served to generate additional revenues, while at the same time decreasing the amount of overhead to operate a club. Black clubs, like the Gorhams and Keystones, benefited from this arrangement.[10]

If this regional arrangement proved to be an effective way of operating, then why would a distinguished black club that had developed a good reputation risk the chance of losing it, not to mention increasing their overhead expenses by expanding their travel itinerary? Throughout its organizational stage, black clubs from Cleveland and a more notable one, the St. Louis Black Stockings, sent letters pledging interest, but never sent delegates to any organizational meetings. Why would the Black Stockings travel east and play Boston, without the assurance of a substantial guarantee to cover their travel expenses? Moreover, if Boston were a poor team, the chances of attracting gate receipts to turn a profit and pay the guarantee would be minimal at best. It was just not in the Black Stockings' best economic interest to travel that long a distance, if they could do better in a regional format.[11]

On March 14, 1887, at the National League of Colored Base Ball Players' final convention, a lack of commitment on the part of the club owners became more evident. Both the Washington Capital City club and the Cincinnati team failed to turn in their entry fees and were dropped from the league. As a result, Brown announced that the league would operate in six cities and that it would be divided into two divisions: New York, Boston, and Philadelphia would make up the "Eastern League," while Pittsburgh, Baltimore, and Louisville would constitute the "Western League." All clubs would have open dates between league games, to enable them to take advantage of any opportunities to schedule exhibition games. The inaugural season would be classified as an "experimental" one.[12]

In addition to this noncommittal status by the league's entrepreneurs, early indications of some of these black teams' competitiveness against black and white clubs were mixed. On April 20, 1887, a minor league club from Reading, Pennsylvania, soundly beat the Keystones, twenty to four. The following day, the Keystones played Reading tough, although they lost fourteen to twelve. In a brief two-game series with Wilkes-Barre, the Philadelphia Pythians were defeated by scores of twenty-nine to two and eleven to one. However, the Pythians won a close game with the Red Stockings of Norfolk, Virginia, a notable black independent from the South, by a score of ten to nine at Recreation Park in Philadelphia. Results against the Cuban Giants by Colored League clubs were also discouraging. The Keystones and the Pythians lost to the Cubans by respective scores of twenty-one to three and ten to two.[13]

Early attendance figures at Colored League games were also not encouraging. The poor attendance was, in part, owing to the inclement weather. In Baltimore, the NCL Lord Baltimores attempted to play the Mutuals, a black independent from the same city, several times in April. Finally, on April 26, the long-awaited contest was played. According to the *Baltimore Morning Herald*, about 200 people attended the game, and nearly half of them were white. Considering that Baltimore's black population was approximately 67,296, this low fan turnout had to be disappointing to the club's organizers. Major league owners permitted NCL clubs to operate within their territorial markets, and the Lord Baltimores operated in American Association territory. With Baltimore represented in the AA, whites did not appear to be anxious to patronize an all-black league. Of the Colored League games reported in the press, the average attendance was 200 fans.[14]

The final factor attributed to the low fan turnout was a piece of federal legislation. On February 4, 1887, President Grover Cleveland signed into law the Interstate Commerce Act, an enabling act of federal legislation designed to regulate the railroads. On April 24, the *Chicago Inter Ocean* reported that the Colored League had "come to a halt," owing to the Interstate Commerce Act making railroad travel too expensive. Railroad operators charged customers low rates when they were in competition with one another. They also charged high rates when they were not compensated for losses. Therefore, rates were contingent more upon the interest of management, and less upon the length of the journey. The railroads charged less on competitive runs, such as from Chicago to New York, than on noncompetitive ones. Another practice was to favor some customers over others. No doubt this discriminatory practice favored white baseball clubs over their Afro-American counterparts.[15]

The impact of the Interstate Commerce Act upon the NCL goes beyond the scope of this study. What is important here is the NCL officials' perception of this legislation. Ironically, the intention of the act—to ensure that rates were "reasonable and just," and to make rebates and discrimination between places, persons, and commodities illegal—would work in favor of the NCL. Nevertheless, Colored League operators perceived, and possibly misread, that this legislation would adversely affect their operations.

Despite these obstacles, the NCL began its inaugural season on May 5, 1887. The Lord Baltimores opened their season by playing a two-game series against the Philadelphia Pythians at Huntington Avenue Park in Baltimore. The Lord Baltimores won both games, by scores of fifteen to twelve and eleven to three. On May 6, the Keystones of Pittsburgh opened their season against the Gorhams of New York. According to the *Pittsburgh Daily Post*, one thousand spectators attended the game, and "leading politicians of both cities were among the white citizens present." The Gorhams defeated the Keystones, eleven to eight.[16]

Four days into the season, some of the league's financial difficulties became evident. The Resolutes of Boston were stranded in Louisville on May 8 and could not meet their obligation to play Pittsburgh two days later. Prior to their opening game with the Falls City club, the Resolutes had embarked on a fifteen-day barnstorming tour. Unfortunately, eight of those days were washed out by rain, leaving the Resolutes short of money. Resolutes manager Marshall Thompson telegraphed home for money, but none had arrived. To ease the financial strain, the game with Pittsburgh was canceled, and the league rescheduled the Resolutes to play Baltimore, the league club within the closest proximity, but Boston could not fulfill that obligation, either.[17]

By May 25, only three clubs remained in the NCL: New York, Philadelphia, and Baltimore. Three days later, Walter Brown announced that the Na-

A pair of Cuban Giants season tickets. *Courtesy of the Trenton Public Library.*

tional League of Colored Base Ball Players had disbanded. According to Brown, low fan turnout and the Interstate Commerce Act were the prime reasons for failure.[18]

The collapse of the NCL did not result in the collapse of black baseball. New York, Philadelphia, Baltimore, and Pittsburgh continued the season as independents, barnstorming the nation for gate receipts. More important, the rise and fall of the NCL provided black baseball with national attention in the baseball world. As the *Sporting Life* accurately pointed out, many in the baseball fraternity had closely observed the NCL's progress. From as far north as Toronto and as far west as Chicago, newspapers gave this Colored League sporadic coverage in their sports sections. Moreover, the NCL further exemplifies the efforts of Afro-American entrepreneurs advancing their own economic interests. Clearly, Reach's investment in the league served to open doors into the white baseball world, but it was Afro-American entrepreneurs who shaped the governance, devised the schedule, and made the necessary connections with park managers to make this enterprise possible. In addition, if the NCL had been successful, operating this segregated league within the structure of organized baseball would also have served as a means of "elevating the race."[19]

"The Happiest Set of Men in the World"

While the NCL went through its organizational phase, the Cuban Giants' management team made several moves to improve the club's profitability. First, in addition to re-signing the ballplayers, S. K. Govern secured leases on the Long Island Eastern League grounds in Brooklyn, New York, the old Polo Grounds, and the Elysian Field in Hoboken, New Jersey. This achievement enabled the Giants to schedule Sunday games against the top clubs in those areas. Next, Walter Cook and John "J. M." Bright leased the East State Street cricket grounds, a location more preferable to Cook, and built a large new grandstand to seat from fifteen hundred to two thousand people. Having access to the Long Island grounds, the old Polo Grounds, and the Elysian Field, along with Trenton's strategic location between New York and Philadelphia, enabled the Giants' management to schedule more games with both major and minor league clubs. Furthermore, Govern sought to expand the Giants' territorial market by promoting the club in the greater New York area.[20]

Although the Cuban Giants' home attendance did not fulfill expectations, the club's relocation was significant enough to schedule more games with teams from the National League, American Association, International League, National Colored League, and Eastern League. On April 12, 1887, the *Trenton Times* reported, "The new and handsome grounds on East State Street were crowded with ladies and gentlemen." The *Times* praised Cook's effort to provide Trentonians with a roomy and comfortable park with easy access. Twenty-five hundred spectators witnessed a one-sided contest, as the New York Metropolitans of the American Association demolished the Cubans, nineteen to seven. On May 7, the Cuban Giants played the Metropolitans for a second time, avenging their early loss with an eleven-to-four victory.[21]

Another promotional strategy utilized by the Cubans' management team had its roots in baseball's amateur era: the home-and-home championship series. On May 11, the *Trenton Times* reported that Govern had challenged the Newark club of the International League "for the championship of the State." Simultaneously, Newark was in first place in the IL and was considered "the strongest team in Jersey." The first game of the series was played on Newark's home grounds. The game also marked the first time the Trenton press acknowledged the showmanship for which the Cubans were becoming noted. Giants catcher Clarence Williams led off the game with a single to center field. After reaching first base, the *Trenton Times* reported, "Considerable amusement was created by Williams's antics in playing off the base and the ineffectual attempts made by the Newarks to put him out." Whatever "antics" Williams was up to were not necessary, as the Cubans destroyed Newark, fourteen to one. The second game of the series was played at the East State Street grounds the following day. The Cubans took the second game, eight to two, and won the state championship series.[22]

Reaction from the Newark press was predictable. According to the *Trenton True American*, both the *Newark News* and the *Newark Journal* cited poor umpiring as the reason for the IL club's defeats. The *True American* sportswriter sympathized with "the sorrowing Newarks" but added: "We know it's pretty hard to [be] beaten so crushingly by a city one-fourth your size but then Trenton is an exceptional city." The *True American* issued a challenge to the Newark club and encouraged them to bring their own umpire, "and the Cubans will 'do you proper' once more."[23] The Giants' victory over Newark represented a source of community pride among Trenton baseball fans.

Trenton fans would also see two notable National League clubs visit their city. On May 25, the Cuban Giants hosted the Detroit Wolverines, who would eventually win the 1887 National League pennant. Sport historian David Voigt points out that "Detroit had cornered the batting market with its purchase of the big four": Dan Brouthers, Jim White, Dave Rowe, and Hardie Richardson. The Wolverines' hitting exploits on the diamond made them an attractive club to schedule when they were on the road. The Cubans played the Wolverines tough, taking a four-to-three lead into the eighth inning, but a five-run rally in the ninth inning resulted in a Wolverine victory.[24]

On June 20, the New York Giants invaded the East State Street grounds. The Giants' visit to Trenton occurred at a time when the team was becoming one of the premier clubs of the late nineteenth century. Most of the team's success was due primarily to the promotional acumen of its owners, the Metropolitan Exhibition Company. Jim Mutrie managed the Giants; he was a colorful field manager who, in 1884, led the American Association Metropolitans to a pennant. Having a reputation as "the shrewdest and most successful [manager] in the baseball arena," an example of Mutrie's managerial flair was inventing the name "Giants" for the NL club. As sport historian Glenn Moore points out, the name had an aura, and its "value to the club over the years could only be guessed at." The driving force behind the Giants was their shortstop and captain, and later labor agitator, John Montgomery Ward. As team captain, Ward ran the game on the field.[25]

The Cubans were no match for the NL club on this day, as New York drubbed them seventeen to six. But what was more significant about this game was the increasing showmanship that was occurring at Cuban Giants games. Many of the Trenton fans came to see New York Giants pitcher and center fielder Mike Tiernan, a native Trentonian. When "Silent Mike" stepped to the plate in the first inning, the Cubans' captain, Clarence Williams, left his position in right field and dashed into the dressing room under the grandstand. A moment later, Williams returned with a beautiful bouquet in his hand and presented it to Tiernan. The Giants pitcher expressed his appreciation and promptly struck out at the plate. Another surprise awaited Tiernan when he came up again in the third inning. This time, S. K. Govern stepped onto the diamond, on behalf of a loyal Trenton fan, and presented Tiernan with a silk umbrella. Once again, Tiernan expressed his appreciation. Although Silent Mike did not fare well at the plate, he did shut the Cubans out for four innings, giving up only two hits.[26]

The relocation to the East State Street grounds, combined with the challenge for state supremacy, resulted in the Cuban Giants scheduling more home games with major and minor league clubs. However, the Cubans' management team was not pleased with the overall home attendance. Even the press encouraged the fans to come out to the ballpark to show their appreciation for the diligent work of Walter Cook and S. K. Govern. Yet the fundamental problem of scheduling remained for this black independent club. There were only a limited number of games an independent could schedule with major and minor league clubs, because of the latter's commitment to playing league games. The Cubans' inability to schedule exhibition games with the most prominent club of the era—the Chicago White Stockings—further complicated their plight. This match was not an option because of Anson's racial bias toward blacks and Spalding reinforcing his manager's behavior. In essence, the Giants still had to schedule games on open dates with semiprofessional and college baseball teams, who were no match for the Trenton nine. When major league clubs came to Trenton, the fans supported the Cuban Giants, even when they lost by lopsided scores. In terms of profitability, much of the low fan turnout at home was augmented by the weekend games played in New York and Hoboken.[27]

The Cuban Giants' subpar attendance at home was not problematic enough to join an organized league. For the second straight year, the Eastern League attempted to lure the Giants into its circuit, replacing one of its disbanded clubs. According to the *Trenton True American*, the Giants would assume the won-lost record of the defunct New Haven club and, if possible, secure grounds and fan support in Bridgeport, Connecticut. The paper speculated whether the Cuban Giants were about to leave Trenton, but as a member of the National Agreement, the Eastern League adopted the National League's policy of prohibiting the scheduling of Sunday games. League affiliation would mean that the Giants would lose lucrative games in the New York and New Jersey area. Because the Eastern League was once again asking the Giants to replace a disbanded franchise, which obviously illustrated the loop's economic instability, this move was not in the Giants' best interest. Nothing illustrates the importance of Sunday games to the Cubans more than Walter

Cook's statement in the *True American*. He said that league affiliation "would interfere with the Cuban Giants' games at Long Island and Hoboken, every Sunday, and these games are too profitable to be abandoned." Thus, the Cuban Giants' rejection of the Eastern League's offer was understandable.[28]

The low fan turnout did not impact the Cuban Giants' aspirations of going on an extended barnstorming tour at the end of the season. On October 19, the *Sporting Life* reported that the Cubans would make their first road trip west, playing against Louisville; Indianapolis; Wheeling, West Virginia; Cleveland; Pittsburgh; and Cincinnati. Games scheduled against the American Association's Cincinnati club and Indianapolis of the National League were in response to the contests played in Trenton. The Cubans beat both clubs on their home grounds. In Pittsburgh, the Keystones defeated the Giants, a victory that salvaged an otherwise disappointing season for Walter Brown.[29]

Although they did not fulfill their expectations in terms of home attendance, it appears that the Cuban Giants' management team did improve the club's profitability. They scheduled more games with major and minor league clubs, and the team also played lucrative weekend games in New York and New Jersey. Their extended barnstorming tour is further evidence of the club's improved financial status over the previous year. Moreover, neither Walter Cook nor J. M. Bright would have invested their money in a new grandstand unless the Cuban Giants were a potential moneymaker.

Yet the players were still the most important commodity to ensure success. From 1886 to 1889, Govern was able to keep intact a nucleus that made the Cuban Giants the top independent club in the East. Clarence Williams, catcher; Jack Fry, first base; George Williams, second base; Abe Harrison, shortstop; Ben Holmes, third base; outfielders Billy Whyte, Ben Boyd, and Arthur Thomas; and pitchers Shepard Trusty, William Selden, and later George Stovey constituted the ball club that was the pride of Trenton, New Jersey. It is understandable why Sol White stated that the Cuban Giants during this time were "the happiest set of men in the world."[30] But another black club from Manhattan would challenge the Cubans for eastern supremacy.

A Black Baseball Rivalry and Baseball Comedy

On August 15, 1886, the *Trenton True American* reported that the Gorhams of New York had challenged the Cuban Giants for the "colored championship of the United States." Gorhams owner Ambrose Davis had wanted to arrange a series of three games with the Trenton nine, but Walter Cook declined the offer until the Gorhams "had shown what stuff they were made of." Cook's reservation proved accurate; the Cuban Giants demolished the Gorhams, twenty-five to four.[31]

Davis's efforts to arrange a series with the Cuban Giants illustrate the sole constant that linked black baseball to its amateur era: the Colored Championship series. In the 1880s, the battle for black supremacy on the diamond was transformed into a source of market promotion, serving the economic needs of black baseball entrepreneurs. The Colored Championship series also shows how the black theatrical profession affected the evolution of black clubs, and provides the best explanation of the origins of the name "Cuban Giants."

The move to establish the Colored Championship series between the Gorhams and the Cuban Giants appears to have been the efforts of one man, John "Bud" Fowler. Prior to joining the Gorhams, Fowler was a member of the Binghamton Bingos of the International League, but he left the club because of the racial hostility of his white teammates. After leaving the Bingos, Fowler joined the Gorhams' management team. On August 10, 1887, the *Sporting Life* reported the following item:

> The Gorham Club of New York City has leased grounds [in Newburgh, New York] and will make this its headquarters during the remainder of the season. Under the management of J.H. Fowler, late second baseman of the Binghamtons, the Gorhams have become the champions of the State Colored League.
>
> Who ever heard of a New York Colored League; and when and where did the Gorhams win the championship title? There is but one colored organization now in existence that can lay claim to superiority over all other clubs of its race and that is the Cuban Giants Club. They can knock the sox out of any colored club that could be pitted against them.

Fowler had a knack for generating publicity, and he no doubt concocted the notion that the Gorhams had won the "State Colored League." On November 18, 1885, the *Sporting Life* reported that the famous colored second baseman had traveled through the Northwest, performing walking and running exhibitions. In any event, the insinuation that the Gorhams were Colored Champions could not go unchallenged without a contest on the field.[32]

Championship contests personified the cultural characteristics that linked the game to both the social galas of the Civil War-era Philadelphia Pythians and the emerging popular culture of the Gilded Age. Sol White, an outstanding black player of the late nineteenth century and later an entrepreneur, stated, "When teams travel to a far section of the country to meet for a championship struggle, there is always given to the visitors a most hearty welcome." In what could best be described as a booster coalition, an aggregate of fans escorted the visiting team to their hotel and then showed them "a good time while they [were] in the city." In the New York area, such a good time could be found in an area known as "Black Bohemia."[33]

In the 1880s, blacks frequented clubs in New York's Tenderloin district. The neighborhood was surrounded by the striped shadows of the El on West Fifty-third Street. Whether centered in Joe Stewart's Criterion, Johnny Johnson's, or Ike Hines's, black theatrical and sports professionals created for themselves a congenial atmosphere. This congeniality was one of emulation and guildship, an environment in which artistic ideas were born and developed. Of these clubs, the best known and most popular was the one that belonged to Ike Hines. Its walls were lined with pictures of black historical figures, sports personalities, and theatrical performers. Entertainers used part of his club for rehearsing their acts.[34]

Many of the personalities who frequented Black Bohemia were drawn from the baseball field. When the Cuban Giants were in town, they generated a great deal of enthusiasm and, according to James Weldon Johnson, who later became a famous author and NAACP official, "were always good story material for sports writers because they introduced baseball comedy." The Cubans' connection to Black Bohemia posed the question of where the name "Cuban Giants" originated. Previous scholars of black baseball suggest that the players sought to avoid, to some extent, the onus of being American Negroes in their native land. By "passing" as Cubans, speaking gibberish that sounded like Spanish on the field, they would somehow appease the white spectator and ease racial tension. This perspective was derived from a 1938 Sol White interview, in which he claimed that this explanation was given to him by the original players. The notion of easing racial tension was a valid one. The bigotry of white players had gained a wider acceptance by the late 1880s and was instrumental in forcing black players, like Bud Fowler, out of organized baseball. However, white owners in the major and minor leagues saw no problem playing a segregated club when economic remuneration was at stake. What is often overlooked is the impact of the business structure under which professional baseball emerged, particularly the independent clubs.[35]

Baseball must stimulate interest to maintain consistent patronage. The unpredictable outcome of a game has always been its most appealing characteristic. Because independents at times had to schedule contests with teams that were not of high caliber, alternative measures were obviously developed to stimulate fan interest if a game became too one-sided. As we shall see later, during the winter months, the Cuban Giants played in the hotel industry. Thus, the Cuban Giants were cast in the dual role of competitors and entertainers. The social interaction with theatrical performers had obviously influenced their vaudevillian flair on the diamond. Observing Bert Williams or George Walker, two of the biggest black comedians of the era, or watching the top minstrel performers trying out a new act at Ike Hines's undoubtedly provided insights for the Cubans to create their own comic style. More important, Govern's brief acting career undoubtedly influenced the Cubans' vaudevillian style on the diamond. Surely, he encouraged the club to engage in their comic routines when games became too one-sided. The Giants developed a series of comedy routines, including a pantomime that would later be referred to as "shadow ball." This act involved simulating an imaginary game on the field without the use of a baseball. Ben Holmes, the Cubans' third baseman, became renowned for his horseplay around the bag and for doing the cakewalk up and down the sidelines. The cakewalk was a dance in which two couples, sometimes of the same sex, danced to unaccompanied singing around a table laden with two cakes. Apparently, the third-base bag served as a substitute for the table, as Holmes modified this fancy step to fit the environment on the diamond. The *New York Sun* reported that when the umpire made a close decision during the game, the Giants would drop to their knees and clap their hands. Contingent upon the tenor of the game, the Cuban Giants were either fierce competitors or vaudevillian entertainers.[36]

Finally, where did the name "Cuban Giants" originate? In addressing this question, the emphasis should be placed upon the fact that the Cuban Giants were both competitors and entertainers. It is a testament to the players' ability that they could function at a peak level under these circumstances. One clue lies in the makeup of the management and the players. There are two characteristics that linked them to the mulatto elite: occupational status and skin color. Both Frank Thompson (a headwaiter) and Bud Fowler (a barber) worked in occupations commonly associated with the black middle class. Their abilities to self-promote were evident, owing to their connections with white businessmen who either financed their club or leased grounds to them. In terms of skin color, virtually every player, not to mention the ones who played in organized baseball, was a light-skinned black. Thus, the name "Cuban" could have referred to their mulatto status, a stage name exemplifying their vaudevillian flair on the diamond instead of signifying their racial or ethnic heritage. The name "Giants" could have possibly evolved because of their consolidation. Interestingly enough, this merger occurred at the same time Jim Mutrie devised the name "Giants" for the National League club. In any event, the merging of three teams into one black elite club made the Cubans giants among the black independents, as their record against white clubs attests. In essence, the name "Cuban Giants" was a stage name that illustrated their vaudevillian flair and their fierce competitiveness on the field.

The notion that the Cuban Giants sought to avoid the onus of being American Negroes is somewhat problematic. In some ways, this notion suggests that the Cubans were cowards and ashamed of their cultural heritage. The evidence suggests the reverse is true. The sporting press commonly referred to them as "colored," the socially constructed euphemism commonly attributed to Afro-Americans. If the Cubans spoke gibberish on the field, it was no doubt part of their showmanship that was a response to the low fan turnout at home games and to some of the lopsided contests that occurred. Whether the Giants were winning a one-sided contest or losing it, vaudevillian baseball served as a means of entertaining the fans in the stands. According to the *Trenton True American*, some people in upstate New Jersey found the Cuban Giants' "antics" amusing. The *New York Age* reported that the Giants' "comical coaching" would drive any amount of blues away, but the paper was also quick to point out the club's high caliber of play.[37] It should be noted that the Cubans' clowning antics went against the protocol of achieving race respectability. No doubt this buffoonery alienated some Afro-American leaders who sought to construct a more positive image of the race. Such were the kinds of compromises Govern and the players were willing to make to advance their economic interests. More important, there is no evidence that suggests the Cuban Giants sought to disguise their identity. The Giants, as well as the Gorhams, were still subjected, in some situations, to racial hostility from both fans and players, but they, like Jackie Robinson sixty years later, endured. The Giants symbolized the mulatto elite's expectation that by creating a successful enterprise, like the Cuban Giants, they would be accepted into the mainstream of American society.

In 1887, Ambrose Davis, with the help of Bud Fowler, was successful in arranging a three-game series with the Cuban Giants for the "colored championship of the United States." Three games were scheduled with the Cubans at the Gorhams' home grounds in Newburgh, New York. In the first game, the clubs were tied going into the ninth inning. Oscar Jackson of the Gorhams forced Cubans catcher Clarence Williams to drop the ball in his attempt to block home plate. The Gorhams won the game, four to three. The Cubans and Gorhams split the final two games, and the club from Gotham became the Colored Champions.[38]

The Gorhams' victory over the Cuban Giants marked the start of a fierce rivalry between these two Afro-American clubs. It occurred at a time when both clubs were developing a fan following throughout New York, particularly at the old Polo Grounds, and the Elysian Fields in Hoboken, New Jersey. But just when it appeared that these black clubs were making inroads into the white baseball world, white hostility on the field against blacks escalated.

Racial Hostility: A Fundamental Undercurrent

Despite the numerous interracial contests that had occurred in the post-Civil War era, white players were not eager to see a large number of Afro-Americans within their ranks. Since Cap Anson voiced his opposition to playing against Moses Fleetwood Walker in 1883, major league owners did not wish to risk player unrest on their team rosters, or alienate white middle-class spectators, by signing Afro-American players. On the other hand, minor league owners did not fully embrace their major league counterparts' discriminatory practice of excluding blacks, because their uncertain existence made it difficult to carry this plan out. Nevertheless, the plight of the International League reinforced the major league owners' fear that signing black players would lead to player unrest.

No league illustrates the minors' precarious existence more than the International League. The IL evolved out of the Eastern League of 1884. When the Eastern League collapsed, the *Sporting Life* suggested that the circuit consolidate into eight clubs from New York, New Jersey, and Pennsylvania. When league organizers were unable to accomplish this goal, clubs from New York organized into the New York State League. Six cities composed this upstate New York league: Albany, Binghamton, Oswego, Rochester, Syracuse, and Utica. With the exception of Albany, each club finished the 1885 season.[39]

Simultaneously, a group of clubs from Canada formed the Canadian League. This league was primarily made up of cites from the province of Ontario: Toronto, Hamilton, London, and Guelph. On December 16, 1885, the Canadian League sent two representatives to the New York State League's winter meeting in an effort to consolidate the two circuits. At first, the proposal was met with stiff opposition. However, by March 24, 1886, the International League was formed.[40]

The new league established an eight-team format with clubs in Toronto, Hamilton, Buffalo, Oswego, Binghamton, Rochester, Syracuse, and Utica. The IL displayed remarkable stability in 1886. For the first time, a minor league remained intact with its original clubs and finished the season. Each team played nearly one hundred games, resulting in an optimistic forecast for the upcoming season.[41]

In 1887, the International League expanded to ten teams, adding two New Jersey teams, Jersey City and Newark. League officials had high aspirations for the ensuing season and even boasted that they would rival the major leagues in caliber of play. These aspirations were short-lived, as the IL experienced a chaotic season. The expanded-league format placed all of its franchises on a weak economic footing. League officials were unwilling to discipline clubs for breaking league rules. A labor conflict arose when the presence of black players led to an increase in racial hostility. By the end of the season, the IL was fighting for its very existence.

Throughout the season, eight Afro-Americans played in the International League, Frank Grant being the first. He began his career in organized baseball in 1886, playing for Meriden, Connecticut, of the Eastern League. The Meriden team folded in early July, and Grant joined the Buffalo Bisons. Grant was referred to as the "Black Dunlap," a comparison to Fred Dunlap, considered the greatest second baseman of the era.[42]

The Newark club signed two black players for the upcoming season. After the Toledo club folded in 1884, Fleet Walker started the 1885 season with Cleveland in the Western League, but the loop folded in June. Walker played the remainder of the 1885 and all of the 1886 seasons for the Waterbury, Connecticut, team of the Eastern League. It was there that Charley Hackett, who later moved to Newark, briefly managed Walker. When Newark was accepted into the IL, Hackett signed Walker to play for him. One of the reasons Walker was signed was to aid in the development of George Stovey. The southpaw was involved in yet another contract dispute between opposing clubs. Prior to the 1887 season, a controversy arose between Jersey City and Newark concerning the rights to sign the talented left-hander. One of the directors of the Jersey City club tried to use his leverage as the owner of Newark's Wright Street grounds to force Newark to relinquish Stovey. Evidently, after careful consideration, the directors came to the conclusion that the Jersey City club should lose Stovey rather than lose the rent of the grounds.[43]

The plight of black players in Oswego, Syracuse, and Binghamton illustrates how both external and structural forces led to them losing their jobs and to their exclusion. Randolph Jackson's career in the IL lasted only one game. He lost his job, not because of any racial hostility by either players or fans, but because less than one month into the season, Oswego folded. Simply put, expenditures, primarily in the form of player salaries, were higher than the revenues accrued. The club's poor showing on the field led to the Oswego community, which had the smallest population in the league, not supporting the team. A club from Scranton, Pennsylvania, replaced them.[44]

The plight of black players on the Syracuse Stars was connected to events that occurred at the end of the 1886 season. The Stars' ownership was reorganized after a lengthy and costly court battle. The club was liable for the injuries of a fan, John A. Cole, who fell from the grandstand. Additionally, the new owners were concerned over the poor showing on the field, as the Stars fell to sixth place. In direct response to this dismal finish, the club signed seven players from the defunct Southern League after the 1886 season. The move appeared to backfire when rumors began circulating that the Southern League players had formed a clique to force their opinions on management. The directors wanted to sign Charley Hackett, but the clique insisted that they would play for the Stars only if Jim Gifford was named manager. Although the directors deemed Gifford too lax, they conceded to the players' demands. The move proved ill-advised, and Joe "Ice Water" Simmons replaced Gifford.[45]

Along with the southern clique, the Syracuse directors signed two black players, Dick Male and Bob Higgins. After Male was signed in November 1886, reports began to circulate that he was actually a black player name Dick Johnson. In an effort to thwart these rumors, Male mounted a personal public relations campaign denouncing them. However, Male's performance on the field, rather than his identity, led to his release in early May. Simmons, in one of his first moves as the Stars' new manager, signed Higgins. The nineteen-year-old flame-throwing left-hander came highly recommended from Memphis, Tennessee, where racial prejudice limited any career aspirations in the South. In addition to his pitching prowess, Higgins was also a good hitter and excellent base runner.[46]

The signing of both the southern clique and Bob Higgins brought national attention to the International League's race relations. On May 23, Higgins made his pitching debut in the league against Toronto. In an article titled "Disgraceful Baseball," the *Toronto World* asserted that the southern contingent in the Stars' lineup blatantly attempted to make Higgins look bad. Players deliberately muffed fly balls and threw wildly, and Higgins's catcher had three passed balls in a lopsided defeat, losing twenty-eight to eight.[47]

Two weeks later, on June 5, the Stars were summoned to pose for a team photo. During the photo shoot, Dug Crothers, a native from St. Louis who had strong southern ties, and left fielder Harry Simon asked to be excused. They refused to be in the same picture with Higgins. Manager Simmons informed Crothers that he would be suspended for the remainder of the season if he failed to comply. Crothers accused Simmons of leaving debts in every city he managed and then decked him. Crothers's suspension lasted only until June 18; he apologized to the manager and was reinstated. On July 2, Syracuse released Crothers, and before the season ended, he played for the rival Hamilton club and in Eau Claire, Wisconsin. The controversial right-hander was threatening to sue the directors for $125.[48]

No disciplinary action was taken against Harry Simon, a Utica, New York, native. He did not add insult to injury by engaging in an altercation with Simmons. The *Toronto World* suggested that because Simon was "such a valuable player, his offense [against Higgins] seems to have been overlooked." The press emphasized that Crothers's failure to pose with Higgins, as opposed to his fight with Simmons, had led to his suspension.[49]

The plight of Afro-American players on the Binghamton club also illustrates the willingness of club officials to concede to white players' demands. The Bingos were marred by economic turmoil. In an otherwise dismal campaign, their star player was Bud Fowler. William Renfroe, a right-handed pitcher who had played in the first black professional league in the South the previous year, joined him. The first incident of racial conflict surfaced in late June. Binghamton defeated Utica, eight to one, although Fowler was not in the lineup. On June 25, both Fowler and Renfroe played, but Milt West, a white outfielder, and Joe Dilworth did not. On June 28, the *Binghamton Daily Republican* indicated that there was a controversy brewing when these white players asked for their release. The *Binghamton Daily Leader* confirmed this report, but also indicated that information was being withheld.[50]

A few days later, there would be more controversy that would be "amicably settled." On July 1, West was reinstated and played against Utica. The following day, Bud Fowler asked for his release; the club agreed, as long as he signed a contingency clause—he had to agree not to sign with any other International League club. It was a sign of things to come. The second baseman stated that he had received a flattering offer to play for the Cuban Giants.[51] However, Fowler did not play for the Giants that year, and the public would not get the whole story until after the Binghamton club disbanded.

Milt West had led an antiblack campaign in Utica. In an effort to appease this slumping club of predominantly white players, Fowler, and later Renfroe, was released. Fowler's play on the field (and at the plate) and Renfroe's pitching had far outclassed these white players, no doubt shattering any notion of racial superiority. Management's decision to reinstate West no doubt was a tactical implementation to hasten Fowler's departure. On August 8, the *Binghamton Daily Leader* reported that the ballplayers were guilty of insubordination for circulating and signing a petition requesting Fowler's release. This petition was also followed by a telegram stating that the white players would refuse to go on the field unless their demands were met. Within weeks of the telegram, both black players were released.[52]

The International League's problems in race relations were further complicated by the presence of Cap Anson. On July 14, Newark scheduled an exhibition game with the Chicago White Stockings. Anson refused to take the field if Stovey and Walker played. Newark manager Charley Hackett complied with his request. The loss of gate receipts that the White Stockings could generate outweighed any stance for social justice. The IL clubs could ill-afford to alienate major league teams because of their economic condition.[53]

Anson's familiar stance of refusing to take the field against blacks was somewhat less significant in the International League's predicament. What was more important was Binghamton's contingency clause when the club directors released Fowler. On the day of the Anson incident, the league directors held a secret meeting to discuss the "question of colored players" and to transfer the Utica franchise to Wilkes-Barre, Pennsylvania. According to the *Sporting Life*, many of the IL's best white players were ready to leave the league, owing to the "colored element." As a result, the board of directors instructed the league secretary to approve no more contracts of black players.[54]

By the end of the season, the economic turmoil was more than the International League could bear. At the league's winter meeting, speculation arose regarding a proposal to rescind the color line. League clubs were divided into two camps. Those clubs with black players—Buffalo, Newark, and Syracuse— had a vested interest in nullifying the color barrier. The other clubs—Toronto,

Rochester, Wilkes-Barre, Scranton, and Hamilton—were opposed or at least neutral on the color question. The issue would never be resolved, marking the beginning of the end of black players in the International League.

On November 16, 1887, the International League dissolved, and a new organization, the International Association of Professional Baseball Clubs, was formed. Buffalo, Toronto, Hamilton, Syracuse, and Rochester tendered their respective resignations to the International League. Minutes later, the directors of these clubs formed the new association. Because of this drastic action, the color question was never addressed. The International Association maintained the policy of not approving the contracts of black players. However, three black players were reserved for the 1888 season. Buffalo retained the services of Frank Grant, whereas Syracuse re-signed Bob Higgins and Fleet Walker. By the end of the 1888 season, however, Bob Higgins had endured all the racial hostility he could withstand. He returned to Memphis and ran a barbershop. At the beginning of the 1889 season, Frank Grant held out for more money, indicating he would not play for less than $250 a month. His demand enraged white players who indicated they would jump the club if team directors agreed to it. Grant was not re-signed, and the second baseman signed with the Cuban Giants. Moses Fleetwood Walker finished the 1889 season with the Syracuse Stars. The following year, Walker was not on the reserve list.[55]

The racial hostility of white players toward blacks led to the latter's exclusion from the International League. It was a central issue that influenced the club owners' decision-making process. Ironically, when the IL began forcing black players out of their circuit, the Eastern League was trying to entice the Cuban Giants to join its loop. But as the careers of Bud Fowler, Fleet Walker, and Frank Grant illustrate, black players were sometimes victimized by organized baseball's maturation process. A league collapsing or reorganizing, or a franchise folding or joining a new league, resulted in blacks either playing in a new organization or losing their jobs. The early minor leagues struggled to achieve a system that would place their organizations on a sound economic footing. The constant franchise shifting of clubs disrupted playing schedules and detracted from interest. The culmination of economic and structural weaknesses and the racial hostility of white players exemplifies the fundamental undercurrent that worked against black players who played in white leagues.

Fundamental Undercurrent: The Incident at West Farms

The Cuban Giants were not immune to the bigotry of white players toward blacks that had gained wider acceptance in the late 1880s. On September 12, 1887, the *New York Sun* reported that approximately six thousand to seven thousand spectators went to West Farms, New York, to witness an exhibition game between the Cuban Giants and the St. Louis Browns. St. Louis president Chris Von der Ahe had reached an agreement whereby the Giants' management would pay a guarantee of $250, or half the gate receipts if they exceeded that amount. However, the Browns failed to appear, and a game was played between the Cubans and the Danbury club of the Eastern League.[56]

The Browns' boycotting their game with the Cuban Giants represented the first time a major league club reportedly refused to play the Trenton nine. It also illustrates the ambiguous evolution of organized baseball's race relations. On the one hand, club owners were giving in to the white players' bigotry that led to excluding blacks from the player force. On the other hand, as the large reported crowd attests, the notion of alienating white middle-class spectators proved unfounded. The Cuban Giants were a good gate attraction. This fact was the central reason that white clubs scheduled games with them. In an era when white clubs and leagues struggled to survive, a black club who could generate gate receipts was too difficult to turn down. One game with the Cubans could possibly have met the weekly payroll of a struggling white club. Yet the boycott highlights an economic dilemma that impacted the business relationships the Cuban Giants attempted to establish with major league clubs.

Sport historian David Voigt states that Chris Von der Ahe and his St. Louis Browns exemplified a sorely needed "Samson to champion [the American Association's] cause against the league Philistines [the National League]." A hard man to evaluate, Von der Ahe is classified as a "tragic genius" by some. He built the St. Louis Browns into the most profitable major league franchise, only to fall because of fate. Others marginalize his wisdom, judging his success as accidental, and crediting him only for hiring his talented manager, Charles Comiskey. Nevertheless, Von der Ahe did have an innovative side, and in 1886, he challenged the National League pennant winner, the Chicago White Stockings, to a "World Championship Series," a precursor to the modern World Series. He suggested that the entire series be played on the two home grounds as a way of ensuring gate receipts. Von der Ahe was at the height of his fortune and influence, as his Browns had won the American Association pennant in four consecutive years, from 1885 to 1888. As Harold Seymour points out, the Browns' president recognized the publicity value of the World Series, and he welcomed postseason games as an opportunity to illustrate his flair for showmanship.[57]

The majority of the Browns' success on the field was owing to the efforts of one man, Charles Comiskey. The son of a politician, "Commy" developed his baseball skills in college, where he met Ted Sullivan, who signed him in 1879 to his first professional contract. That same year, Comiskey helped Sullivan's team win the pennant. When Sullivan became manager of the Browns in 1881, he signed Comiskey and put him at first base. Von der Ahe also recognized Comiskey's potential, and when the Browns' president dismissed Sullivan in 1883, he chose Commy as team captain, and a year later as manager. On the field, Comiskey developed his own style, which stressed base running and fielding, along with excellent pitching. He also emphasized the psychology of heckling opponents into blind anger. A contributor to the *Sporting Life* described the Browns as: "vile of speech, insolent in bearing. . . . [T]hey set at defiance all rules, grossly insulting the umpire and exciting the wrath of spectators."[58]

Assisting Commy in his unconventional playing style was his difficult-to-manage third baseman and coach, Walter "Arlie" Latham. Latham was the mastermind behind the boycott of the Cubans game at West Farms. A merciless heckler who could talk his opponents into fits of anger, Latham's coaching methods and "free tongue" made him a loyal fan favorite. His controversial style also won him a lot of enemies, and, according to Voigt, the third baseman once found himself scheduled for twenty postseason fights, including five with teammates. Latham's badgering prowess masked his skills as an ordinary player, but won him a large following of fans, though many also condemned his style as being offensive to fans.[59]

In any event, the unconventional playing styles of both clubs provided fans with an interesting contest to watch. The Browns' flair for heckling their opponents was countered by the Giants' antics and spontaneity. If the game became too one-sided, the fans could still enjoy Latham's heckling or Ben Holmes's comical coaching. No doubt Von der Ahe and Govern encouraged such actions from their respective clubs, especially if it resulted in an increase in gate receipts.

However, at West Farms, there would be no gate receipts for these entrepreneurs to divide. According to the *Sporting Life*, Von der Ahe received a telegram indicating that his ball club was "in a crippled condition," and unable to play. Later that same day, the players sent a letter to the Browns' president, signed by everyone, except Charles Comiskey and pitcher Fred Knouff, refusing to take the field against an all-black nine. As a result of the boycott, only a portion of the crowd watched the game between the Cubans and Danbury.[60]

The boycott outraged Von der Ahe and Cuban Giants co-owner J. M. Bright. Bright threatened to file suit against the Browns for damages. Von der Ahe fined Latham $100 for masterminding the boycott. The Browns' owner added, "The failure to play the game with the Cuban Giants cost me $1,000." Von der Ahe was only slightly exaggerating this loss in revenue. If, for example, seven thousand fans had shown up at West Farms, paying an admission fee of $0.25, the game would have amassed $1,750 in ticket revenue. Von der Ahe's percentage would have been $875, but because the game was boycotted, he berated his ball club in the press, stating that it had "been [his] experience that a [baseball] player is the most unappreciative of any class."[61]

What was also of interest were the efforts of two New York papers to marginalize the issue of race in the Browns' boycott. The *New York Tribune* stated that local baseball enthusiasts laughed at a story from Philadelphia claiming that the Browns had refused to play the Giants because they were "colored men." The *New York Clipper* reported that the Browns' refusal to play the Cubans was mere "subterfuge for the champions backing out from their engagement." The *Clipper* also pointed out that when St. Louis had come to Trenton in 1886, the Browns had voiced their objection to playing the Giants, but the game had still been played.[62]

What was overlooked was the prejudice of white players gaining wider acceptance in the baseball world. Because the Cuban Giants were not affiliated with the American Association, there were no threats of reprisals by the other league clubs if the Browns boycotted the game. Therefore, alleging that the club was "in a crippled condition" served as a means of masking the Browns' prejudice. No doubt these clubs' unconventional playing styles clashed with each other. If the Browns attempted to enrage the Giants into fits of anger, the Cubans, no doubt, devised routines to counter this ploy. One tactic could have possibly been speaking gibberish on the field that sounded like Spanish, to diminish the Browns' psychological strategy. The Browns had possibly met their match when it came to showmanship on the diamond, and this club of white players could not accept being outclassed by colored ballplayers.

From the club owners' standpoint, the Browns' boycott highlighted an essential dilemma when it came to scheduling interracial contests. Although Bright threatened to file suit against the Browns, his declaration was probably an emotional outburst at best. Games with St. Louis meant a big payday, and Bright could ill-afford to alienate Von der Ahe with threats of litigation. On the other hand, Von der Ahe could not afford to lose lucrative games with the Cuban Giants, either. The boycott occurred at a time when internal dissension among the American Association's club owners started the organization's decline and eventually led to its demise.[63] Moreover, the white players' racial hostility toward blacks was making it difficult to maintain a business arrangement between black and white clubs. Scheduling exhibition games with the Cuban Giants made good business sense, but white owners allowed racial prejudice to override this economic imperative, illustrating how race prevailed over sound judgment.

Despite the fundamental undercurrent of racial hostility and the economic instability of the minor leagues, the 1887 season highlights the significance progress that black professional baseball had made. Although the National Colored League folded, it placed a national spotlight upon black entrepreneurs' efforts to advance their economic interests in the national pastime. Furthermore, the collapse of the NCL did not mean the end of black baseball. The league clubs continued to operate as independents.

Although the Cuban Giants' management team did not fulfill their expectations in terms of home attendance, they did improve the club's profitability. The relocation to the East State Street grounds resulted in scheduling more games with major and minor league clubs. Combined with securing leases in New York and New Jersey, and extending their barnstorming tour to the South and West, the Cuban Giants expanded their territorial market and thus became an elite touring team. According to the *New York Clipper*, by September 10, the Cuban Giants had played 143 games, winning 130 of them.[64] The incident at West Farms in no way hindered the Giants' efforts to become interwoven within the fabric of organized baseball. In other words, the Cubans continued to go where the money was. Moreover, the increasing showmanship at Cuban Giants games served as a source of market promotion, a means of entertainment when games became too one-sided, and a response to the low fan turnout at home games. However, there was a new frontier to conquer, and Frank Thompson once again played a pivotal role. Florida awaited the Cuban Giants.

5

A New Frontier and New Challenges, 1888–1889

Despite the changing racial climate in baseball, the Cuban Giants and Gorhams of New York continued to operate their businesses as usual. A fundamental underpinning of their operations was to create a demand for their clubs in several locales. The Gorhams emerged as one of the top black baseball clubs of the East, and they challenged the Cubans for supremacy. The Cubans for their part sought new ways to expand their territorial markets during the off-season by establishing a home base in Florida.

In 1889, both the Cuban Giants and the Gorhams of New York played in the Middle States League. The league consisted of six teams: Harrisburg, Lancaster, Philadelphia, Reading, York, and the Cuban Giants. League officials admitted the Cubans in order to capitalize upon the novelty of a black club playing at a big league level. Affiliation with this minor league proved to be an ill-advised move on the part of both the Cubans and the Gorhams. Joining the MSL altered the way the teams conducted business. The issue of race came to the forefront, as the Giants were accused of failing to follow league policy. They also proved to be too superior to MSL clubs on the diamond in the early months of the season. The Cubans' plight was further exacerbated by the league officials' unwise move to expand the league structure and schedule, and by several clubs disbanding less than two months into the season, which resulted in constant franchise shifting and league instability.

This constant franchise shifting, a direct consequence of poor attendance owing to the ballparks' poor locations and a weak bureaucratic structure, resulted in the Gorhams joining the MSL. Because the Gorhams played the majority of their games in Hoboken and New York, Ambrose Davis agreed to move his club to Pennsylvania to alleviate travel and overhead expenses. The relocation proved unworkable, and Davis pulled his Gorhams out of the MSL by late August. In response to the low fan turnout and the inept MSL officials, the Cubans and Gorhams were consolidated into one superclub, with the intent to barnstorm the nation for gate receipts. However, the culmination of the Cubans' leadership transition, the MSL's economic instability, and the rise of internal dissension within the ranks of the Cuban Giants resulted in both clubs dramatically altering the way they did business in the upcoming years.

On June 25, 1888, Walter I. Cook died. The *Trenton True American* described Cook as "a most liberal patron" who took on the task of bringing the Cuban Giants to Trenton, "thus giving the city the best base ball it ever had." [1] Cook's death led to a transformation in the way the club operated during the regular season. The Giants lost a wealthy financial investor who had the team's best interests at heart. Cook's death also led to the dissolution of the Cubans' corporate structure—the separation of management from ownership—and the club coming under the control of Cook's partner, John M. Bright.

Unlike Cook, Bright did not come from a wealthy family. Sol White described Bright as "a lover of the game and a money getting man," and "the leading spirit of his day in keeping the game before the public." However, the *New York Amsterdam News* probably provided a more objective analysis of the Giants' new enigmatic owner. The *News* described Bright as extremely selfish in financial matters and "naturally shrewd" when it came to devising schemes to promote the Giants.[2] He would develop a reputation for holding up games after his team reached the grounds in order to demand a "boost in his stipulated guarantee" when the grandstand was full. Unlike his former partner, Bright's dealings with his players and with S. K. Govern were stingy at best, leading to dissension.

At first, the ownership transition did not affect the way the Cuban Giants operated during the regular season. Govern continued to schedule games with major and minor league clubs, semiprofessional nines, and college baseball teams. He also continued to manage the club on the field and devised promotional gimmicks to stimulate fan interest. For example, on April 20, 1888, the *New York Sun* reported that champion fighter Jack Dempsey would umpire a Giants game at Atlantic Park, New Jersey. This announcement marked the start of black baseball teams securing celebrities to umpire games to put fans in the stands.[3]

Govern organized and promoted an intrasquad series. According to the *Trenton Sunday Advertiser*, "considerable feeling" existed between two factions within the ball club. To satisfy this internal rivalry, Govern divided the Cubans into two teams. First baseman Jack Frye managed one team, while shortstop George Williams managed the other. A series of three games were scheduled in Trenton in the month of June. As an incentive, Govern offered a purse of fifty dollars to the winning side. Local businessmen also got involved in the series, probably as a means of marketing and advertising their products. The Cubans were showered with gifts, such as a box of "Cuban Giants" cigars, a shaving cup and brush, and a pair of "Kangaroo" shoes. Unfortunately, only one game was reported in the press. On June 15, the *Trenton True American* reported that George Williams's Cuban Giants had defeated Frye's Nine, eleven to eight. The contest was a seesaw affair, and because of the prizes at stake, several disputes occurred throughout the game. According to the *True American*, both clubs contested every close call, and the umpire threatened to leave the field.[4] Undoubtedly, the game somewhat tarnished the Cubans' reputation as a "thoroughly disciplined" and gentlemanly club. More important, securing a celebrity to umpire a game and promoting an intrasquad series were responses to losing their wealthy financial backer. Govern recognized the need to develop new ways to promote the Cuban Giants to ensure a degree of profitability.

An unexpected way in which the Cuban Giants sought to promote themselves was their continuing rivalry with the Gorhams of New York. According to the *New York Age*, there had been some "jealous feelings" between the two clubs for some time. Both Bright and Gorhams owner Ambrose Davis waged a war of words in the press over who had won the most games between the two clubs during the 1887 season. According to Bright, the Cubans had won ten out of eleven games played with the Gorhams. Davis, on the other hand, stated that the Cubans had won only four out of five games. Evidently, this war of words did not include the Colored Championship series, won by the Gorhams the previous season. It was difficult to determine whether this dispute over black baseball supremacy in the East was a ploy to stimulate fan interest. The Gorhams were emerging as a black baseball power, and, according to the *New York Age*, they had played fifty-five games by the end of August, "losing but a fraction of that number."[5]

In September, the Colored Championship was determined by a baseball tournament in New York City and Hoboken, New Jersey. Four clubs entered the tournament: the Cuban Giants, the Keystones of Pittsburgh, the Gorhams of New York, and the Red Stockings of Norfolk, Virginia. The winning club would receive a silver ball, donated by J. M. Bright, in addition to being crowned Colored Champion. A series of games were scheduled at the old Polo Grounds and the Elysian Fields. Inclement weather hampered the series, but the Cuban Giants claimed the Colored Championship by decisively winning every game they played. The Giants' dominance on the field left no doubt as to who was the premier black baseball club in the East.[6]

While the rivalry between the Gorhams and the Cubans continued, there were indications that the two clubs would form a partnership. The *New York Age* reported that the two clubs would combine at the end of the season.[7] The purpose of this consolidation was to provide an opportunity to rest the players. Simultaneously, one team could barnstorm the nation for gate receipts while the other operated as a stay-at-home. In one way, this merger was emblematic of the way in which the National League was supposed to operate. The owners were competitors and partners in both the marketing and the promotion of black baseball. The merger could serve as a way to create a demand for both clubs in several locales, thus expanding their market potential. In other words, one club played within their local region, while the other embarked on an extended tour, thus creating a local-to-regional barnstorming format. The Cubans and Gorhams did not consolidate at the end of the 1888 season, but would the following year. Before this plan was implemented, the Cuban Giants established a home base in Florida during the winter months.

The Cuban Giants and Flagler's Florida

The emergence of the Cuban Giants coincided with the rise of the hotel resort system in Florida. In the summer of 1885, Henry Morrison Flagler made the decision to build the Hotel Ponce de Leon in St. Augustine, Florida. The Ponce de Leon integrated a network of leisure activities designed to attract and entertain a wealthy clientele. Such a commercialized amusement system enticed the elite to spend their winter months away from the cold northern cities and enjoy the warm Florida climate. Moreover, Flagler's vision of making St. Augustine the "Newport of the South" provided Frank Thompson an opportunity to incorporate black baseball as part of this commercialized amusement system.

Newport, Rhode Island, was the most famous of U.S. resorts. It was acclaimed as a retreat for wealthy Americans as early as 1729. Cleveland Amory, the chronicler of American "high society," indicates that Newport was firmly established as a leisure center in what he terms "the Southern Planter era."

Rich cotton planters congregated in Newport during the summer months when the city began to decline as a trade city after the American Revolution. After Reconstruction, Henry Flagler and other entrepreneurs sought to bring the leisure aspects of the Gilded Age to Florida. His first project was transforming St. Augustine into a stylish vacation area by building one of the country's most luxurious hotels.[8]

In December 1883, Flagler visited a city whose history was its major obstacle. Established in 1565, St. Augustine was America's oldest permanent settlement. People commonly referred to it as the "ancient city," and among its tourist attractions were Fort Marion, the Catholic cathedral, and the Huguenot Cemetery. St. Augustine also had a reputation as a coastal town locked in time. John Temple Graves, a southern newspaperman, described St. Augustine as a city adorned with "misty garments," whose ancient ruins were covered with cobwebs. That image changed a decade later, and Henry Flagler was primarily responsible for the transition.[9]

Although St. Augustine had long been a winter mecca for the infirm, Flagler saw the city's pleasant climate as an enticement for the wealthy as well. Joseph W. Howe, a contemporary writer, advised invalids and their families that the city had a pleasant winter temperature, although it had more humidity than inland Florida towns. The accommodations, however, were mediocre at best. The most attractive characteristic of the city was its average yearly temperature of seventy degrees.[10]

The origins of the hotel resort system began with the erection of the San Marco Hotel. Upon his second visit to the city in February 1885, Flagler stayed in the new hotel where he met the builder, James A. McGuire, and the manager, Osborn D. Seavy. Seavy, an experienced New England hotelman, first came to Florida to operate Isaac S. Craft's winter hotel, the Magnolia. Later, he became the manager of the Ponce de Leon. As was the custom with many hotel managers during the Gilded Age, Seavy managed the Magnolia during the winter and Craft's Maplewood Hotel in Bethlehem, New Hampshire, during the summer. Through his efforts, more easterners spent the winter of 1885 in St. Augustine than ever before.[11]

The construction of the Ponce de Leon was completed on May 30, 1887, but it did not open its doors to the public until January 10, 1888. At first, Flagler did not realize that building the plush hotel would lead to further development. A second hotel would cater to people who were not so wealthy; the Alcazar Hotel was built across the street to accommodate this group. He also built a casino that contained a large indoor swimming pool, therapeutic baths for treatment of various illnesses, a bowling alley, billiard rooms, and a ball-room. There were also adjacent tennis courts.[12]

The hotels offered a variety of entertainment. Exhibitions in the casino were popular. Horsemanship tournaments were held regularly. Guests enjoyed both tennis and golf. Some of the more ambitious guests visited the antiquated rink in town to watch cakewalks sponsored by Afro-American bellhops and hotel waiters. The evening began with a "back dance," conducted in a brisk, strutting double shuffle with the performers holding their heads back. This part was followed by singing and the cakewalk itself, for which prizes were awarded. In a decade when Jim Crow segregation became more rigid, the cakewalks were an opportunity for blacks and whites to coexist in a cordial atmosphere. Moreover, the resort system created opportunities by which this cordial environment enabled Frank Thompson to bring black base-ball south during the tourist season.[13]

Evidently, Thompson's and Seavy's paths intersected during the summer months in the New England area. The link between them was the Cuban Giants. On January 17, 1889, the *St. Augustine Weekly News* reported that "colored employees of the Hotel Ponce de Leon will play a game today . . . with a pick nine from the Alcazar." The article added that both teams possessed some of the best black talent in the country, composed mostly of Cuban Giants.[14] This club could possibly have been an aggregation of both the Cuban Giants and the Gorhams of New York. Prior to traveling to Florida, the *New York Age* reported that Cuban players Jack Frye and Clarence Williams had been released to teach school during the winter, and the Gorhams' pitcher and first baseman, Sol White, had been released to coach at the Columbia College for boys. St. Augustine could possibly have been the first attempt to consolidate the remaining Cubans and Gorhams into a traveling team. Moreover, this consolidation was another way the mulatto elite utilized economic cooperation as a strategy to advance their economic interests.

Concurrently, Thompson formed an organization called the Progressive Association of the United States of America (PAUSA). On February 23, 1889, the *New York Age* reported a written correspondence by Govern indicating that Thompson had called a meeting "to inaugurate a course of annual sermons to the hotel men that came to St. Augustine each winter, and the citizens in general, upon our [race's] progress the past twenty-five years." A permanent organization was formed, and Thompson was elected president and S. K. Govern secretary. The Cubans' third baseman, Ben Holmes, was also an active member of the association. Thompson lectured his audience on the unpardonable sin of racial prejudice practiced in the dining room of the Ponce de Leon. According to the *Age*, his eloquence received many rounds of applause. At the end of the meeting, Thompson invited men to discuss ways in which racial prejudice could be eliminated.[15]

Thompson's speech typified the race rhetoric that permeated Afro-American thought in the years following Reconstruction. Highlighting race progress was an emblematic way to emphasize economic activity to solve the race problem. This perspective was usually part of a larger complex of ideas that included racial solidarity and self-help. It was grounded in the assumption that by acquiring wealth and morality—attained primarily by their own merits—Afro-Americans would gain the respect of white men and thus be accorded their rights as citizens.[16]

The Cuban Giants exemplified this black enterprise that was a symbol of racial solidarity and self-help. They were lauded for their abilities and showmanship on the field. The Cubans were praised for their gentlemanly conduct and for being a thoroughly disciplined ball club in the white press. They became fan favorites in cities such as Trenton and Hoboken, New Jersey, and New York City and in upstate New York. Such accomplishments should have resulted in the Cuban Giants earning the respect of white men, particularly players and owners.

The formation of the PAUSA exemplifies this notion of black-white cooperation that was prevalent among some Afro-American leaders in the post-Civil War era. Historian Leslie Fishel states that those Afro-American leaders sought to paint "a somewhat idyllic picture of whites and blacks working together for the good of the race and the nation."[17] The racially integrated makeup of the PAUSA illustrates this sense of black-white cooperation that was both practical and ideological. In the case of Frank Thompson and S. K. Govern, the PAUSA served as a means of eliminating racial barriers that hindered efforts to facilitate entrepreneurship. Black ballplayers were to conduct themselves as model employees, waiting tables and entertaining the guests with their diamond skills. In essence, Thompson and Govern's efforts to eliminate racial barriers created employment opportunities for their players during the winter months. At the same time, they also attempted to promote the black game to the white spectator.

The opening of the Hotel Ponce de Leon enabled the Cuban Giants to play baseball year-round. Prior to settling in Trenton, the *True American* reported that the Cuban Giants were undefeated in Cuba and throughout their tour of the South. Govern evidently saw the potential of such a venture on an island where the game had taken root as early as the 1860s. American baseball arrived in Cuba at a time when a transition of the island's foreign relations shifted from colonial Spain to the United States. North American sailors, students, businessmen, and Cubans who had traveled north carried the game back to this Caribbean island as part of their newfound cultural baggage. In 1878, the first official Cuban baseball championship occurred. In addition, an increasing number of clubs from the United States added Cuba to their barnstorming tour during the winter and spring months. The first U.S. team to play in Cuba, the Bitter Hops Baseball Club, arrived in 1881 to play the Alemendares. In 1886, the Philadelphia Athletics played a series of exhibition games against Cuban professional teams. In the following years, various teams and leagues were organized, and "baseball fever" swept the country. This fever pitch made it possible for the Cuban Giants to play baseball in Cuba during the winter months of December and January, and travel to St. Augustine in February just in time for the opening of the resort season.[18]

It is difficult to assess how often the Cuban Giants played in Cuba during the winter months. The limited evidence makes it problematic to suggest that the Cubans even played there in the late 1880s. Furthermore, there is evidence to suggest that the Cuban Giants played in Florida prior to the opening of the Ponce de Leon. St. Augustine was significant because it provided the Cuban Giants a home base in Florida to market and promote black baseball in the South during the winter months. Such a move was consistent with their strategy of creating a demand for the club in several locales. As the 1889 season approached, several events occurred that dramatically transformed the way the Cuban Giants and Gorhams of New York ran their ball clubs.

A Tumultuous Season

On November 19, 1888, delegates representing eight cities in Delaware, New Jersey, Pennsylvania, and Connecticut met to organize the Middle States League. S. K. Govern represented Trenton, New Jersey. Initially, league organizers sought to establish a ten-club circuit with five teams in the East and five in the West. Only one game would be played in each city on a trip, and a cap on player salaries of $75 month was instituted. League organizers admitted the Cuban Giants primarily as a gate attraction. It marked the first time an all-black nine was admitted to a white minor league. Despite its high aspirations, league organizers settled with a six-club format in two states. Five clubs in Pennsylvania—Philadelphia, Reading, Harrisburg, Lancaster, and York—

and the Cuban Giants constituted the new league. In addition, the MSL did not seek National Agreement protection. Thus, the MSL operated outside organized baseball's structure.[19]

The Cuban Giants did not make a smooth transition into the MSL. They did not always follow the league rules, especially if they adversely impacted the Cubans' ability to turn a profit. Playing in the MSL meant sacrificing a number of lucrative weekend games in Hoboken and New York. League membership also meant playing in small Pennsylvania towns, which possessed poorly accessible playing grounds, resulting in poor attendance. Moreover, the Cubans' home attendance continued to fall below expectations.

No event illustrates the Cubans' plight in the MSL better than a two-game series in Trenton with the Reading club. The Giants defeated Reading, ten to three, before a reported crowd of six hundred spectators. With ticket prices set at $0.25, the game amassed $150 in ticket revenue. Because the league rules required an equal division of the gate receipts, or the home team paying the visiting club a $50 guarantee, both clubs received $75 each. The following day, Reading refused to play the second game, so the Cubans scheduled an exhibition game with the Jersey Blues. However, Reading manager Edward Cuthbert asserted that the game was forfeited to his club. In addition, Cuthbert added that he would bring the matter to the Board of Directors, in an effort to make the Giants pay the $50 guarantee.[20]

On May 15, MSL officials called a special meeting to discuss the Reading conflict and other charges brought against the Cuban Giants. The Reading dispute was resolved when the Cubans agreed to pay the guarantee, and the game was rescheduled. The directors then discussed the other charges brought against the Giants. They included not using the official league ball and using players who had not signed regular contracts. After two hours of debate, the charges were dropped. S. K. Govern had promised to follow the rules in the future. Less than two weeks into the season, Govern was called before the directors to address allegations of league misconduct, and the experience left a lasting impression upon him.[21]

On May 22, MSL officials extended the playing schedule from sixty to seventy games and expanded the league format from six to eight clubs. Teams from Norristown, Pennsylvania, and Norwalk, Connecticut, filled the final two berths. These decisions proved to be ill-advised. The league's weaker franchises, both economically and on the field, virtually ruined any chance of achieving a competitive balance. The factors contributing to the weakness of the franchises, including the ballparks' locations, the weather, and Pennsylvania blue laws prohibiting the scheduling of Sunday games, placed the Middle States League in an economic and administrative muddle.

From June 15 to June 25, three clubs—Lancaster, Reading, and Philadelphia—disbanded. The *Philadelphia Press* cited poor patronage, owing to the club's poor showing on the field, as the primary reasons for Lancaster's collapse. The franchise was reported to be $1,000 in debt, and the team's directors deemed it better to fold than run the risk of losing more money. The *New York Clipper* reported that the factors that had sacked Reading included the weather, the distance of the grounds from the city, and the impossibility of scheduling Sunday games because of the blue laws. The Philadelphia Giants management typified the ineptitude of the MSL club owners. Charley Mason, the club's manager, selected his players based on their height, rather than their baseball skills, which is why the club was nicknamed the "Giants." Player heights ranged from six feet to six feet six inches. Furthermore, the Philadelphia Giants operated in National Agreement territory and were doomed to fail. As a result, the MSL was classified as an "outlaw" by the NL and AA and could have been subjected to both territorial and player raids by other agreement leagues or associations without compensation. The Giants' poor play on the field made the club no threat to the major leagues. They had lost all but one of their first twenty-one games. The Giants could not compete for patronage against the National League Phillies or the American Association Athletics.[22]

On June 28, the Gorhams of New York replaced the Philadelphia Giants in the MSL. Their entry into the league exemplified the Gorhams' rise as one of the premier black clubs in the East. Like their rivals the Cubans, the Gorhams had been admitted as a gate attraction. They had also developed their own unconventional playing style and comical coaching. In a game in Connecticut, the *Norwalk Hour* reported that Gorhams catcher and "coacher" Nat Collins would be on hand "to make matters lively" for the Independents, a local semipro club. Initially, the Gorhams played their home games in Hoboken, but because of the travel distance, Davis moved the Gorhams to Lancaster, before finally settling in Easton, Pennsylvania.[23]

The Gorhams' entry into the MSL resulted in race becoming an issue among club owners. According to the *New York Sun*, MSL owners were reluctant to admit the Cuban Giants "principally on account of their color." The owners were further aggravated by the Cubans' superior play on the field. MSL directors admitted that the Giants had been a great drawing attraction in MSL cities. However, league officials also believed that a close pennant race would be a better gate attraction than the novelty of a game with "colored" ballplayers. According to the *Sun,* one league organizer was asked how the Cubans could be forced out of the league. He replied, "On the grounds that Manager Govern [was] violating the League rules by paying salaries beyond the limit which is $75 a month."[24] Govern allegedly paid one player $175 a month. This statement appears to be a gross exaggeration. If pitchers and catchers, the highest-paid players on the Giants, received $18 a week, their monthly salary would have been $72, below the MSL salary cap. Because J. M. Bright was not as wealthy as his former partner, Walter Cook, it is inconceivable that a Cuban player could amass $175 a month in salary.

On June 12, MSL directors held a special meeting, and, according to the *Philadelphia Inquirer,* the club owners denied allegations that the Cuban Giants would be expelled from the league.[25] Clearly, it was not in the MSL owners' best interest to exclude the league's top gate attraction. The controversy over expelling the Cubans occurred prior to three league clubs disbanding in the space of ten days. Economic survival overrode the owners' racial prejudice. In essence, the MSL needed the Cuban Giants more than the Cubans needed the MSL.

In late June and July, both the Cuban Giants and the Gorhams of New York were subjected to character assassinations by the white press—especially from the *Harrisburg (Pa.) Patriot.* Considering that the Harrisburg Ponies were the Cubans' chief rival, the *Patriot* editor's biased reporting was predictable. The *Patriot* editor referred to the Gorhams' entry into the MSL as "an outrage." The editor added, "If [the league] cannot support itself without making it a mixed color arrangement, it would be better to throw up the sponge." The Cubans and Gorhams were characterized as being "dirty foul mouthed ball players," and the editor asked, "[Why] cannot a negro baseball player be just as respectable as a white one?"[26] The *Patriot's* commentary typified the decline in race relations in professional baseball. These Afro-American clubs, once praised for their discipline and gentlemanly character, were now being characterized as immoral and dishonest.

Much of this character assassination could be attributed to the Cubans' and Gorhams' showmanship. On July 18, the Gorhams lost to the York club, nine to six, before a reported crowd of four hundred people. According to the *York Gazette,* the Gorhams disgusted the audience by their conduct. The Gorhams allegedly "waged more objections than the Cuban Giants ever did." Furthermore, Gorhams catcher Oscar Jackson made offensive remarks to the home plate umpire, who threatened to eject him from the game. On the other hand, in a contest between the Cuban Giants and Norristown, the *Philadelphia*

Inquirer reported that the crowd "thoroughly enjoyed the humorous coaching of the Giants and the close score."[27] It is possible that at times both the press and the fans misread the Cubans' and Gorhams' antics on the field and interpreted them as being ungentlemanly and disgusting.

However, showmanship was not enough to consistently fill the grandstands of MSL clubs. The reported average attendance at MSL games ranged from four hundred to six hundred fans. If a league game was canceled owing to inclement weather, the home team was still required to pay a fifty-dollar guarantee. More important, league affiliation limited the number of weekend games both clubs could schedule with nonleague teams. Although Pennsylvania blue laws prohibited the scheduling of Sunday games, the Cubans and Gorhams were expected to fulfill their obligation by playing league games if they were scheduled on Saturdays. Playing a league game on Saturday and then traveling to either Hoboken or Long Island on Sunday would be an expensive undertaking. It would not be cost effective to operate this way. It had become evident to both clubs that league affiliation was adversely affecting their abilities to make a profit. Weekend games in upstate New York were more lucrative than MSL contests.

In response to the MSL's instability, the Cuban Giants and Gorhams consolidated their player forces and formed a traveling team to tour upstate New York. Concurrently, both clubs maintained an affiliation with the MSL. According to the *New York Sun*, neither the Cubans nor the Gorhams were able to accept many dates offered to them by out-of-town clubs.[28] This inability resulted in Bright and Davis merging their clubs and forming the Colored All Americans. It was evident to both these magnates that neither club had to be at full strength to compete in the fledgling MSL. Therefore, in an effort to capitalize on lucrative weekend games in New York state, the Colored All Americans would play there, thus continuing their efforts to create a demand for the Cubans and Gorhams in several locales. The Colored All Americans scheduled a barnstorming tour of upstate New York in mid- and late July. There is no indication of how the gate receipts were divided.

Despite this ambitious undertaking, the result of the consolidation was mixed. On July 13 and 14, the Colored All Americans split a two-game series with a semiprofessional club from Albany, New York. On August 11, the Colored All Americans played the New York Metropolitans before a reported crowd of twelve hundred fans on Long Island. The Metropolitans trounced the Coloreds, twenty-six to four, but even in such a lopsided defeat, twelve hundred fans were a substantial increase over the average attendance at MSL games.[29]

Part of this mixed result can possibly be attributed to the intense rivalry that existed between the Cubans and the Gorhams. In early August, the Gorhams defeated the Cubans in a closely contested game at Easton, Pennsylvania. However, the Giants protested the game because the official league ball had not been used. The following day, the Gorhams defeated the Cubans again, four to three, but there was supposedly a conflict in the schedule because both clubs were slated to play two games on that day. The Gorhams did not show up for the morning contest, and the Cubans claimed a victory by forfeit. Such conflicts undermined any effort on the part of management to cooperate in this undertaking, which, no doubt, impacted player performance.[30]

By late August, the plight of the Cuban Giants in the MSL frustrated S. K. Govern. The Cuban manager voiced his frustration on the pages of the *Trenton Sunday Advertiser:* "[H]ad I to do it over again I'd never enter[ed] the league. We were always in demand in former years, and could go and play where we pleased with a good guarantee. Now it's different. When at home we must pay a guarantee, which we never did, and while away, except in Harrisburg, play for the same sum. Of course, we'll remain in the league according to our agreement, but it is only on that account."[31]

Simultaneously, Ambrose Davis had had enough of the MSL. Rumors began circulating that Davis was going to pull his Gorhams out of the league. It is evident that Davis had gone along with the other MSL officials and relocated to Pennsylvania. Such a decision typified the ineptness of MSL club owners. Both Lancaster and Easton had been affiliated with a minor league prior to the Gorhams relocating there—the former in the MSL and the latter in the Atlantic Association. Evidently, the league directors believed the Gorhams' reputation as a gate attraction would make baseball profitable in these cities. Yet the Gorhams confronted the same obstacles that led to the previous clubs disbanding—the ballpark's poor location, the weather, and Pennsylvania blue laws. Even the Gorhams' prominence and business acumen could not overcome these obstacles.[32]

Whereas the Gorhams may have benefited the MSL by relocating to Pennsylvania, it adversely affected their own ability to turn a profit. No game illustrates this fact more than a league contest between the Gorhams and the newly admitted Lebanon Grays. According to the *York Gazette*, the game accumulated a paltry twenty dollars in ticket revenue. Because field manager Benjamin Butler did not have the full amount to pay the guarantee, the Gorhams' field boss proposed that both clubs divide the gate receipts of the second game. But Lebanon's field manager refused the offer and took his club home.[33] Thus, after compiling a record of fourteen wins and eighteen losses, the Gorhams dropped out of the MSL and returned to New York.

Upon their return to New York, the Gorhams embarked upon their most successful barnstorming tour in their brief history. Davis scheduled several games with the Metropolitans and with the top semipro clubs in upstate New York. On September 17, the *New York Sun* reported that the Metropolitans "had to play hard to win," as the Mets narrowly defeated the Gorhams, five to four. The score was tied at two when the Metropolitans erupted for three runs in the ninth inning. The Gorhams rallied with two runs in the bottom of the inning but fell short. By the end of the year, the Gorhams had played 106 games, winning 73, losing 31, and tying 2. Despite their plight in the MSL, the 1889 season was the Gorhams' best to date.[34]

While the Gorhams completed their successful season, the MSL was engaged in another round of franchise shifting. A club from Hazleton, Pennsylvania, replaced the Reading club, while a team from Shenandoah, Pennsylvania, replaced Lancaster. On August 9, both Shenandoah and Norwalk were expelled, and clubs from the aforementioned Lebanon and Wilmington, Delaware, were added. Finally, on September 9, after losing four straight games to Harrisburg, York disbanded. York's collapse destroyed any hope of a close pennant race at the end of the season. They were one of the strongest teams in the league, challenging Harrisburg and the Cubans for first place.[35]

The constant franchise shifting resulted in the Cuban Giants becoming involved in yet another dispute. On September 14, the *York Gazette* reported that Harrisburg had won the MSL pennant, owing to the Cubans canceling their games with Wilmington to embark on a tour of upstate New York. The *New York Sun* reported that J. M. Bright indicated his Giants would play no more games in the MSL. The last round of franchise shifting triggered this decision. Moreover, gate receipts appeared to be more important to the Giants' owner than the MSL pennant. Two days later, Harrisburg claimed the MSL pennant.[36]

At first, it appeared that Bright had no interest in the MSL pennant. On September 21, however, the *Harrisburg Patriot* reported that league secretary William Voltz had given Harrisburg credit for two games against Hazleton, in which the latter failed to appear. This adjustment gave Harrisburg a record of sixty-four and nineteen (.771), barely ahead of the Cuban Giants at fifty-five and seventeen (.764). However, the *New York Sun* declared the Giants the pennant winner with a percentage of .772 and had Harrisburg finishing at .771.

According to the *Sun*, Harrisburg was credited with two victories they were not entitled to, and should also have been credited with one more defeat. The *Patriot* editor asked the *Sun* to "please tell an anxious public in this neighborhood what two victories Harrisburg is credited with she is not entitled to."[37]

On October 8, J. M. Bright got involved in the dispute. In an open letter printed on the pages of the *New York Sun* and the *Philadelphia Inquirer*, Bright argued why the Cuban Giants should be awarded the MSL pennant. First, he pointed to a two-game series between Harrisburg and the Gorhams of New York. The Cubans' owner stated that the Gorhams had failed to appear for the first game and Harrisburg had claimed a victory by forfeit. The following day, Harrisburg failed to appear for the second game, but still claimed a win by forfeit. This same scenario repeated itself in September when Harrisburg was scheduled to play a two-game series with Wilmington. According to Bright, Wilmington disbanded, and Harrisburg claimed both games in the win column.[38]

Bright now focused on the injustices the Cuban Giants had endured. First, he pointed to two games with the defunct Philadelphia Giants, both of which the Cubans had won. However, both games were thrown out because the official league ball had not been used. The same thing occurred in the aforementioned two-game series with the Gorhams. According to Bright, both games should have been thrown out, but to his amazement one game counted in the standings. Finally, the Cubans had played a four-game series with the Hazleton club in Hoboken, New Jersey. Two of the games were makeup games, and the Giants had swept the four-game series, but the Cubans were credited with only two victories instead of four. It was because of these injustices that the Cuban Giants were not awarded the MSL pennant.[39]

MSL secretary William Voltz responded to Bright's allegations with an open letter of his own. Voltz was not surprised that Bright claimed the pennant for his Giants, but the Cubans were not entitled to it. He first indicted Bright for his Giants playing the majority of their games when and where they wanted to. Games scheduled in Trenton were transferred to Hoboken or postponed to accommodate the Giants on numerous occasions. Voltz added that Harrisburg deserved the pennant because they filled all of their engagements, at great financial loss, and filed only two protests the entire season. On the other hand, the Giants filed nine protests with the league secretary. This assertion appears to be contradictory, considering that the Cubans were charged with numerous allegations of league misconduct less than two weeks into the season. Voltz pointed out that the Board of Directors would decide the protested games at the November meeting, but at the present time those games would not count.[40]

Voltz concluded with some parting shots directed at Bright. The league secretary asserted that Bright's allegations were unwarranted and untrue. He added that if Bright had "any interest in the Cuban Giants, which I doubt, the proper time to make these charges will be when the league convenes [in November]." Voltz alleged that the Giants were not in good standing with the league financially at the close of the season, for the team "had failed to pay its last assessment." All these factors, according to the league secretary, justified Harrisburg's claim to the MSL pennant.[41]

Despite this debate in the press, the dispute over who won the pennant was never resolved. The unwise decision to expand the schedule and league format, constant franchise shifting, and poor leadership made it problematic to render a fair and just decision. By late August, it appeared that crowning a pennant winner was the last thing on the minds of the league directors. Rumors circulated about the need to reorganize the MSL, and press reports called for a league consisting exclusively of Pennsylvania clubs. The call for a state league apparently meant that the Cuban Giants would not be invited back for the 1890 season.[42]

Bright had more pressing problems than the MSL's struggle for economic survival. Since becoming the Giants' sole proprietor in 1888, evidence of internal conflict began to surface among the players. The *Trenton Sunday Advertiser* reported that a fight had broken out between outfielder Ben Boyd and shortstop Abe Harrison during a game with the Brooklyn Athletic Club. Boyd had picked up a bat to hit Harrison when the two were separated and ordered off the grounds. On May 15, 1889, the *Harrisburg Patriot* reported that Govern had suspended Harrison "for conduct unbecoming a gentleman" in a game against the Boston Beaneaters of the National League. Later, Govern reinstated Harrison after the disgruntled shortstop promised to do better in the future. By August, the *York Gazette* reported that Bright was having trouble with catcher Clarence Williams, outfielder Arthur Thomas, and first baseman Jack Frye. According to the *Gazette*, the Cubans' owner suspended one of them as an example to the others. The Cuban Giants were not "the happiest set of men in the world."[43]

On the Verge of a Turbulent Voyage

Although the Cuban Giants attempted to maintain their usual business operations, the death of Walter Cook had dramatically reshaped their enterprise. The Giants continued to schedule games with major and minor league clubs, semiprofessionals, and college baseball teams. S. K. Govern created new ways to promote the Giants to stimulate fan interest. Establishing a home base in Florida exemplifies Govern's efforts to promote the club in several locales, thus expanding their market potential.

Walter Cook's death resulted in J. M. Bright becoming more involved in the day-to-day operations of the ball club. At first, it appeared that daily operations would remain under Govern's control, but by the end of the 1889 season, Bright had become more intrusive in daily affairs. Nothing illustrates this fact more than Bright declaring in early September that the Cuban Giants would play no more games in the MSL. Prior to this declaration, Govern had stated that the Cubans would keep their word and finish the season in the MSL. Undermining Govern's edict no doubt created a rift between the Cubans' manager and Bright. Moreover, the players did not adjust well to Bright's intrusiveness, leading to some player unrest.

Simultaneously, the Gorhams of New York emerged as one of the premier black baseball clubs in the East. The Gorhams expanded their barnstorming tour until it paralleled the Cuban Giants by the end of the 1889 season. The Gorhams promoted themselves through their own unconventional style of play on the diamond. Their consolidation with the Cubans was an effort on the part of both clubs to expand their market potential. Although their entry into the MSL proved unworkable, their year-end barnstorming tour of upstate New York more than made up for their dismal experience in Pennsylvania.

The Cuban Giants and the Gorhams of New York were about to enter another rocky transition period. Both clubs would inadvertently become involved in the MSL's reorganization. Player unrest within the Cuban Giants resulted in rumors circulating that the club would disband. Moreover, while the players in major league baseball were about to revolt against their owners, the Cuban Giants would have a players' revolt of their own.

6

The War over Players, 1890–1891

*I*nternal dissension within the Cuban Giants' ranks fragmented the club, and as a result of the gloomy 1890 season, a war over players occurred between the Cubans and the Gorhams of New York. The Giants lost their co-owner and manager and several of their players, and became inadvertently entangled in the Middle States League's reorganization effort. Recognizing the consequences of losing several of his top players, J. M. Bright began bidding for top players from several black independent clubs. The Gorhams were also unintentionally involved in MSL affairs, losing several of their players. The 1890 season left both clubs in a chaotic situation.

In 1891, Bright expected his former players to return to the fold, but Ambrose Davis had hired S. K. Govern as the Gorhams' new manager. Govern competed with Bright for the best black talent in the East, and successfully persuaded many of the original Cuban Giants to sign with the Gorhams. He devised a sophisticated playing schedule in which the Gorhams would be affiliated with a minor and a semiprofessional league. Govern divided the club into two teams: one to operate as a local stay-at-home, playing games primarily in New York, the other to operate as a traveling team. According to Sol White, the Gorhams of 1891 were "without a doubt one of the strongest teams ever gotten together, white or black." Higher salaries, increased travel and overhead expenses, and the disbandment of semiprofessional and minor leagues destroyed the Gorhams' efforts to operate as a local and traveling club.

A semiprofessional player's contract did not contain a reserve clause, binding him to his club until traded, sold, or released. At the end of the season, a player would have to sign a new contract for the upcoming season. Yet the movement of a black player from club to club, particularly a star player, was minimal. There is no evidence to suggest that black baseball entrepreneurs had a "gentlemen's agreement," in terms of respecting each other's players under contract. Evidently, there was a "general understanding" among these entrepreneurs to discourage players from signing with another team. After all, the Cuban Giants' strength and stability were owing to the fact that Govern had kept the same team intact for four years.

The 1889 season had left a bad taste in the mouths of S. K. Govern and his players. Bright's invasion of the club's day-to-day operations had undermined Govern's influence over the squad, driving a wedge between management and the player force. By the end of the 1889 season, rumors had begun circulating that this great Afro-American club would disband.

On January 2, 1890, the *Trenton True American* reported that J. M. Bright would be the Cuban Giants' sole proprietor and "that Govern has been dropped." Both the *True American* and the *New York Sun* pondered how Bright became the Cubans' sole owner. Several factors suggest that Govern walked away from the club. The Cuban Giants' chaotic season in the MSL constituted the first factor. Govern admitted that if he could have done it all over again, he would have never joined the league.[1] The Cubans' manager did not adjust well to operating the Giants within the context of a league structure. Because of the loss of the club's wealthy investor, Walter Cook, the effort to affiliate with a minor league was understandable. Unfortunately, the Cubans joined a league that was poorly managed by its club owners and lacked strong leadership.

Second, the decline in race relations within organized baseball could have also influenced Govern's decision to leave. By 1890, white player hostility toward blacks had gained wider acceptance. This situation, undoubtedly, made several owners in the National League and American Association reluctant to schedule exhibition games with the Cuban Giants. It influenced minor league operators as well. There were fewer games reported in the press between the Cubans and major and minor league clubs.

The Middle States fiasco, Bright's meddling in the daily operations of the club, and the decline in race relations were more than Govern could bear. Combined with the infighting among the players themselves, it became difficult to hold the Cuban Giants together. Undoubtedly, Govern was the glue that held the organization together. A contemporary wrote in the *Trenton True American* that Govern was a "colored man" with exceptional ability, and that the club would miss his services. He described the former Giants manager as a disciplinarian, which made him unpopular with the players, but this quality was viewed as an asset. After all, "who ever heard of a ball club that amounted to anything without good discipline"?[2]

Despite this transition in management, J. M. Bright began to make plans for the 1890 season. He hired M. E. Fitzgerald as the Cubans' new field manager. Bright adopted what he called "a new system of traveling." In the first week of each month, the Cubans would play exclusively in New York state. In the second, third, and fourth weeks of each month, the Giants would play in Connecticut, Pennsylvania, and New Jersey, respectively. However, Bright's plans would be ruined by the Middle States League's reorganization efforts.[3]

The Cuban Giants' unexpected involvement in MSL affairs began when an attempt was made to place a second club in Harrisburg to compete against the pennant winners. A group of investors, known as the Harrisburg Athletic Association, was well financed and had made plans to secure a new playing facility located in the center of the city. Their biggest acquisition was securing James Farrington, Harrisburg's field boss in 1889, as the club's field manager. The old Harrisburg club, led by Samuel Crook, Fred Ebel, and J. Monroe Kreiter, was outraged by this obvious invasion of their territory. Judging by their actions, they were not about to go away quietly and had every intention of operating a club in the upcoming season. They had renovated the grandstand of their playing facility, and purchased uniforms, bats, and other essential equipment.[4]

On December 2, 1889, at Harrisburg's Leland House, the Middle States League was reorganized and renamed the Eastern Interstate League (EIL). The new league was initially composed of eight cities: Allentown, Altoona, Easton, Harrisburg, Scranton, Lebanon, and Wilkes-Barre, Pennsylvania; and Wilmington, Delaware. Two applications were received from Harrisburg: one from the Harrisburg Athletic Association and one from the old club. League organizers conducted a secret ballot to determine which application would be accepted. Fifteen votes ended in deadlocks. At the evening meeting, a final vote was taken, and the new Harrisburg club was admitted into the league. It is unclear why league organizers chose the Harrisburg Athletic Association over the old club, but the evening vote set in motion the Cuban Giants' unexpected involvement in EIL affairs.[5]

Despite their exclusion from the reorganized league, the old Harrisburg club was determined to operate a team in the state capital for the 1890 season. From their perspective, league affiliation, particularly one under National Agreement protection, was essential to compete against the better-financed

Athletic Association. Furthermore, the old club would have to field a team of equal or better talent, in an effort to lure patronage away from the new club. Although it may not have been known to them, the time was right to sign a disgruntled group of players from the Cuban Giants' roster.

From as early as December 5, 1889, rumors circulated that the old Harrisburg club had filed an application to join the Atlantic Association, which had a better circuit, fielding clubs in Washington, D.C., Baltimore, and Newark. In addition, the association was under National Agreement protection. If the old club were admitted, EIL president William Voltz's plan to have the league under agreement protection would have been hampered. Two clubs could not operate within a five-mile radius of each other. Furthermore, no league or association under agreement protection would schedule exhibition games in that city. Although the old club had every intention of gaining admission into the Atlantic Association, it is also evident that this move was a ploy to cripple the EIL.[6]

From February to April 1890, a series of events occurred that led to the dismantling of the Cuban Giants. First, the old Harrisburg club directors failed to gain entry into the Atlantic Association. The association was experiencing internal division within its own ranks and never considered the old contingent's application. Furthermore, if the old club directors intended to field an all-black team, this decision, as we shall see later, possibly influenced the association directors not to consider their application. If the old Harrisburg contingency had aspirations to run a club in 1890, an alternative plan would have to be devised.[7]

Simultaneously, a change occurred in the EIL's original plans. Allentown could not secure a franchise and was replaced by Lancaster. The league directors decided to operate without Scranton and Wilkes-Barre owing to the travel distance and lack of commitment from these cities' delegates. Wilmington withdrew its application; no reason was given. Although York did not send delegates to the February 24 meeting, it did send a telegram stating its commitment to the enterprise.[8]

At the March 25 meeting, an effort was once again made to place a second franchise in Harrisburg. Although James Farrington stated no objection to a second club operating in the state capital, the application angered the Harrisburg manager, who left the meeting until the issue was settled. It was finally agreed to reject the application so that the league would have only one club in Harrisburg. The league was now complete with six Pennsylvania clubs: Altoona, Easton, Harrisburg, Lancaster, Lebanon, and York.[9]

Although the old Harrisburg contingent failed to place a second club in the state capital, they had secretly entered into an agreement with the York delegates. In late April, the York Base Ball Club filed an application in the court of York County, Pennsylvania, for a charter of incorporation. Historian Jerry Wright states that "Harrisburg Group, Inc.," put up fifteen hundred dollars in capital, allowing York representatives William Whorl to sell five hundred dollars' worth of stock at fifteen dollars per share. With the stock arrangement, Harrisburg Group, Inc., had controlling interest in the York Base Ball Club. The *York Gazette* reported, "Harrisburg people have obtained grounds here and plan to place a team of colored players in a new league." Sol White reinforced this assertion, stating, "A party of gentlemen who backed the Harrisburg Club of 89, secured the grounds in York, and sign[ed] the Cuban Giants as representatives of the Eastern Interstate League." [10] By mid-April, Crook and his associates had secretly signed several of Bright's Cuban Giants and began scheduling exhibition games in York.

Local boosters made several civic improvements in order to make the York Colored Monarchs a paying proposition. They renovated the grandstand and made efforts to improve transportation to and from the playing facility. Captain Lanius, a streetcar company magnate, began running extra cars to accommodate spectators at the exhibition games. Local boosters sold commutation tickets, which enabled a customer to ride the streetcar and gain admission to the game. Five dollars purchased a book of twenty-five tickets, which could be bought at various stores within the York community. These boosters' investment in the York Colored Monarchs exemplifies a phenomenon that became more prevalent in the post-World War II era—civic improvements to lure a professional franchise to their growing city. [11]

On May 7, 1890, the boosters held a town meeting to discuss the Colored Monarchs' financial state up to that time. The early turn on their investment looked promising. According to the *York Gazette*, the Colored Monarchs were worth two hundred dollars "in hard cash," and they had been playing to large audiences. They added that if a former York club, known as the Keystones, had "started out as propitiously as did this club it would have been a very successful venture in a pecuniary sense." Efforts were made to improve the club's profitability. Club officials agreed to sell fifty shares of stock to the public at a par value of twenty-five dollars per share. [12] In essence, the Colored Monarchs had become a community-based venture. It was an ironic business arrangement in the late nineteenth century: a town that had a heavily German-influenced population financially supported an Afro-American ball club.

Selling stock to the public to raise funds served as a means of signing more talented black players. York officials targeted Frank Grant, one of the most talented black players of the late nineteenth century. However, Harrisburg was also interested in signing Grant, resulting in a controversy between the two clubs. York filed a protest with league president William Voltz, and filed suit in Harrisburg's municipal court before Judge Joseph Simonton. On May 19, Voltz ruled in favor of Harrisburg; Judge Simonton reinforced this decision on June 7 by ruling in favor of the Ponies. In response to losing Grant, York officials persuaded several players on the Gorhams' roster to jump their contracts. They signed Sol White, Andy Jackson, Oscar Jackson, and catcher William Jackson of Detroit. As a means of operating a ball club, Harrisburg Group, Inc., had completely dismantled the rosters of both the Cuban Giants and the Gorhams of New York.[13]

This business arrangement between Harrisburg Group, Inc., and the York boosters, however, ended in failure. Several factors contributed to its demise. First, attendance at York home games did not reach expectations. On June 16, 1890, the *York Gazette* reported that the Colored Monarchs could possibly be transferred to Reading if attendance did not improve. According to published attendance figures in the press, York's average attendance was 829 fans. With ticket prices set at $0.15, the Colored Monarchs amassed on average $125.35 in ticket revenue. The league required the home team to pay either 40 percent of the gate receipts or a $65 guarantee. After deducting the visitor's share, York's average revenue was $60.35 per game.[14] In essence, the club was operating at a loss. It is evident that York officials had to pay higher salaries to lure these talented black players away from their old clubs. It is also apparent that the York community was not ready to patronize a club of colored ballplayers. More important, the York situation illustrates how problematic it was for a city with a small urban base to sustain a commercialized amusement.

To add insult to injury, the Colored Monarchs played to larger crowds on the road. The Monarchs averaged 1,550 fans at away games, generating $232.50 in ticket revenue, with tickets priced at $0.15 each. York received 40 percent of this gross ($93.00), while the home team kept $139.50. The Monarchs made more money on the road, and they generated more revenue for the other league clubs. Higher salaries and travel and overhead expenses diminished any profits the club could realize.

York was also plagued by the EIL's overall instability and weak administration. For the second straight year, several clubs disbanded in a short period, hampering the league. On May 26, Lancaster disbanded and was replaced by

Allentown. By July 6, both Allentown and Easton disbanded. Allentown's manager, Charley Mason, mysteriously left town owing his players a month's salary. (This Charley Mason was the same one who had chosen his players based on their height, instead of their playing ability, when he managed the Philadelphia Giants the previous season.) All these clubs pointed to poor attendance as the reason for their demise. EIL club owners were dissatisfied with President William Voltz's administration of league affairs. According to the *Philadelphia Inquirer*, a meeting was called on June 8 for the purpose of deposing him. Voltz was allegedly more concerned about his salary than rehabilitating the league, but because the league was falling apart, no successor was named.[15]

Finally, the Harrisburg Ponies' jump to the Atlantic Association constituted the final factor leading to York's demise. The loss of Harrisburg led to the Eastern Interstate League folding. York fans felt Harrisburg had jumped to the association to be saved from the embarrassment of possibly losing the pennant. By late July, the Monarchs were in first place with only Harrisburg still challenging them for the pennant. Harrisburg, however, had filed an application with the Atlantic Association in late June. But because of the club's black players, Clarence Williams and Frank Grant, the association was reluctant to accept the Ponies. To remedy the situation, Harrisburg's directors negotiated a compromise whereby they would retain Grant and release Williams.[16]

In response to the EIL disbanding, the York Colored Monarchs completed the 1890 season as an independent. York fans were incensed when Crook and his associates elected to move the club to Harrisburg. From the state capital, they maintained their York affiliation and barnstormed the state of Pennsylvania for gate receipts. Efforts were made to schedule weekend games in New York City, but met with no success. By the end of the season, the Monarchs had reportedly traveled more than six thousand miles in Pennsylvania and New Jersey, compiling a record of eighty-eight wins and twenty-seven losses.[17]

Salvaging a Turbulent Season

Although the majority of the player force that once composed the Cuban Giants languished in York, Pennsylvania, J. M. Bright managed to field a club for the 1890 season. Much like his York competitors, Bright engaged in the same activity of encouraging black players to jump their contracts, no doubt at great expense. Paying higher salaries substantially reduced any profit Bright might have realized. The Cubans' owner signed several top players from the Boston Resolutes and the Keystones of Pittsburgh. Apparently, persuading these players to jump their contracts marked the end of those black clubs. With this revamped club, Bright scheduled games throughout New York and New Jersey, winning eighty games and losing twenty-four.[18]

On the other hand, the Gorhams' season was a total disaster. Decimated by player jumping, the Gorhams were relegated to a weekend enterprise. Evidently, this dismal campaign resulted in a rift between Ambrose Davis and Benjamin Butler. By September, the *New York Sun* was referring to Butler as the Gorhams' ex-manager. To salvage something from this tumultuous season, Butler challenged the Cuban Giants to a three-game series. The Gorhams "ex-manager" wrote the *New York Sun* and stated that he would "match the Gorhams against the Cuban Giants to play the best two out of three games for $100 on the Polo Grounds." In response, Bright asked Butler why he had waited until the end of the season to challenge the Cubans when most of his players had gone home. According to Bright, Butler should have challenged the Cubans a week sooner, or waited until spring when the Giants were intact. Despite Bright's reluctance, the Cuban Giants did play one game with the Gorhams at Monitor Park. The contest was over by the fourth inning when the Cubans erupted for seven runs en route to an eleven-to-two victory.[19] For the Gorhams, the defeat was a fitting conclusion to a season where nothing went right for this once prominent black club.

By the end of the 1890 season, the future of both the Cuban Giants and the Gorhams of New York was mired in uncertainty. Would the players who played in York return to either the Giants or the Gorhams? Would Bright or Davis attempt to field a club for the upcoming season? Finally, would they operate as an independent or attempt to join a white minor league?

Warring Factions in 1891

With the dismal 1890 campaign behind him, J. M. Bright made preparations for the upcoming season by devising a unique scheduling arrangement. He proposed a scheduling format in which the Giants would play on five different grounds, one for each day of the week except Saturday and Sunday. Weekend games were reserved exclusively for Long Island grounds. Bright also attempted to secure a playing facility in Connecticut, so the Cubans could "hustle the clubs in that state for the semiprofessional championship."[20]

Simultaneously, local boosters in Altoona, Pennsylvania, attempted to lure the Cuban Giants to their city. Altoona was one of the only EIL cities that drew well at home. A group known as the Driving Park Association believed that baseball could be a profitable enterprise if it could persuade the York Colored Monarchs to relocate to Altoona. The association proposed to renovate the grounds and grandstand and retain the revenue generated from them. Bright and his new associate, E. K. Myers from Harrisburg, would furnish the club and collect all gate receipts other than the grandstand. The deal was contingent upon Bright's ability to re-sign the original Cuban Giants and the city of Altoona improving the rapid transit to and from the playing grounds.[21]

While Myers attempted to negotiate this deal with Altoona's civic boosters, Bright made preparations to join the newly formed New York Semi-Professional League (NYSPL). The NYSPL was composed of six clubs: the Flushings, Senators, Allertons, Monroes, Cuban Giants, and Gorhams. Ambrose Davis represented the Gorhams. According to the *New York Clipper*, the Cubans and Gorhams were admitted because both clubs had secured playing grounds in the New York area. Each club was required to pay a deposit (one hundred dollars for clubs with playing facilities, fifty dollars for teams without them) to ensure that each team played the entire season. As an incentive, the deposit would be returned at the end of the campaign. Ticket prices were fixed at twenty cents, and no league club was allowed to play exhibition games during the season.[22] The latter stipulation would be a source of controversy for the Cubans and Gorhams.

While these New York clubs organized into a semipro circuit, delegates representing several cities in the state of Connecticut came together to form a minor league. From the outset, these delegates were a divided group, resulting in two leagues being organized: the Connecticut State League (CSL) and the Central Connecticut League (CCL). On March 4, three clubs—Waterbury, Hartford, and Bridgeport—formed the Connecticut State League. On the same day, delegates from Meriden, West Haven, New Britain, Portland, and Wallingford formed the Central Connecticut League.[23]

The central issue that divided these delegates into two minor leagues was gate receipts. Delegates that organized the CCL favored an equal distribution of gate receipts. On the other hand, in the CSL a plan was proposed whereby the visiting team received 40 percent of the gate receipts and the home team 50 percent, and the remaining 10 percent would be sent to the league as an incentive to play out the season. Waterbury delegates emphatically rejected this plan. Such an arrangement was out of the question.[24]

The Cuban Giants became a member of the Central Connecticut League within this context of disharmony and uncertainty, which ironically led to both leagues merging. Concurrently, longtime Cubans rival the Metropolitans joined the CSL, and they would later join the NYSPL. In any event, the Cuban Giants would at first represent Norwich in the CCL, before finally settling in Ansonia. On April 29, both the CSL and the CCL consolidated into the Connecticut League. It is unclear why both leagues decided to merge. According to the *Sporting Life*, the CCL possessed "several desirable towns" that the CSL coveted. Both leagues were unstable from the outset, and the CCL made advances to the CSL to discuss a possible merger. After a short debate, both leagues agreed to merge, and J. M. Bright served on the scheduling committee.[25]

By May, it appeared that Bright's plans were going to materialize. He had secured grounds in the New York area and become affiliated with a semipro league in Gotham and a minor league in Connecticut. Bright still had aspirations of securing grounds in Altoona, thus establishing a territorial market in which the Cuban Giants would play games in New York, Pennsylvania, and Connecticut. But whatever bliss the Cubans' owner may have experienced was short-lived.

On May 2, the *New York Sun* reported that S. K. Govern had become the Gorhams' manager.[26] Govern quickly made arrangements whereby the Gorhams would represent Norwalk in the Connecticut League. As the Gorhams had already joined the NYSPL, Govern then began scheduling additional games with the top semipro clubs, to the dismay of NYSPL officials. In order to reach this objective, the best black talent in the East would have to be acquired, particularly the players who had once constituted the York Colored Monarchs.

At first, it appeared that Bright and Govern had signed an equal number of the original Cuban Giants to their respective clubs. Clarence Williams, Ben Boyd, and Ben Holmes re-signed with the Cubans. In addition, Bright had signed Sol White, George Stovey, William Jackson, and Frank Grant. Govern signed George Williams, William Selden, and William Malone. Former Gorhams players Andy Jackson, Oscar Jackson, Nat Collins, and George Evans were also re-signed.

By May 20, rumors began circulating that several Cuban Giants players would jump to the Gorhams. According to the *New York Sun*, George Stovey had already jumped to the Gorhams, and Clarence Williams and Frank Grant intended to give Bright the "razzle dazzle." When asked to respond to these rumors, Williams and Grant were puzzled. They had no intentions of jumping to the Gorhams. The following day, the *Sun* stated that they had exposed Williams and Grant's scheme "to pull the wool over their [manager's] eyes." Reportedly, Bright was surprised by the news that both players planned to leave his club.[27] Williams did jump to the Gorhams, and Grant soon followed.

Without question, S. K. Govern persuaded these players to jump their contracts. Such action was in retaliation for the Gorhams manager's past relationship with Bright that had gone sour before the 1890 season began. Moreover, the players' relationship with Bright was a negative one, a central reason they jumped to York in the first place. If the players had an opportunity to play for another club, particularly one that offered a higher salary, they would play for that team. Govern recognized this fact, and he capitalized on the opportunity. By July, he had secured the services of the best black talent in the East. It is understandable why Sol White stated that this Gorhams club was one of the best, "black or white."[28] It was an impressive list that included the original Cuban Giants: Clarence Williams, George Williams, Arthur Thomas, Ben Holmes, William Selden, and William Malone. Govern also signed the Gorhams' top players: Andy Jackson, Oscar Jackson, Nat Collins, Sol White, and George Evans. When George Stovey and Frank Grant were added, Govern attempted to field both a local stay-at-home and a traveling team, in an effort to maximize the profit potential of such a talented club.

Convincing these players to jump their contracts had an adverse effect upon the Cubans' and Gorhams' scheduling arrangements. Obviously, Bright's business arrangement with Altoona's Driving Park Association fell through when he could not deliver the original Cuban Giants. The Cubans and Gorhams angered the member clubs of the NYSPL because of the constant quarreling over players. Evidently, the league had a reserve list, and both clubs had a tendency to play ineligible players, the Cubans being the worst offender. According to the *New York Sun*, in one game the Giants had a player named "Washington" playing left field in a league game.[29] It was learned later that "Washington" was actually Gorhams infielder George Evans, playing under an assumed name. Such actions resulted in other league clubs filing protests against the Cubans and Gorhams.

Simultaneously, things were not going well in the Connecticut League, either. The Cubans and Gorhams were playing to small, practically nonexistent crowds, and both clubs threatened to relocate, but the constant internal dissension and ineptitude among the club owners tarnished this league. League directors failed to discipline players or team officials for breaking league rules, and club owners refused to follow the schedules they had established. By June 15, the Connecticut League club owners voted to disband.[30]

By mid-July, the New York Semi-Professional League collapsed. Much like the Connecticut League, club owners had failed to abide by their own league rules. Both the Metropolitans and the Gorhams were expelled, and when "trouble" arose with Bright's Cuban Giants, the league disbanded on July 19. Because the club owners did not follow their own league rules, it is unclear why the Metropolitans and Gorhams were targeted for expulsion. Using ineligible players probably led to both clubs' quick exodus from the league. Nevertheless, less than two and one-half months into the regular season, the Cubans and Gorhams once again operated as independents. It marked the end of both clubs' efforts to affiliate with either a minor or a semiprofessional league.[31]

Upon their return as an independent, the Gorhams, according to the *New York Sun*, had won forty-one straight games. However, winning did not ensure profitability. Throughout the 1891 season, the Gorhams' average attendance in the New York area was 1,089 fans. With ticket prices set at $0.20, the club from Gotham amassed an average revenue of $217.80. After subtracting the visitor's share ($87.12), the Gorhams brought in $130.68 in ticket revenue.[32] The Gorhams' 1891 season illustrates the importance of scheduling a significant number of games in a metropolitan area. Black baseball clubs, like their white counterparts, needed a large urban base to sustain their economic viability.

Playing games outside the New York area told a different story. If the Gorhams' plight in Harrisburg was any indication, road trips became an expensive undertaking. For example, the Gorhams played a single game with the Philadelphia Athletics and two games with the Cuban Giants at Harrisburg's Island Grounds. The three games averaged 600 fans, amassing $120.00 in ticket revenue. After subtracting the visitor's share ($65.00), the Gorhams earned $55.00 in ticket revenue, resulting in the club operating at a loss.[33]

Higher expenses also marred the Gorhams' profitability. They had to pay higher salaries to keep their talented club together. Attempting to operate as a local club and traveling team resulted in increased travel and overhead expenses. Road trips could also be a frustrating experience if the Gorhams had to endure the racial prejudices of hotel owners. Sol White stated that black players confronted "great inconveniences, at times, while traveling." He added that it was "common for [black clubs] to arrive in a city late at night and walk around for several hours before getting a place to lodge."[34] Part of this inconvenience could possibly have been attributed to management's inability to pay for hotel accommodations. In any event, the Gorhams also had to pay for uniforms, equipment, and rent for playing facilities. Incurring these expenses no doubt eroded any profits this black club could realize. Although the concept of simultaneously operating as a stay-at-home and traveling team was commendable in theory, it turned out to be economically unfeasible. More important, the Gorhams' plight in 1891 would be typical of many great black clubs in the early twentieth century who accumulated tremendous won-lost records. An impressive winning record did not always translate into a profitable season.

Aftermath: Toward the Age of Accommodation

The Cuban Giants' and Gorhams' return to independent ball marked the end of an era that Sol White referred to as "the money period." Afro-American entrepreneurs who organized black independent clubs developed business ties by scheduling exhibition games with major and minor league clubs, semiprofessionals, and college baseball teams. They followed a simple business strategy of going where the money was to advance their economic interests. Black entrepreneurs managed to sustain a commercial enterprise in spite of the numerous obstacles they confronted, but by the end of the 1891 season, the window of opportunity, in terms of maintaining business ties with major and minor league clubs, began to close. Moreover, the fundamental obstacle—race—continued to cripple the ways black and white clubs conducted business.

It is well documented that racism has run like a dark thread throughout U.S. history, tarnishing the lives of many Afro-Americans. Racial animosity, however, has varied in intensity over both place and time. Its effects have been channeled in distinctive ways, particularly in the evolution of baseball's development into a commercialized amusement.

The issue of race becomes even more complex and confusing when it is examined within the context of a developing commercial enterprise. The Cuban Giants exemplified this complexity. In many ways, the Cubans were the exception to the black clubs that emerged in the 1880s. Their partnership with a wealthy white investor enabled manager S. K. Govern to capitalize upon certain advantages that other black clubs did not have. Walter Cook's civic ties with the Trenton community allowed Govern to establish a home base, while at the same time barnstorming the nation for gate receipts. Undoubtedly, white ownership was essential for the Cubans to schedule games with major and minor league clubs. They would, more than any other black club of the era, play more games with organized baseball clubs. This situation was due primarily because the Giants could ensure a higher guarantee than most black clubs. None of these aspirations could have been realized without the financial support Cook provided. Although this business relationship disintegrated after Cook's death, it did mark the start of white influence in the ownership of black clubs.

The Gorhams of New York typified the black clubs of the 1880s. The Gorhams began as a traveling team, and at times they attempted to establish a home base by securing a leasing agreement for a playing facility in a particular city. But this arrangement would turn out to be a bad business move if the city did not have adequate transportation to and from the facility. The arrangement was further exacerbated if the Gorhams scheduled subpar teams at home. Therefore, barnstorming became the Gorhams' lifeblood in terms of their economic existence, and a precarious one at that. Furthermore, because the Gorhams were black-owned and -operated, they were considered a second-class club. Despite their record against top-level white clubs, such as the Metropolitans, the Gorhams were never recognized on the same level as their rival, the Cuban Giants.[35]

White player hostility toward blacks and organized baseball's maturation process resulted in severing the business ties between black and white clubs. This statement is not to suggest that white owners did not have racial animosity toward blacks. After all, at no time did National League clubs have black players on their rosters. White owners fought wars over white players, especially if they would help win a pennant and generate profits. Simultaneously, they conveniently allowed the white players to shape their policy on race relations. It was acceptable to play black clubs as long as there was no outcry from the white players. The owners' behavior was further influenced by the plight of the black players in the International League in 1887. From the owners' perspective, it was not in their best economic interest to employ blacks or schedule games with black clubs. Thus, it was race, not economics, that dramatically influenced this policy.

The players' revolt of 1889 and the subsequent National League war with the American Association further severed the business relationship between black and white clubs. The rise of the Players League was in response to the hated reserve clause. When the NL owners crushed the Players League, a second war over players emerged between the National League and the American Association. The second association war resulted in both major leagues raiding the minor leagues of their top players, causing several leagues to disband or end up in a crippled state. The association was in no position to endure a second war over players and eventually capitulated. The NL absorbed four association clubs—St. Louis, Baltimore, Washington, and Louisville—and formed a twelve-club National League. Combined with the internal problems occurring between the Cuban Giants and Gorhams, in terms of their ownership transition and war over players, hardly any games were scheduled with major league clubs after the 1891 season.[36]

Yet it was still race, not economics or structural development, that dramatically influenced the business relationship between black and white clubs. Nothing illustrates this fact more than club ownership. As the Gorhams' and Cubans' plight in the minor leagues illustrates, many white club owners were inept and lacked the business acumen to run a baseball club. Their incompetence affected the way the Cubans and Gorhams operated within a league format. S. K. Govern and Ambrose Davis would have never become major league owners, even though the former partnered with a wealthy white businessman. Both men demonstrated their business savvy over a period of years when some clubs or leagues did not last three months. These Afro-American owners confronted obstacles that most white major or minor league owners never endured. As the emergence of baseball comedy illustrates, Govern and Davis had to be more innovative in their marketing and promotion of black baseball.

In spite of Davis's and Govern's business acumen, white owners (in the major or minor leagues) never accepted or recognized these black owners as good businessmen. White owners were well aware of these Afro-Americans' competence, and some had even done business with them. However, in many ways the acceptance of Davis and Govern as competent businessmen would have suggested that a sense of equality existed between black and white men. White owners in the late nineteenth century would never come to terms with such an assertion. More important, baseball's pattern of race discrimination and exclusion illustrates the kind of systemic racism that could occur within a business or industry. The collusive nature of organized baseball's business practices fostered an environment in which institutionalized racism could thrive.

Govern's and Davis's success, however, would also lead to their demise. Developing these successful teams would, for the first time, attract white interest to the ownership of black teams. Despite the numerous obstacles, a top-level black club proved to be a potentially lucrative enterprise. Throughout the 1880s, black owners had to seek out white park owners, or businessmen with civic ties, to secure playing facilities. White owners in Harrisburg seized the opportunity to lure the Cuban Giants away from J. M. Bright at a time when the club was mired in internal strife. Moreover, the Cubans' experience in York reinforces Steven Riess's assertion regarding traction magnates having the necessary capital to sponsor professional baseball.[37] York's traction magnate, Captain Lanius, attempted to assist the Colored Monarchs with subsidies and favors, but clearly this business relationship, as well as the one in Altoona, was due primarily to the Monarchs' white ownership. It is problematic to suggest that such an arrangement would have even been considered if S. K. Govern were the sole owner of the club. As the Gorhams' manager, Govern reassembled the original Cuban Giants, a feat Bright did not accomplish.

The fact that all-black clubs materialized in the nineteenth century exemplifies how race shaped the dimension of their evolution. Black baseball was birthed from the womb of community building, at a time when segregation shaped the relationship between black and white people. The black game was influenced by a generation of Afro-Americans who made it clear that in spite of their exclusion from mainstream America, they would develop their own institutions and shape their own sporting patterns. Black baseball entrepreneurs transformed the game into a commercialized amusement, and simultaneously sought to advance their own business interests and symbolically "elevate the race" through their success. More important, black baseball entrepreneurs were determined to compete in the marketplace, regardless of the obstacles they confronted. The efforts of black baseball entrepreneurs were consistent with those Afro-Americans who sought inclusion in mainstream America through economic advancement.

The entrepreneurial efforts of Frank Thompson, S. K. Govern, Ambrose Davis, and to a lesser degree Benjamin Butler and Bud Fowler shaped the dimension of black baseball in the nineteenth century. They marketed and promoted their game by advocating white middle-class values, and created an unconventional playing style that made their product inherently Afro-American. Black players were cast in the roles of both competitors and entertainers. They skillfully utilized the press to schedule games and advertise their prominence throughout the East and, at times, in the South and Midwest. However, the plight of the early black baseball entrepreneur highlights the essential dilemma of the emerging black middle class: no amount of fame or success could shield any black person against the fundamental and all-pervasive subordination forced on blacks of all backgrounds and occupations during that time.

As the 1892 season began, black baseball would enter a new era. Afro-Americans continued to advance their economic interests, while at the same time, white influence became more prevalent in the ownership of black clubs. Regardless of whether the owner was black or white, these magnates emulated the mode of operation developed by the aforementioned black entrepreneurs. But black clubs would not be promoted as a means to elevate the race. The black entrepreneurs of the 1890s would operate their clubs within the parameters of a biracial institutional structure and scheduled games primarily with white semipro clubs and college baseball teams, and among themselves.

7

The Lean Years, 1892–1895

$\mathcal{F}$rom 1892 to 1895, black baseball, particularly in Chicago and New York, underwent a period of decline and reorganization. The changing attitude of business toward baseball and the efforts of local businessmen to organize the Windy City's amateur clubs contributed to the emergence of the Chicago Unions as the West's premier Afro-American club. The Unions began as a local stay-at-home, playing games on Chicago's prairie land and passing the hat to meet expenses. By 1890, the Unions' management team made their initial efforts to transform their amateur club into a full-time operation, signing top-level players and barnstorming the nation for gate receipts. By 1894, their nominal success resulted in the Unions splitting into two clubs.

This same period was grim for both the Cuban Giants and the Gorhams of New York. The Cuban Giants were relegated to a local stay-at-home, rarely scheduling games outside the New York area. The Gorhams' decline was much swifter. Neither Ambrose Davis nor the players fully recovered from their disappointing 1891 season. Although Davis continued to operate the club, primarily as a weekend enterprise, throughout the 1890s, the Gorhams would never again duplicate their peak year of 1889. Although the Cubans maintained their playing schedule, playing more than a hundred games annually, a fundamental change occurred in their day-to-day operations, in terms of the relationship between management and the player force. J. M. Bright, however, could not divorce himself completely from the club's day-to-day operations. By 1894, Bright returned to running the daily affairs.

By 1895, two Afro-American entrepreneurs laid the foundation that resulted in elevating the black game in the West. Drawing from the early success of the Cuban Giants, Bud Fowler formed the Page Fence Giants in Adrian,

Michigan, around the familiar concepts of showmanship, comical coaching, and top-level baseball. What made Fowler's scheme unique was the presence of private business interests providing the necessary start-up capital to form this club around the notion of product promotion, entertainment, and competition. At the same time, William Peters began initial steps to improve his Unions' profitability through the creation of rivalries with the top white semi-pro clubs in Chicago. In addition, Peters began to book as many as three games on a single Sunday to maximize profits. By the end of the 1895 season, the Page Fence Giants and Chicago Unions were ready to challenge the Cuban Giants for black baseball supremacy.

The Rise of the Chicago Unions

Sol White stated that the Chicago Unions emerged as the leading amateur club in the West in 1886. They won every game they played in their inaugural season. The Unions began initially as a weekend enterprise, playing primarily against local white clubs. By the mid-1890s, under the direction of William S. Peters and Frank Leland, the Unions were transformed into a full-time semi-professional club. They played games throughout the states of Indiana, Illinois, Iowa, Michigan, and Wisconsin, returning on Sunday to play games in Chicago. According to White, throughout the 1890s the Chicago Unions won 613 games, lost 118, and tied 12.[1]

To understand the Unions' meteoric rise to prominence, it is necessary to examine the various forces that led to the emergence of semiprofessional baseball in Chicago. The changing attitude of business toward baseball constituted the first factor that influenced Chicago's local baseball scene. The Windy City embodied Harold Seymour's contention that baseball play among workers was altered from self-generated play to company-sponsored teams in the late nineteenth century. Players on the city's amateur teams frequently came from the same occupations or the same firms. Employees in a particular line of work challenged others in like occupations, and organized leagues soon followed. By 1889, the Chicago press covered several amateur leagues: the Garden City League, Commercial League, City League, Market Street League, and Mercantile League.[2]

Second, it was within this context that the Chicago Amateur Baseball Association (CABA) was formed. The CABA was organized in 1882 and served primarily as a booking agent for the local clubs. The association secured leasing agreements with several parks throughout the city and organized playing schedules for each of them. By 1887, the *Chicago Inter Ocean* reported that the CABA had obtained leases on four enclosed ballparks: the South Side grounds, located at Portland Avenue and Thirty-third Street; the Southwest Grounds, at Rockwell Street and Ogden Avenue; the Northwest Grounds, at Division Street and Oakley Avenue; and the North Side Grounds, at Clybourn and Sheffield Avenues. Each park possessed an enclosed ground with a seating capacity of three thousand. A member club that wished to play any games at one of the enclosed parks would have to pay a flat fifty-dollar annual fee.[3]

Evidently, some of the amateur clubs were not satisfied with this arrangement, and in 1887, the City League was formed. Before the start of the 1887 season, the Whitings club signed an agreement to use the White Stockings' West Side Park on any open Saturday. The rest of the league games were played "on the open prairie," as the city's regular parks were often referred to. Less than a month into the season, the CABA and the City League reached an agreement that allowed the latter to resume use of the enclosed ballparks. However, three years later, clubs that made up the City League were still unhappy with the way the CABA dictated terms to the local clubs. As a result, eight clubs—the Whitings, West Ends, Aetna, Garden City, Stars, Franklins, Picketts, and Diamonds—secured control of several parks and began the 1890 season as a separate institution. Games were played primarily on Sundays, and City League clubs rarely played teams outside of their organization.[4]

The City League provides the best evidence of Chicago's local baseball scene. According to the *Chicago Inter Ocean*, the clubs were composed of clerks, "and [included] some of the best element in the city." City League clubs promoted the ideal of baseball as a means of advancing healthful exercises, while simultaneously adding a few dollars to the small salaries received from their employers. Operating expenses included fifteen dollars per week for both the rent and the maintenance of the playing grounds, and two dollars per day for the services of two policemen to provide security. In addition, the City League paid an umpire's fee of three dollars each and a scorekeeper's fee of one dollar, which also covered the cost of baseballs for each game. City League officials provided the fans with refreshments, nothing stronger than lemonade, and distributed scorecards free of charge. A score book, patterned after the one sold at National League games, was sold for five cents and provided fans with information on teams, individual players, and league standings.[5]

The Chicago Unions emerged within this context of the evolution of the organization of white semipro clubs into leagues and associations. The Unions' principal organizers were William S. Peters, "Abe" Jones, Henry

Chicago Unions owner William S. Peters. *Courtesy of the New York Public Library.*

"Teenan" Jones, and Frank Leland. Little is known about the backgrounds of William Peters and Abe Jones. Teenan Jones would later make his fortune in the saloon and gambling business, supporting black cultural and athletic enterprises, while using his influence and financial resources to help aspiring Afro-American politicians. Jones's contribution to the Unions appears to be in a financial capacity, as his name does not appear in any of the team's box scores. Frank Leland was born in 1869, graduated from Fisk University, and was on the roster of the Washington Capital City Club of the National Colored League in 1887. When the colored league disbanded, Leland moved to Chicago and along with Abe Jones, Teenan Jones, and Peters formed the Union Base Ball Club. The club's name was later changed back to its original name, the Chicago Unions.[6]

Much like the entrepreneurs of the Philadelphia Pythians of the National Colored League, the Cuban Giants, and the Gorhams of New York, the Unions' organizers formed their club around the business strategy of economic cooperation. Unlike the Pythians and Cubans, however, the Unions did not seek a white partner. But at the same time, these Windy City entrepreneurs followed the same business approach of going where the money was to be made. This strategy meant scheduling games with several Chicago white semipro clubs, as well as securing leasing agreements with white park managers.

The business relationship between black and white baseball entrepreneurs that arose in the 1890s could best be described as a "general understanding." Black baseball clubs were promoted less around the notion of race elevation. Instead, black baseball entrepreneurs accommodated racial prejudices by de-emphasizing any potential conflict with racist overtones. In other words, black baseball entrepreneurs had a vested interest in downplaying any possible racial clashes, to advance their economic interests. Throughout the 1890s, the white press rarely reported any incidents in baseball that had racial implications. This statement is not to say that conflicts that arose were not racially motivated. As we shall see later, Afro-American entrepreneurs and ballplayers would make compromises with white individuals who would not associate with blacks, except to maximize profits.

From 1887 to 1890, the Unions operated as a weekend enterprise, passing the hat to meet expenses. Nevertheless, the Unions did offer additional incentives to attract the top white semipro teams. Besides dividing gate receipts, the Unions offered a side bet—ranging from twenty-five to fifty dollars, and sometimes as high as one hundred dollars—to the team that won the game. In one game between the Brightons and the Unions, the Afro-American club promoted a footrace among players from each club. The winner received fifty dollars plus an extra ten dollars from the CABA. In another game between the Unions and Models, the winner received a gold ball and a silver-mounted ebony bat.[7]

In 1888, the Unions played the P. B. S. Pinchbacks of New Orleans for the Colored Championship. The Pinchbacks were named after P. B. S. Pinchback, who sat in the Louisiana's governor's chair for forty-three days during Reconstruction. The Pinchbacks were considered the best Afro-American semiprofessional club from the South, and during the 1888 season they underwent a barnstorming tour of the North and West. A three-game series was scheduled, and in the first game the Unions surprised the Pinchbacks, winning four to one. In the second game, a reported crowd of eighteen hundred fans watched the Pinchbacks even the series, scoring two runs in the top of the ninth inning and winning six to five. The third game was never played.[8] Evidently, the Unions were tougher opponents than the Pinchbacks had expected, and probably left town to save face. More important, playing these two closely contested games established the Unions' reputation as one of the "crack" teams in Chicago.

The following year, a series of games was played among the Pinchbacks, Unions, and Resolutes. The Resolutes were a black club from Chicago that had acquired William Renfroe, the black pitcher who had played with Bud Fowler on the Binghamton Bingos of the International League in 1887. Renfroe went down in defeat, nine to five, to the hard-hitting Unions. The following day, the Pinchbacks hit Renfroe hard and early en route to a seventeen-to-eleven victory. Although there was no box score in the press, the Pinchbacks defeated the Unions, much to the dismay of Abe Jones. Jones challenged the Pinchbacks to another contest, the winner to receive the entire gate receipts. He was turned down. Jones then challenged the Pinchbacks to a three-game series for a side bet as high as $150 before the club from New Orleans returned south.[9] The challenge was never accepted, marking the end of a potential West-South rivalry between these clubs.

On April 2, 1890, the *Chicago Inter Ocean* reported that the Unions would open the season as a full-time operation. They elected the following officers: Abe Jones, president; F. Scott, vice president; H. Elby, secretary; and Teenan Jones, treasurer. Frank Leland was appointed field manager and was responsible for signing the best available talent. The main objective was to elevate the Unions to the same plateau as the Cuban Giants and compete for the Colored Championship. The Union organizers attempted to construct a barnstorming pattern around the parameters of a local-to-regional format. The Unions would play Sunday games in Chicago and barnstorm Illinois, Indiana, and Michigan during the week.[10] Much like the Cuban Giants and Gorhams, these black baseball entrepreneurs sought to expand their market potential by creating a demand for their club in several locales. Undoubtedly, this move was motivated by the club's performance against the Pinchbacks the previous two seasons.

A second factor that could have possibly influenced this decision to go full-time was the effort to reorganize the CABA. Local businessmen affiliated with amateur clubs sought to organize the uniformed clubs into one central organization. G. S. Cusack, a railroad magnate who would eventually become the association's president, attempted to create a governing body patterned after the National League. In addition to Cusack, Louis Houseman of the *Chicago Inter Ocean* and J. P. Reilly, manager of the Water Street West Ends ball club, spearheaded this organizational effort. In actuality, the reorganized CABA was more similar to the National Association of Base Ball Players of the late 1850s and 1860s. CABA organizers proposed several broad objectives that included scheduling games, assigning players, and establishing a governing body to resolve disputes and formalize rules.[11]

The CABA's first objective was to organize an event known as "Base-Ball Day." The fundamental underpinning of the event was to create an awareness of all the numerous uniformed amateur clubs in the greater Chicago area. These local clubs would be part of a parade that marched through the streets of downtown Chicago. The Unions were one of the several uniformed clubs that marched in this parade. The procession was divided into three divisions, and the parade proceeded down Wabash Avenue, Franklin Street, and Randolph Street and eventually ended on Pacific Avenue. From there, the clubs boarded a train at the Lake Shore Railroad depot and departed for the South Side grounds. The uniformed clubs watched an exhibition game between the Whitings and the Garden Citys, two City League clubs. The Whitings led four to two going into the sixth inning when the Garden Citys erupted for nine runs in the bottom of the frame, and won eleven to four.[12]

Undoubtedly, being a part of Base-Ball Day resulted in some valuable publicity for the Unions. The event highlighted the hierarchy emerging among Chicago's amateur clubs. At the top of the ladder was the City League, followed by the various leagues under the CABA's umbrella. The Unions were affiliated with the Prairie League, which played its games primarily on Sunday. This plan proved to be a nice fit for the Unions' organizers, in their attempt to become a full-time operation.

Despite the eternal optimism of these black baseball entrepreneurs, their efforts to become a full-time enterprise yielded only marginal results. Several factors contributed to this limited success. The first, and probably the most important, factor was the sporadic press coverage. Unlike S. K. Govern, Unions organizers devalued the importance of press coverage, using the print medium mainly to issue challenges and announce upcoming games. Important games, such as the aforementioned Colored Championship, received extensive coverage. Yet the Unions were not alone in marginalizing the importance of press coverage. With the exception of the City League, local amateurs rarely reported their games to the city newspapers on a consistent basis. The newspapers that did participate printed only line scores of the games. The *Chicago Inter Ocean*'s sports editor reminded the amateur clubs from time to time to turn in the results of their games for publication.[13]

This sporadic press coverage makes it problematic to ascertain the Unions' profitability. The 1892 season provides the best evidence of the club's barnstorming efforts, because the tour received extensive press coverage. Throughout the months of late June to August, the Unions played a group of clubs that made up the Michigan-Wisconsin Association. The association was composed of six clubs from northern Michigan and Wisconsin: Ishpeming and Marquette, Michigan; and Green Bay, Marinette, Menominee, and Oshkosh, Wisconsin. The Unions played games with this minor league during the week, returning to Chicago for Sunday games. Travel distance ranged from as close as 177 miles to Oshkosh, to as far as 398 miles to Marquette. The Unions' average attendance with clubs from the Michigan-Wisconsin Association was 980 fans. Attendance varied from as low as 300 to as high as 3,000, for the Fourth of July. With ticket prices set at $0.15, the Unions' games took in on average $149 in ticket revenue. After subtracting the home team's share, the Unions took in $73.50. Their weekly revenue would be approximately $367.50, with a potential monthly take of $1,470.[14]

It is difficult to estimate how much the Unions' operating expenses impacted their generated revenue, but because the club's organizers signed the best players available, it is safe to say that these entrepreneurs paid higher salaries. The farthest city from Chicago—Marquette—undoubtedly resulted in higher travel expenses than they were accustomed to paying. Like the Cuban Giants and Gorhams, the Unions' organizers had to pay for hotel accommodations, uniforms, and equipment. Because few box and line scores reported attendance figures for Sunday games, it is difficult to determine how much of these operating expenses were offset by the revenue generated at Windy City games. Moreover, by the end of August, the Michigan-Wisconsin Association disbanded.

Evidently, the Unions' organizers were disappointed with the outcome of their attempt to become a full-time operation. On April 29, 1894, the *Chicago Inter Ocean* reported that William Peters had formed a partnership with Al Donigan and secured a lease on a playing ground on Thirty-seventh and Butler Streets, on Chicago's South Side. Frank Leland also remained with the club and served as the secretary and traveling manager on road trips. The new location was easily accessible by either the State Street or the Halsted Street cable-car lines. On May 6, Peters organized a dedication ceremony for the new grounds and scheduled a game with the Edgars, a top-level white semipro club. In 1893, the Unions and Edgars played a nine-game series, and according to the *Inter Ocean*, a "bitter rivalry" existed between the two clubs. The Unions won the series, five games to four. The following year, a five-game series was scheduled between the two teams.[15] The series typified the sporadic press coverage that was common among amateur clubs. There were no box or line scores published on the sports page.

The Unions combined good hitting, pitching, and fielding with their own brand of vaudevillian baseball and comical coaching. Harry Buckner, Robert Footes, Al Hackley, George "Gus" Hopkins, Harry Hyde, Willie Jones, and William Joyner formed the nucleus that made the Unions the elite among black clubs in the West. Sol White acknowledged that the Unions were "hard hitters and good fielders." The *Chicago Inter Ocean* declared that large crowds witnessed the Windy City club's "many fine plays and their coachers are considered the funniest and best in the business." William Joyner's "fog-horn voice [could] be heard clear out of Cook County." Buckner was clearly the club's most versatile player. He pitched, caught, and played in the infield and outfield. Willie Jones was the Unions' team captain, and was also described as the "pride of the team."[16] Together these men provided Chicago with some excellent baseball at the semiprofessional level.

Although the Unions' 1894 season began optimistically, it ended in internal division. On July 20, the *Chicago Inter Ocean* reported that an individual by the name of Ward had signed five of the original Unions. Ward, no doubt, offered higher salaries to these players to encourage them to change teams. To avoid confusion, the club was referred to as Ward's Unions. Ward proceeded to schedule a series of games with the Edgars. This fact could have been the reason that no games were reported in the press between the Chicago Unions and the Edgars; the series may have never occurred. Ward's Unions provided no competition for the top semipro clubs. In two games against the Edgars and the Dalys, Ward's Unions were soundly beaten, seventeen to two and nineteen to eight, respectively.[17] Also, Ward's Unions proved no threat to William Peters. Moving to a new location that was easily accessible by the streetcar lines marked the start of Peters establishing a barnstorming pattern designed to exploit the largest baseball market in the West.

A Conservative Operation: The Decline of the Gorhams

From 1892 to 1895, J. M. Bright constructed a moderate barnstorming pattern for his Cuban Giants, rarely playing games outside the New York area. Although Bright secured a leasing agreement to play games in Norwalk, Connecticut, he coveted more the Sunday games on the Long Island grounds. On May 15, 1892, twelve hundred fans witnessed the Cuban Giants shut out the Senators, seven to nothing, behind the excellent pitching of John Nelson. A thousand spectators watched a closely contested game between the Cubans and the Manhattan A. C., the former winning seven to four, capped by a three-run rally in the seventh inning.[18] Throughout this period, the Giants played almost exclusively white semiprofessional clubs. The Cubans' rivalry with the Gorhams had ended, and because of their inability to pay a heavy guarantee, the Giants scheduled no games with either the National League or minor league clubs. The Cuban Giants were only a reflection of their former selves.

The 1892 season marked the beginning of the end for the Gorhams of New York. Only Ambrose Davis remained from the original entrepreneurs who had made up this cooperative enterprise in 1886. S. K. Govern did not return for the 1892 season and was now out of black baseball. The Gorhams did begin the season with some top-level players: Andy Jackson, Oscar Jackson, George Stovey, William Malone, William Jackson, and Sol White.

The Gorhams' contest with the New York Giants illustrates the club's fall from prominence. On April 7, 1892, the *New York Sun* reported that the Gorhams had strolled into the Polo Grounds in a cakewalk. They were adorned with new uniforms and "swallow-tail coats," an ensemble that "gave them a very attractive appearance." However, the *Sun* added that two hours later, "the Gorhams dragged themselves out of the grounds looking as though they had been engaged in an unsatisfactory argument with a tornado." The game was over in the third inning when the Giants scored thirteen runs! They went on to score nine in the sixth, one in the seventh, and seven in the eighth, winning thirty-six to one. The game was mercifully stopped after eight innings because both clubs were totally "exhausted" by the occasion. To add insult to injury, only five hundred spectators witnessed the fiasco.[19]

From that time on, the Gorhams wandered through the rest of the season in a daze. They began losing to semipro clubs they had once dominated. For example, on June 17, the Gorhams were shut out, five to nothing, by the Acmes on Long Island grounds. The Olympics of Paterson, New Jersey, soundly beat them, fifteen to four.[20] More important, the Gorhams began to disappear from the *New York Sun*'s sports page.

In addition to declining press coverage, the Gorhams had a significant turnover in their player force. Andy Jackson, Oscar Jackson, George Stovey, and William Jackson jumped the Gorhams for the Cuban Giants in late July and early August. These defections were based upon an economic motive. Davis was in no position to pay these players the salaries to which they were accustomed. Bright was better able to compensate them due largely to the crowds the Cubans drew on Long Island grounds on Sundays.

Despite this poor season, Ambrose Davis continued to operate the Gorhams throughout the 1890s. They were relegated to a weekend enterprise, passing the hat to meet expenses. The Gorhams of New York would never again reach the plateau they had achieved from 1886 to 1889, but Ambrose Davis's business acumen enabled them to operate for several years in an era when some clubs did not last a month.

With the Gorhams operating as a local stay-at-home, the Cuban Giants became the only full-time Afro-American club operating in the New York area. Despite being only a shadow of their former selves, the Cubans were still one of the elite semipro clubs in the East. They began the 1893 season with an impressive array of player talent: Andy Jackson, Oscar Jackson, Clarence

Williams, Frank Grant, Abe Harrison, George Stovey, Sol White, and William Jackson. Bright also signed some new players that contributed to the Cubans' success. John Patterson was a second baseman and outfielder, who later became a black baseball entrepreneur. Dan Penno was a utility player who played in the outfield and at second base and on occasion pitched. James Robinson was a pitcher who was known as the "Black Russie," a comparison made to New York Giants' pitching ace, Amos Russie.[21]

On April 20, 1893, the *New York Sun* reported that J. M. Bright had hired a new field manager. According to the *Sun*, Frank Grant would "have full control of the men."[22] What was significant about this announcement was how race shaped the business relationship between black players and white owners. Although several of the original Cuban Giants continued to play for Bright, the players had an estranged relationship with their enigmatic owner. But the players confronted a fundamental dilemma. If they wanted to sustain their elite status in baseball's semipro circles, not to mention receiving adequate economic remuneration, their best-case scenario was to play for a white owner. In addition, if top-level white semipro clubs, and at times local boosters and civic leaders, had to choose between doing business with a white or a black owner, a white magnate would win every time.

Bright's proposed Altoona deal before the 1891 season illustrates this preference of doing business with whites, as opposed to Afro-Americans. Local leaders were aware of Bright's underhanded ways of doing business, but these executives were still willing to renovate the grandstand, at the expense of local business interests, and made efforts to improve transportation to and from the grounds. Yet the deal was contingent upon Bright signing the original Cuban Giants. Bright failed to accomplish this feat, and even when S. K. Govern reassembled the original Cubans, no deal was forthcoming. The Altoona deal exemplifies how uneven, and often irrational, racial prejudice could be.[23] To be sure, an argument can be made that white park managers and local leaders negotiated leasing agreements with Ambrose Davis in the late 1880s. However, there is no evidence to suggest that investments would be made to improve either the grounds or transportation. After all, a central reason for the Gorhams' constant movement from city to city was the poor accessibility of the playing grounds.

No doubt Bright recognized the need to compromise if he desired to operate the Cuban Giants at an elite level. Therefore, Grant as player-manager served as a liaison between this white owner and his black players. Management and the players recognized that both sides needed each other in order to function. For the time being, both sides were willing to maintain this "general understanding" to continue operations. This complex relationship between white ownership and a black labor force continued to play out among black clubs well into the twentieth century.

This partnership almost ended before it began. On May 8, 1893, the *New York Sun* reported that police had stopped a Sunday game between the Giants and the Xaviers at the Long Island grounds. Before the blue laws were abolished in 1919, professional ball clubs were forbidden to schedule games on Sunday. To circumvent this law, it was customary for professional and semiprofessional clubs not to sell tickets of admission to games. Instead, they admitted fans free if they purchased programs or magazines for fifty or seventy-five cents, or if they volunteered a "donation." Baseball magnates generally received cooperation from the police, who rarely arrested violators. Furthermore, magistrates seldom convicted anyone tried in their courts. Bright asserted that Police Justice William Monteverde had exceeded his authority in stopping the game. The Cubans' owner indicated he would attempt to rectify the situation, but evidently made no headway because the following Sunday game was also prohibited. Both incidents led the *Sun*'s sports editor to speculate that Bright could lose several players, owing to police officials prohibiting Sunday games. Furthermore, it meant Bright would lose a big payday, a luxury the Cubans' owner could ill-afford.[24]

The Sunday dilemma was soon solved, and the Cuban Giants enjoyed an excellent 1893 season. A solution was reached whereby semipro clubs could play Sunday games at Leo Park in Queens County. Semipro magnates probably made a deal with the local police and the magistrate. This concession allowed the Cubans to continue to play Sunday games in the New York area, a critical factor in devising a successful barnstorming pattern. By August, the Cuban Giants played 112 games, winning 99, losing 12, and tying 1.[25]

Despite the excellent season, J. M. Bright could not separate himself from the day-to-day affairs. On April 24, 1894, the *New York Sun* reported that Bright had named himself as the club's manager, and he would also accompany the club on road trips for the next two years.[26] After only one year of allowing Grant to manage the club, Bright could not totally relinquish this responsibility to his player-manager. However, this decision proved ill-advised. By 1896, the Cubans' owner would face his most serious challenge in the presence of another white owner from Brooklyn.

An Innovative Enterprise

After leaving the Gorhams in 1887, Bud Fowler continued his itinerant ways, playing on white minor league clubs that offered the opportunity. He played in minor leagues throughout the West and Northwest in cities such as Santa Fe, New Mexico; Terre Haute, Indiana; Burlington, Iowa; and Lincoln, Nebraska. By 1894, Fowler played on an independent club based in Findlay, Ohio.

Fowler met Grant "Home Run" Johnson in Findlay, and they devised a scheme that became an innovative means of market promotion. A native of Findlay, Johnson was a college-educated long-ball hitter. He began his career as a shortstop for the Findlay Sluggers in 1894 and reportedly hit sixty home runs, thus the nickname "Home Run." Sol White stated that Johnson in connection with Fowler conceived an idea of a "colored team traveling in a private car and giving street parades prior to every game."[27]

By the 1894 season, Fowler and Johnson made their initial effort to make their vision a reality. Evidently, Fowler sparked interest for his idea in Adrian, Michigan, a small agricultural-industrial area sixty miles west of Detroit. According to the *Adrian Daily Times and Expositor*, "Local baseball enthusiasts are much interested in the enterprise." The paper added that it was "not impossible that Fowler's scheme may succeed." On September 21, 1894, the Page Fence Giants were formed. Fowler and two white businessmen, L. W. Hoch and Rolla Taylor, entered into an agreement with the Page Fence Wire Company and an unidentified Massachusetts bicycle company for the purpose of funding a black professional baseball club. The unidentified bicycle company may have been the Overman Wheel Company, which had introduced the safety bike in 1887 and had branch offices in Detroit, Denver, San Francisco, and Los Angeles. Additionally, Overman had a riding school, which is where the ballplayers possibly trained for the proposed cycling exhibitions they gave prior to the games.[28]

Why would the wire company and the bicycle firm finance this plan at a time when U.S. race relations were deteriorating? Concurrently, neither company would share in the club's profits. Two factors contributed to these businessmen supporting this scheme. The bicycle craze from about 1889 to 1895 constituted the first factor. Entrepreneurs capitalized upon the spectators' enthusiastic reaction to the speed and excitement generated at bicycle races. Substantial fortunes were being made in the production, distribution, and retail sale of bicycles and their components. Every major city had its "bicycle row," where retailers competed for the sale of nationally advertised brands such as

The Page Fence Giants were cosponsored by the Page Fence Wire Company. Undoubtedly, this was a promotional photo to promote the ball club and their sponsor's product. *Courtesy of the National Baseball Hall of Fame Library, Cooperstown, N.Y.*

the Rambler, the Crescent, and the Victor—the latter being marketed by Overman in 1895.[29]

The final factor dealt with the use of a private railroad car for travel. The railroad car served two purposes. First, it was a response to the declining race relations in the 1890s. Instead of looking for hotel accommodations in a particular city, an activity a black club may engage in for an entire night without success, players lodged in the railroad car. This specially designed car possessed a lavatory, kitchen, and combined dining-sitting-sleeping room, capable of accommodating twenty people. A porter and a cook were also hired to service the players and railroad car. Combining transportation and lodging in this private car served to reduce any potential conflicts along racial lines.

Second, this specially built railroad car also provided a means of market promotion. Fowler's vision combined the national pastime with a wire company and a bicycle firm, developing a marketing plan commonly used by the modern sports industry: brand equity, the value added to a product by virtue of name recognition. Moreover, Fowler's scheme also exemplified a crude form of integrated marketing—the culmination of advertising, public relations, and promotion collectively and systematically used to market a product or service.

With the Giants playing in middle-size cities—such as Grand Rapids, Michigan, and Oshkosh, Wisconsin—the Page club marketed their sponsors' products to expand their market potential. This integrated marketing scheme of product promotion, entertainment, and competitive baseball was ahead of its time in the sporting world.[30]

The Page Fence Giants' management team consisted of a player-manager, team captain, and business manager. Fowler served as player-manager, while Grant Johnson assumed the role of team captain. Augustus S. "Gus" Parsons was the club's business manager in charge of scheduling games. Parsons, a clerk at the Hotel Emory in Adrian, was also the team manager of the Adrian Light Guard club in 1894. Parsons probably met Fowler when the Light Guard club played Findlay in August that same year. The hotel clerk could possibly have introduced Fowler to Hoch and Taylor. His brother H. B. Parsons served on the Page Company's board of directors, but Fowler was clearly the driving force behind the enterprise.[31]

Much like the Cuban Giants of the late 1880s, the Page Fence Giants were expected to maintain an acceptable moral image that exemplified white middle-class values. No doubt Fowler sold his plan to these white businessmen on the premise that his players were morally respectable individuals. Fowler boasted that only two players used tobacco and nobody drank alcohol. Twelve of the players were college educated, and five had graduated. Most of the players came from other black professional teams, such as William Malone, Sol White, and John Patterson from the Cuban Giants. Two players were recruited from the Wilberforce and Oberlin campuses.

Founded upon the concept of product promotion, the Page Fence Giants were exclusively a traveling team and made no effort to establish a home base. A two-game series with the National League Cincinnati Reds illustrates the pattern of events that occurred at Giants games. Parsons placed an advertisement in the Cincinnati newspapers announcing the Page Fence Giants' arrival in their city. The *Cincinnati Enquirer* reported that the Giants would conduct "a street parade on bicycles and put up a good article of ball." On game day, Parsons distributed souvenirs to the fans with a picture of the Giants on one side, and a picture of the Page Wire Company on the other. The words PLAY BALL PLAY BALL were above the picture, while *We Are Playing Ball* appeared below it. The Giants played a spirited contest against the Reds in the first game before losing eleven to seven. The *Enquirer* reported that every "colored barber, wine boy, and palace car porter" who could get the day off attended the game. The second game was a different story. The game was over in the first inning, when the Reds erupted for eleven runs and won sixteen to two. The Page club started poorly in the month of April, winning only two of eleven games.[32]

However, by late June, the Giants caught fire and went on several winning streaks for the remainder of the season. They began to dazzle fans with their showmanship, comical coaching, and competitive baseball. Grant Johnson once executed a cartwheel around the bases after hitting a home run. Giants pitching ace Billy Holland was once described as "funnier than an end man in a minstrel show."[33] Even the servants occasionally got involved. Will Gaskin, the cook, rapped five hits against the Romero club. The Page club also played many close games against top-level semipro clubs, illustrating their ability to play top-level ball when needed. Thus, the Page Fence Giants, like the Cubans, were both competitors and entertainers.

The Giants barnstormed throughout Ohio, Indiana, Illinois, and Michigan in their inaugural season and exhibited an ability to turn a profit. Average attendance at Giants games was 1,175, reportedly ranging from as low as 500 to as high as 2,800. Games generated revenue in the amount of $235, which the Page club split with the home team. A particularly impressive figure was the revenue generated at a three-game series between the Giants and the Grand Rapids Goldbugs of the Western League. The average attendance for the three games was 1,533, with a gate of $306.60.[34] It is hard to assess the impact the pregame bicycle exhibitions had on attendance, but clearly the club's sponsors were pleased with their investment.

Fowler had greater aspirations for his Page Fence Giants. By mid-July, rumors circulated in the press regarding the Giants embarking upon an international barnstorming tour. The *Detroit Free Press* reported that the Page club, along with Minneapolis of the Western League, would play forty games in England at the end of the regular season. The *Adrian Daily Times and Expositor* reported that a pick nine from various clubs of the Michigan State League would travel with the Giants to Honolulu, Hawaii, and play for an entire month. Both clubs would then barnstorm the countries of Australia and New Zealand for approximately three months. Five players from the Cuban Giants would accompany the Page club.[35] No evidence was uncovered to indicate that either of these tours ever occurred, but the proposed tours do illustrate Fowler's uncanny ability to generate publicity, in an effort to promote the black game.

The Page Fence Giants concluded their 1895 season with a benefit game for Detroit players. The club, known as the Detroits, was composed of players from the Western League and major league players who made Detroit their home. The Detroits consisted of major league players such as Sam Thompson—who played on the champion Detroit club of 1887—Washington shortstop Frank Scheibach, and Boston pitcher Ed "Kid" Nichols. Unfortunately, inclement weather marred the series, and only one game was played, resulting in many of the star players refusing to play. Only 150 fans watched the Giants drub the Detroits sixteen to two.[36]

The Page Fence Giants became Bud Fowler's crowning achievement in promoting black baseball in the late nineteenth century. Fowler did not return for the 1896 season for reasons that are unclear. He endured the gnawing dilemma that confronted black baseball players and entrepreneurs in the late 1880s and 1890s. The systemic racism that had become widely accepted by the 1890s left Fowler with few options but to play on all-black teams. Judging by his behavior, Fowler wrestled with the reality of playing on an all-black club, a form of self-segregation. To Afro-Americans who advocated the integrationist position, any type of separate black institution smacked of segregation and represented a compromise of principle. However, at times a black institution, like the Page Fence Giants, might be necessary as a temporary expedient. A segregated black club operating within the fabric of the white baseball world could never be regarded as a substitute for the ultimate goal of integration, though. Therefore, it was problematic for Fowler to pass up the opportunity to play on white minor league clubs when the situation presented itself. In any event, Fowler returned to the Findlay Sluggers and played for the next three years.[37]

Bud Fowler left a legacy in black baseball that carried into the early twentieth century. The private railroad car became the mode of transportation for elite black clubs, such as Andrew "Rube" Foster's Chicago American Giants, to barnstorm the nation for gate receipts. Black baseball entrepreneurs continued making concerted efforts to expand their winter barnstorming tours nationally and internationally. In 1899, the *Sporting News* reported that Fowler had attempted to organize an all-black club to barnstorm the Pacific Coast.[38] Bud Fowler continued to promote black baseball until his death in 1913.

The Emergence of William Peters

William Peters began a concerted effort to improve his Chicago Unions' profitability. Baseball entrepreneurs sought to create rivalries with other semipro teams to sustain their economic viability. A seasonal rivalry, particularly on Sundays, meant a big payday for semipro clubs. Club owners attempted to de-

velop seasonal rivalries with at least two or three independent clubs throughout the year.

In 1895, the Chicago Unions developed rivalries with two of the top white
semiprofessional clubs in the Windy City: the Edgars and the Dalys. Tom Far-
ley managed the Edgars and, like Peters, booked several games with top semipros, including the Page Fence Giants. In April, the Edgars played the Page
club to a tie at five, the latter promising to return in May to play off the tie.
Upon their return, the Giants demolished the Edgars, fourteen to five, breaking the game open in the seventh inning with a twelve-run rally.[39] Much like
the previous two seasons, the Unions-Edgars rivalry received sporadic press
coverage. The two games that received coverage resulted in Unions victories.

The Dalys were the Unions' fiercest rivals for the 1895 season. The Dalys
were supported financially by local businessman James M. Daly and Thomas
Carey, a political boss of the stockyards. A three-game series was scheduled,
the winner receiving a purse worth five hundred dollars. The Unions took the
first game, eighteen to nine, but lost the second game, twelve to eight. The
final game of the series was played on September 15 at the South Side grounds.
Unions center fielder Al Hackley, who won the Douglass Cycling Club cup for
most hits in the series, led his club to a nine-to-eight victory. Neither Daly nor
Carey, however, was satisfied with the series outcome, and they challenged the
Unions to another three-game series, the winner to receive a one thousand-
dollar purse. The Unions declined the challenge, but the reported crowd of
thirty-six hundred in the series finale illustrates the importance of seasonal rivalries for independent clubs.[40]

The creation of Sunday doubleheaders was the second way Peters sought
to improve the Unions' profit potential. On June 15, the *Chicago Inter Ocean*
reported that the Unions would "meet all comers" every Sunday. Peters scheduled two games, the Schroeder Brothers in the first game and the Cranes in the
second; both ended in Unions victories. On August 7, Peters booked three
games at Unions' Park with the Schroeder Brothers, the Lake Views, and the
Altmans.[41] Unfortunately, the results were not reported in the press.

Herein lies the fundamental flaw in Peters's plan to improve his Unions'
economic viability: sporadic press coverage. Peters failed to recognize at first
the importance of consistent press coverage to generate publicity and stimulate fan interest. Unlike the National League, semipro clubs did not have the
advantage of a cooperative press providing extensive coverage. As Harold Seymour accurately points out, newspapers sold baseball and baseball sold newspapers.[42] More accurately, major league baseball sold newspapers, resulting in

the National League receiving top priority in terms of news coverage, particularly in the large urban cities. Therefore, it was the semipro club operator's responsibility to ensure his team remained on the sports pages.

The Unions continued to receive valuable publicity from their affiliation with the CABA in general and participating in "Base-Ball Day" in particular. The CABA officially declared August 31 as amateur Base-Ball Day. According to the *Chicago Inter Ocean*, several businesses consented to give their employees who played baseball for recreation a holiday to participate in the festivities. The activities included a cruise on the steamboat the *Christopher Columbus* to Milwaukee, Wisconsin, to witness a five-inning exhibition game. The rest of the day was reserved for the players to show "their sweet hearts the sights of the great city where the beer comes from."[43]

The Unions' affiliation with the CABA was instrumental in Peters's improvement of his club's economic status in Chicago. Several Unions opponents, such as the Schroeder Brothers and the Mandel Brothers, evolved from the CABA's ranks. Moreover, the aforementioned clubs' evolution occurred at a time when Peters sought to create seasonal rivalries and schedule two or three games on a particular Sunday.

However, by late September, the CABA's informal hierarchy began to crumble. The *Chicago Inter Ocean* reported that the City League had disbanded. For two years, the league had been experiencing financial difficulties. Early in the 1895 season, the league dropped two of its clubs, the Whitings and Brands, and operated as a four-club circuit. Club officials could not secure enough playing grounds to permit those teams to play every Sunday.[44]

League officials pointed to the National League Chicago White Stockings playing Sunday ball as the primary reason for the City League's demise. National League owners had relaxed their policy on Sunday games when their circuit merged with the American Association. Each team determined its own Sunday policy. At first, Chicago did not schedule Sunday games because Spalding's South Side lease prohibited Sunday amusements and the West Side middle-class community strongly opposed it. On December 23, 1892, White Stockings president James Hart announced a new policy of Sunday games for the forthcoming season. He asserted that the new policy was the result of a changing public opinion toward Sabbath entertainments. On May 14, 1893, the White Stockings played their first professional Sunday game at their new Polk Street Grounds, drawing 13,500 fans, making Sunday ball an immediate success. The *Chicago Inter Ocean* reported that receipts from City League games ran from $350 to $500 per game prior to the White Stockings playing

Sunday games. By 1895, gate receipts ran as low as $33, and the largest atten-
dance of the season netted only $88.[45]

The City League's demise goes beyond the scope of this study. Competing
for Sunday patronage against the Chicago White Stockings does not adequately explain why the league collapsed. But the City League's collapse does
raise the question of why the White Stockings playing on Sunday did not have
the same effect upon the Chicago Unions' attendance. After all, Peters was attempting to schedule more games on Sunday in order to maximize profits.
Moreover, the Unions' chief rivals, the Edgars and Dalys, were also not affected by the White Stockings' competition.

A fundamental answer to this question is that the Unions, Edgars, and
Dalys secured their own leasing agreements for playing grounds. This strategy
enabled these clubs to develop a home base, an essential element in sustaining
the seasonal rivalries with each other. Furthermore, these clubs were full-time
operations, and they probably played a higher caliber of baseball than the City
League. The rise of Chicago's elite semipro clubs occurred simultaneously
with the National League expanding to twelve clubs, because of the peace settlement with the American Association. The White Stockings had been adversely affected by the second association war. From 1892 to 1894, Anson's
club finished no higher than seventh place. It should also be noted that
Chicago's elite semipros played every Sunday in the Windy City, and the
White Stockings, because of their NL affiliation requiring them to make several road trips, did not. Furthermore, semiprofessional clubs benefited from
the NL's dismal decline throughout the 1890s. Contemporary sports editor
Frank Richter remarked that the NL's governance was characterized by the
magnates' "gross individual and collective mismanagement, their fierce fac-
tional fights, their cynical disregard of decency and honor, their open spolia-
tion of each other, their deliberate alienation of press and public, their flagrant
disloyalty to friends and supporters, and their tyrannical treatment of the players." It was evident that the NL was not putting a good product on the field.
Chicago's semipros charged only twenty-five cents for their games, giving the
fans a choice to determine whom they wanted to patronize. This decision was
made easier for some because of America's economic decline in the 1890s. In
any event, the City League found itself competing against the White Stockings and these independent clubs for Sunday patronage in the Windy City.[46]

The fact that the Unions survived during these lean years attests to
William Peters's business acumen. His Unions endured a transition in management and a brief breakup of their player force. Peters endeavored to im-

prove his club's profitability in the midst of an economic downturn. No doubt the Chicago Unions endured racial animosity from both white clubs and white fans, which could possibly explain why the Unions received sporadic press coverage. Peters probably did not report such games in order to maintain the business contacts he had established, and to accommodate racial discrimination in this era of "general understanding." This concession represented the kinds of compromises black baseball entrepreneurs made in order to operate within this biracial institutional structure.

The Chicago Unions and Page Fence Giants made considerable progress in their efforts to become full-time operations. Both clubs elevated the black game in the West to the point that they were ready to challenge the Cuban Giants for black baseball supremacy. This challenge would be made possible by the emergence of a new entrepreneur from Brooklyn, whom the original Cuban players found more to their liking.

8

The Search for a Colored Champion

From 1896 to 1898, black baseball's premier clubs in the East and West underwent a significant change in their barnstorming tours. A fundamental undercurrent that ignited this change was the quest for black baseball supremacy. The rise of the Cuban X Giants resulted in J. M. Bright abandoning his stay-at-home barnstorming ways, and for the first time since the late 1880s, a black club from the East toured the West for gate receipts. The rise to prominence of both the Page Fence Giants and the Chicago Unions made the trip west economically feasible. Reviving the Colored Championship series would, once again, bring national attention to black baseball, but the series also marked the start of petty disputes between the club's entrepreneurs.

In 1897, the Colored Championship series became the foundation in which several black baseball entrepreneurs marketed their respective clubs, particularly against each other. Cuban Giants owner J. M. Bright attempted to organize a tournament to determine the "real" Colored Champion. When the tournament failed to materialize, William Peters and the Cuban X Giants organized their barnstorming tours to include playing the top black clubs from the East, West, and South. Each series with these black clubs was billed as a Colored Championship series, but the number of games within each series was contingent upon the agreement reached by the entrepreneurs prior to it.

Although the 1897 season provided valuable publicity for black baseball, it was evident that a repeat performance would not occur the following season. E. B. Lamar and J. M. Bright continued their verbal battles in the sporting press. Their dispute was partially responsible for the creation of a barnstorming rivalry between the Cuban X Giants and the Chicago Unions. At the same time, the Unions began the 1898 season with a series of games with Western League clubs. By the end of the season, however, the seeds of decline that would decimate this prominent black club emerged.

The Rise of the Cuban X Giants

On March 15, 1896, the following advertisement appeared in the *New York Sun:*

> Cuban Giants will be known as the X Cuban Giants [*sic*]. The following well-known ball players have signed: Clarence Williams, O. Jackson, A. Jackson, B. Jackson, Selden, Nelson, Sol White, and Terrell. Clubs wishing games can address Manager E. B. Lamar, Jr., northeastern corner 134th Street and St. Ann's Avenue
> —Yours Truly E. B. Lamar, Jr.

Little is known about Edward B. Lamar Jr.'s background. Previous scholars of black baseball, such as Jerry Malloy, state that Lamar became the manager and booking agent of the Cuban X Giants. Lamar's brother, Pete, supposedly christened this team of ex-Cuban Giants as the Cuban X Giants. But how could Lamar emerge from obscurity and suddenly become the manager and booking agent of the premier semipro club of the late nineteenth century? No evidence has been uncovered to suggest that Lamar ever managed a ball club at any level. Yet every indication would suggest that Lamar was part of a cooperative enterprise formed by the players.[1]

Two factors allude to the Cuban X Giants being a cooperative enterprise. First, according to the *Pittsburgh Courier,* Sol White stated that the players had chosen Lamar to act as manager. Lamar, a Frenchman, was characterized as a "sportsman," and his primary responsibility was bookkeeping. In addition, the Cuban X Giants operated on the co-op plan, equally dividing the gate receipts among the players and their administrator.[2]

A core of veteran players who had been in baseball since 1885 composed the Cuban X Giants' roster. Clarence Williams, William Selden, Andy Jackson, Oscar Jackson, and Sol White had witnessed the administrative efforts of S. K. Govern, Ambrose Davis, and Benjamin Butler. As a former player-manager, Clarence Williams had undoubtedly accumulated some administrative skills over the years. No doubt these players had gleaned some organizational expertise from their predecessors. Furthermore, these players' reputations alone had created a significant degree of brand equity. They were well known in the baseball world.

Finally, in this era of the "general understanding," these Afro-American players recognized that business dealings went smoother with a white manager at the helm. In Lamar, the players found an alternative to J. M. Bright and his underhanded ways. Their new "manager" would serve as a figurehead in their dealings with white semipro clubs and park managers. In addition to his book-keeping responsibilities, Lamar also handled the press releases. In this way, both Lamar and the players created a cooperative enterprise: the Cuban X Giants.

Bright's initial response to the formation of the Cuban X Giants was to ig-nore them. In order to avoid confusion, he renamed his club the "Genuine Cuban Giants" or the "Wonderful Cuban Giants." According to Bright, he had released some of his players owing to their poor performance in 1895, which led him to replace them with "younger blood." On March 17, Lamar challenged Bright to a series of games. Because Bright considered his club to be superior, Lamar proposed a series of games to be played either in Brooklyn or at the Polo Grounds. The winner would receive all of the gate receipts. Bright did not respond to the challenge.[3]

Despite Bright's refusal to accept Lamar's challenge, the Cuban X Giants began the season playing clubs in the Atlantic, Eastern, and New England Leagues. They performed poorly against these minor league clubs. For exam-ple, in a two-game series against Newark, Giants pitching surrendered thirty-two runs. Pawtucket destroyed the Giants, twenty-four to three. The Cuban X Giants did manage a close nine-to-eight victory over Bridgeport.[4]

The Cuban X Giants and Cuban Giants maintained their dominance over white semipro clubs throughout the 1896 season. Their excellent season re-sulted in a fan, calling himself "Admirer," to call for a season-ending series be-tween these clubs. Such a series would have been a fitting conclusion to a fine year. Moreover, the fan also suggested that part of the proceeds be donated to some hospital of the players choosing. In response, Lamar stated that he had made several attempts to arrange a series between the two clubs with no re-sults.[5] Once again, Bright snubbed the X Giants.

While J. M. Bright continued to ignore Lamar's request for a series, the Cuban X Giants would make their first extended barnstorming tour since the late 1880s. The rise of the Page Fence Giants and the Chicago Unions, in con-junction with the emergence of the top white semipros in the Windy City, made the trip economically feasible. Moreover, the Western League, the precursor to the American League, was willing to play games with black clubs when their schedules permitted. The Cuban X Giants, organizing a series of games for the Colored Championship, would also bring national attention to the black game.

Reviving the Colored Championship

The Page Fence Giants began the 1896 season without their founder and innovator, Bud Fowler. According to the *Adrian Daily Times and Expositor,* Fowler had formed a black baseball club in Muncie, Indiana, with the intention of "wrestling the laurels from the Page Fence Giants." In Fowler's absence, Gus Parsons and Grant Johnson formed the Page club's management team that barnstormed the nation for gate receipts.[6]

The Giants opened the season with a three-game series against the Grand Rapids Gold Bugs of the Western League. Although it was somewhat one-sided, a fierce rivalry developed between the two clubs. The first game of the series typified the Gold Bugs' dominance, as the Giants went down in defeat, ten to two. Despite this lopsided victory, a reported crowd of twenty-seven hundred witnessed the Gold Bugs win a close contest, six to five. What made this game significant was that the contest was played on a Sunday. According to the *Detroit Free Press,* the game marked the first time a Sunday contest was played within Grand Rapids's city limits, an apparent test of their blue laws. The *Free Press* added that there was no interference from the police, but it was "more probable that some of the Sunday observance people will take the matter up." Although the Gold Bugs swept the series, the Page Fence Giants continued to exhibit their ability to draw substantial crowds.[7]

The Giants embarked on a long barnstorming tour throughout Wisconsin, Minnesota, Illinois, and Indiana. According to the *Detroit Free Press,* the Page club won thirty-five straight games against clubs within this region of the country. In June, the Giants began a forty-game schedule throughout Michigan, beginning in Hillsdale with a fifteen-to-five victory. Unlike the previous season, Parsons scheduled more games in Adrian, and the Giants' birthplace served as the club's home base. On July 1, fifteen hundred fans watched the Grand Rapids Gold Bugs defeat the Giants, twelve to five. A month later, the Page club avenged their home loss by defeating the Gold Bugs, six to four. According to the *Free Press,* the Giants had to beat both the Gold Bugs and the umpire, as several close calls favored the Western League club.[8]

By late July, press reports announced the series between the Page Fence Giants and the Cuban X Giants for the Colored Championship of the United States. A seventeen-game series was scheduled that had both clubs crisscrossing the state of Michigan, with stops in South Bend, Indiana; and Lima and Montpelier, Ohio. The series was significant for two reasons. For the Cuban X Giants, the series elevated their status to a touring team for the first time since the late 1880s. In addition to making this extended barnstorming tour, the Cuban X Giants established a home base in North Adams, Massachusetts. The series also justified the players leaving J. M. Bright and forming a cooperative enterprise with E. B. Lamar. The players demonstrated their business acumen by handling matters on the field as well as off. Second, the series served as a litmus test for the Page Fence Giants. Previously, they had established a home base in Adrian and extended their barnstorming tour. By defeating the Cuban X Giants on the diamond, the Page Fence Giants would elevate their status as one of the premier black clubs of the late nineteenth century.[9]

However, the series almost did not occur. According to the *Adrian Daily Times and Expositor,* a dispute emerged between Gus Parsons and one of his pitchers, Joseph "Kid" Miller. In 1895, Miller compiled a seven-and-four record and also played in the outfield, amassing a .231 batting average. Miller was charged with allegedly "throwing" a game in order to obtain his release. He was reportedly offered $125 a month to play for a semipro club in Bryan, Ohio. Upon his release from the Giants, Miller claimed that Parsons owed him $25 and threatened to attach the gate receipts from a scheduled game between the Page club and the Bryan club. Parsons canceled the game. Two days before the series began, the Cuban X Giants signed a pitcher named Miller. If the player in question turned out to be Kid Miller, Parsons could have possibly withdrawn from the series. But the conflict was averted when the X Giants' new player turned out to be Frank Miller, who also pitched and played in the outfield.[10]

With the prospective controversy resolved, the series began poorly for the Page Fence Giants. They lost a close game in the opener, eight to six, and then were manhandled, twenty to thirteen, behind the poor pitching of Billy Holland. In game three, the Page club demolished the X Giants, winning twenty-six to six, and proceeded to win the next three games. After ten games, the Page club led the series six games to four. They proceeded to win five out the next six games and won the series eleven games to six. The Page Fence Giants received a commemorative silver medal engraved with the inscription: "1896 Page Fence Giants Champions." More important, although the coverage was sporadic, the series did receive national press coverage in the *New York Sun*, the *Detroit Free Press*, the *Adrian Daily Times and Expositor*, and the *Sporting Life*.[11]

Crowning the Page Fence Giants as Colored Champions, however, was premature. According to the informal parameters that determined the Colored Champions, neither club had played the top black club within its respective region of the country. Bright refused to play the Cuban X Giants, while the Page club did not play the Chicago Unions. As we shall see later, another series billed as the Colored Championship took place in the Windy City.

Reorganization, Rivalry, and Conflict

The demise of the Chicago City League resulted in a reorganization of the Windy City's informal amateur baseball hierarchy. At the top of the ladder were several independents that included the Chicago Unions, Dalys, Edgars, Mandel Brothers, and Schroeder Brothers. The remaining clubs were in an assortment of leagues and associations that resided under the Chicago Amateur Baseball Association's umbrella. Ironically, there was no indication that these independents sought to form their own league. The rivalries between these clubs became very lucrative. The Cranes, Franklins, or Careys could have been a sixth club in a prospective league. Evidently, these club operators were satisfied with the barnstorming patterns they created. All these clubs barnstormed the midwestern states for gate receipts during the week, returning to Chicago for Sunday games. Moreover, the precarious existence of Chicago's amateur clubs may have also influenced these club owners' decision to remain independent.

The Unions in particular appeared to have mastered this mode of operation by the 1896 season. Frank Leland functioned as the Unions' traveling manager, handling administrative duties on the road, while Peters remained in Chicago. The Unions barnstormed during the week throughout Illinois, Indiana, and Michigan. The *Chicago Inter Ocean* reported that during one stretch, the Unions went on a seven-game winning streak against "the best teams in Michigan." A strong rivalry emerged between the Unions and the Whiting Grays of Whiting, Indiana, and an aggregate of fans from Chicago traveled with the club to root for the "colored champions." The *Inter Ocean* reported that "interested parties" desiring to see these two clubs play in Whiting should meet at Unions outfielder Al Hackley's shop on Thirty-sixth Street.[12]

The 1896 season provided the best evidence of the Unions' ability to generate revenue from Sunday games in Chicago. Average attendance at Union Park

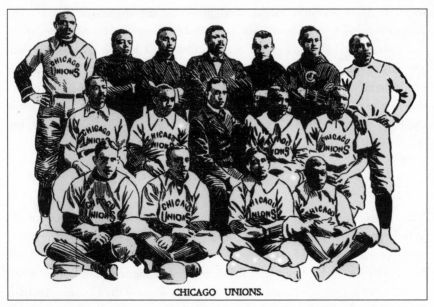

CHICAGO UNIONS.

By 1897, the Chicago Unions were the premier black club in the West. *Courtesy of the Illinois Historical Society.*

for Sunday games was 3,680 fans, generating $736.00 in ticket revenue. After subtracting the visitor's share, the Chicago Unions made $368.00 for Sunday games. Gate receipts became even more impressive when both clubs arranged a winner-take-all series plus a side bet, ranging anywhere from $100 to $500. For example, the average attendance for a three-game series between the Unions and the Edgars on consecutive Sundays might be approximately 11,040 fans. The series could generate $2,208 in ticket revenue. If the side bet was $500, the winner could realize a profit of $2,708. In addition, the Unions continued to periodically schedule two or three games on a single Sunday, further exploiting the weekend profit potential. Scheduling additional games became a way to cover side bets and minimize the loss of revenue if the Unions lost the series. The Unions had established themselves as the premier gate attraction in Chicago's semiprofessional world. This fact was not lost upon the other white semipro clubs, not to mention black clubs such as New York's Cuban Giants and Cuban X Giants. Furthermore, William Peters and Frank Leland had devised an innovative way to facilitate entrepreneurship in the national pastime.

Nothing illustrates the demand Peters created for his Unions more than a challenge made by an anonymous fan in the *Chicago Inter Ocean*. The fan, referred to as "Unknown," proposed a best-two-out-of-three, winner-take-all series in which he would cover a side bet ranging from $100 to $500. A further stipulation was that the Unions play the Auburn Parks, Schroeder Brothers, or Dalys in the series. The following day, Peters responded by stating his Unions would play any club under the aforementioned terms. Peters added, "If that party that calls himself 'Unknown' is willing to back his favorites, why doesn't he put his money up or shut up, and further sign his name in place of disguising his identity?"[13] It was problematic to tell whether this suggestion was a ploy by one of the aforementioned clubs to arrange such a series. In any event, there is no indication that this series took place.

Interestingly enough, a series was arranged between the Unions and the Dalys for the "Chicago Baseball Championship." A winner-take-all series was scheduled that included a $100 side bet. A reported crowd of 4,350 fans witnessed the Dalys edge the Unions, one to nothing, in the series opener. Unions pitcher Harry Buckner gave up a solo home run to "Dad" Traynor that proved to be all the Dalys needed for victory. In the second game, the Dalys erupted for six runs in the fourth inning and won easily, thirteen to six. The third game was marred in controversy. Dalys manager and CABA president G. S. Cusack accused the Unions of using an "illegal" baseball, resulting in the game being held up for several hours. It is problematic to determine what Cusack meant by an "illegal baseball." The CABA may have possibly adopted the Spalding baseball to be used in association games, but the illegal ball did not provide an advantage for the Unions. The heavy-hitting affair ended with the Dalys scoring one run in the top of ninth, leading to an eleven-to-ten victory. A fourth, and rather meaningless game, also ended in a Dalys win. The Dalys became Chicago's "Amateur Baseball Champion," and avenged the close defeats by the Unions the previous two seasons.[14]

On September 26, the *Chicago Inter Ocean* reported that a triangular series had been organized among the Edgars, Unions, and J. M. Bright's Cuban Giants. It marked the first time since 1888 that Bright toured outside the New York area. The unwanted competition from the Cuban X Giants, not to mention their much publicized Colored Championship series with the Page Fence Giants, led Bright to break from his conservative barnstorming ways. The series was based on the proposition that the Cuban Giants could not win a two-out-of-three-game series with either the Unions or the Edgars. According to the *Inter Ocean*, the three clubs and "several local followers" had contributed a purse worth $1,000. The series between the Cuban Giants and the Chicago Unions was for the "world's colored championship."[15]

The series began with the Unions playing the Edgars at the latter's home base at Elgin Athletic Park. The Edgars took a three-to-two lead into the ninth inning. In the bottom of the ninth, Unions shortstop William Joyner hit a double and then scored on Gus Hopkins's game-winning home run. The four-to-three victory typified the close games the Unions and Edgars played against each other, fueling the fire of their fierce rivalry.[16]

However, the Unions performed poorly against the Cuban Giants. The Unions took an early five-to-two lead into the sixth inning when the Giants broke the game open, scoring four runs in the sixth, seven in the seventh, one in the eighth, and two in the ninth, and won sixteen to five. The Unions were their own worst enemy, committing nine errors in the contest. The following day, the Giants knocked Unions pitcher Harry Buckner out of the box early and took a ten-to-three lead into the seventh inning. The Unions mounted a comeback in the later innings but eventually lost, eleven to nine. The Cubans had also swept the Edgars in their series and claimed the $1,000 purse. The Cuban Giants put on an impressive performance. Even in defeat, however, organizing this triangular series exemplified the business acumen of Edgars owner Tom Farley and Unions owner William Peters. The Unions did get some satisfaction by defeating the Edgars in the other half of the triangular series.[17]

The Unions' 1896 season was the most successful in their brief history. Peters had developed a local-to-regional barnstorming pattern that enabled the Unions to become a profitable enterprise. The Unions' three-game series with the Cuban Giants elevated their status among the ranks of the elite black clubs, despite their disappointing defeat. The Unions concluded their season on a positive note when they defeated the Minneapolis club of the Western League.[18]

But who were the "real" Colored Champions? Both the Page Fence Giants and the Cuban Giants were spectacular in their respective series, but no evidence was uncovered to suggest that J. M. Bright or Gus Parsons attempted to arrange a Colored Championship series between their respective clubs. Efforts would be made to resolve this dilemma in the upcoming season.

The Cuban X Giants' Finest Hour

J. M. Bright made his initial preparations for the upcoming season that included an ambitious undertaking. The *Sporting Life* reported that Bright had signed George Williams, an original member of the Cubans in the late 1880s, to manage the club. Bright planned a western barnstorming tour throughout

Ohio, Indiana, Michigan, and Canada. The Cubans would also play the Page Fence Giants, but it would not be for the Colored Championship. According to Bright, a Colored Championship series could occur only "when all the crack colored clubs enter into a tournament." [19]

Bright proposed to organize a colored baseball tournament to determine the "genuine colored champion." No doubt hiring Williams to manage the club on the field allowed Bright to organize the tournament. He secured a lease for a playing ground in Gloversville, New York, a small town located approximately two hundred miles north of New York City. Bright invited several black clubs to travel to Gloversville that included the Page Fence Giants; Pinchbacks of New Orleans, Louisiana; Red Stockings of Norfolk, Virginia; Chicago Unions; and Cuban Giants. The Cuban X Giants were not invited to the tournament. Given the antagonistic relationship between Bright and his former players, the Cuban X Giants' exclusion was predictable. The plan would have these clubs barnstorm their way to Gloversville, compete in the tournament, and barnstorm their way back to their respective regions of the country. Bright had also secured a lease for a playing ground in Brooklyn, and some of the tournament games would be played there.[20] The proposed baseball tournament typified the kinds of grandiose schemes Bright was known for. Although the plan was commendable in theory, Bright failed to obtain agreements from the invited clubs, and the tournament never took place.

Whereas Bright's attempt to organize a colored baseball tournament failed, E. B. Lamar and his Cuban X Giants embarked on one of the most successful extended barnstorming tours of the late nineteenth century. The tour was scheduled in such a way that the X Giants would play several black clubs in Colored Championship series. Simultaneously, the Cuban X Giants played the top white semipro clubs of Chicago, the National League's Cincinnati Reds, and clubs in smaller cities and towns such as Marion, Ohio. This way, the Cuban X Giants marketed and promoted themselves utilizing the same strategy devised by S. K. Govern in the late 1880s—creating a demand for their club in several locales.

Concurrently, William Peters continued his innovative ways of marketing and promoting his Chicago Unions. He booked several Sunday games with the top black clubs of the South and East and billed them as Colored Championship series. With Leland traveling with the Unions on the road, Peters organized a junior semiprofessional club, consisting of young men from the ages of fourteen to sixteen.[21] In May, the Unions began the Colored Championship series by playing the Page Fence Giants. A reported crowd of fifty-four hundred fans watched the Unions nip the Giants behind the pitching and hitting of Harry Buckner. Chicago trailed, four to three, going into the sixth inning, when the Unions broke the game open with four runs in the seventh and won seven to six.

In June, the Cuban X Giants invaded Unions' Park. A three-game series was scheduled that included a Sunday doubleheader. The Unions became their own worst enemy throughout the series. In the first game, the Unions committed five errors and were easily defeated, fourteen to five. The Unions won the second game behind the excellent pitching of Billy Holland, but their poor defense proved their undoing in the third game. Union fielders committed eleven errors and lost the game, fourteen to nine, thus allowing the Cuban X Giants to claim victory over the Colored Champions of the West.[22]

The Cuban X Giants continued their extended tour of the West and South. The tour took them through St. Louis, southern Illinois, and Indiana. By late June, the X Giants scheduled a two-game series with the National League Cincinnati Reds. After losing the first game, three to one, the X Giants took a seven-to-three lead into the eighth inning of game two. According to the *Cincinnati Enquirer*, the Giants began taunting the Reds with their vaudevillian style of play, but this time their unconventional playing style worked against them, as the Cubans eventually lost the game, eight to seven. The most important games on the tour took place in Louisville, Kentucky. The Cuban X Giants played a two-game series with the Brotherhoods, the self-proclaimed Colored Champions of the South. The Cuban X Giants swept the series. By July 1, the Cuban X Giants played thirty-five games on their extended western tour, winning twenty-eight of them.[23]

Meanwhile, in Chicago, William Peters continued booking the top black clubs from the South and East. Colored Championship series were scheduled with the Cliffords of Memphis, Tennessee, and J. M. Bright's Cuban Giants. Peters also attempted to schedule games with the Brotherhoods of Louisville and the Kansas City Unions. However, Peters was unable to book games with these clubs. A best-two-out-of-three series was scheduled with the Cliffords, who also claimed to be the Colored Champion of the South, during the Fourth of July holiday. The first game was a slugfest, with the Cliffords taking a six-to-four lead after one inning. Unions second baseman Gus Hopkins became the hitting hero, belting two home runs en route to an eighteen-to-thirteen win. The Cliffords were never in the second game; the Unions, scoring eight runs in the second inning, won easily, seventeen to five.[24]

In late August, J. M. Bright's Cuban Giants made their way to the Windy

City. From the outset, the Unions were waiting for this rematch after their poor performance the previous season. Unions catcher Robert Footes and pitcher Harry Buckner hit a pair of home runs and led a twenty-two-hit attack against the Cubans. Although the Giants mounted a late-game rally, they fell short and lost, twenty-one to twelve. Game two was a much closer affair, but the Unions prevailed, eleven to nine. Game three was also a heavy-hitting affair. The Unions jumped to a big lead early and led fourteen to seven going into the ninth inning. Once again, the Giants mounted a late-game comeback, but they still came up short and lost, fourteen to twelve. Although Chicago had previously lost to the Cuban X Giants, the Unions found some satisfaction in avenging their poor performance against the Cuban Giants the previous year.[25]

On September 19, the *Chicago Inter Ocean* announced the formation of a player benefit ceremony for former Chicago White Stockings star Fred Pfeffer. Often called "Unzer Fritz" by the sportswriters, Pfeffer was a star second baseman for many years who later wrote a book titled *Scientific Baseball*. In 1881, Pfeffer was one of several players who walked off the field during Moses Fleetwood Walker's warm-up in Louisville. He was part of the legendary White Stockings infield that included Cap Anson at first base and Ed Williamson at shortstop. In 1894, Pfeffer, along with former Louisville manager Billie Barnie and former Pittsburgh manager Al Buckenberger, was involved in an attempt to form a rival league, a new American Association, to compete against the National League. The senior circuit ruthlessly squelched the idea in the planning stage. Because of their role in attempting to organize the new league, Pfeffer, Barnie, and Buckenberger were "suspended" and ruled "ineligible to be employed" until they proved their innocence to the satisfaction of the National League. Barnie and Pfeffer were invited to appear before the league board, but the latter sent a letter instead. Pfeffer explained that when he was injured toward the end of the season, he had secured his release from Louisville by forfeiting the balance of his salary, and it was only then that he had decided to connect with the association. This alibi did not convince the board members, and they turned him down because his letter was "extremely indefinite and unsatisfactory." Pfeffer signed on as a baseball coach at Princeton University, but he let it be known that he would rather play in the big leagues, and the fans came to his rescue. According to Harold Seymour, approximately ten thousand fans signed a petition asking for his reinstatement and promised to boycott National League parks if he did not get it. The league compromised and reinstated the star second baseman after levying a five hundred-dollar fine against him.[26]

As part of the festivities, the Unions played the Marquettes in an exhibition game that Pfeffer umpired. The Unions' participation in this benefit typified the kind of compromises black entrepreneurs made in the white baseball world. Although Pfeffer was a fan favorite, he also had an obvious disdain for black players. In addition to the Louisville incident, Pfeffer was also a member of the White Stockings team in 1883 when Cap Anson reportedly told Toledo manager Charlie Morton to "get that nigger [Moses Fleetwood Walker] off the field." Black baseball clubs had customarily used celebrities as umpires in their games as gate attractions. From the Unions' perspective, participating in Fred Pfeffer Day was a business decision. The former White Stockings star possessed the kind of appeal that put fans in the stands.

While the Unions participated in Fred Pfeffer Day, J. M. Bright finally relented to a championship series with the Cuban X Giants. No doubt Bright's capitulation was in response to the proposed baseball tournament that had failed to materialize. Three games were scheduled on consecutive Sundays in Weekhawken, New Jersey. After winning the opening game, eleven to nine, the Cuban Giants lost the next two games, enabling the Cuban X Giants to proclaim themselves as the "world's colored champions." According to E. B. Lamar, the Cuban X Giants had defeated the Chicago Unions (champions of the West) and the Brotherhoods of Louisville (the southern champions). By defeating the Cuban Giants, the X Giants had defeated all the top black clubs of the West, South, and East. However, during the course of the series, R. L. White, manager of the Chamberlain Baseball Club of Old Point, Virginia, issued a challenge to the winner of the series between the Cuban Giants and the Cuban X Giants. According to White, his players were the "champions of the South."[27]

Clearly, these informal standards for determining the Colored Champion were flawed and served as a source of confusion rather than clarification. Yet this conflict generated valuable publicity for the black game. Several black clubs, particularly from the South, began to surface and sought to challenge the Cuban Giants or the Cuban X Giants for black baseball supremacy. Defeating one of these clubs elevated a black club's status, as the Page Fence Giants and the Chicago Unions could attest. Competition brought out the best in the Cuban X Giants, who probably had their finest season since 1888, but at the same time, determining who was the "true" Colored Champion led to petty disputes among the club owners that carried into the next season.

Seeds of Transition

E. B. Lamar and J. M. Bright continued squabbling with each other. This time, their dispute included the alleged signing of several black players. Although signing top-level players ensured a semipro club's competitiveness, black stars with a reputation brought a significant degree of brand equity to a club. A black player with vaudevillian flair on the diamond or one with a comical coaching routine put fans in the stands. A black player whose skills were comparable to a white major league star also improved a black club's appeal. On March 26, Lamar reported in the *Sporting Life* that James Robinson, the "Black Russie," had signed with the Cuban X Giants. Lamar charged Bright with claiming to sign black players that he did not have under contract. Moreover, Lamar was unsure why Bright was engaging in such a false advertisement.[28]

Concurrently, a controversy arose over an effort to schedule a series of games between the two clubs. Lamar offered to schedule a ten-game series: five games to be played on the X Giants' home grounds in North Adams, Massachusetts, and five games to be played in either Weekhawken, New Jersey, or Albany, New York. To make the offer more attractive, Lamar would pay one hundred dollars for every game the Cuban Giants won. In addition, every game the Cuban X Giants won, Lamar would donate fifty dollars to the *New York Journal* Monument Fund.[29]

Bright took issue with Lamar "dictating" terms to him. The Cubans' owner pointed out that he did not have a say in which grounds the game would be played on. According to Bright, it was owing to the five prospective games scheduled in North Adams that Lamar could make a donation to the Monument Fund, if the X Giants won. Instead, Bright proposed that all ten games be played on neutral grounds, possibly in Philadelphia or Washington, D.C. To somewhat evade the issue, Bright asked where had the Cuban X Giants won the Colored Championship of the "East or anywhere else?"[30] This obvious subterfuge allowed Bright to avoid scheduling this ten-game series with the Cuban X Giants.

Instead, the Cuban X Giants devised what could best be described as a barnstorming rivalry tour with the Chicago Unions. From the beginning, only the reported games in Chicago were billed as a Colored Championship series. A series of games were scheduled throughout Wisconsin, Illinois, and Michigan. Simultaneously, both clubs scheduled games with white semipros on open dates. In Chicago, the Unions secured the services of Fred Pfeffer to umpire the games. Harry Buckner and James Robinson dueled to a three-all tie in the first game. After the Cuban X Giants won the second game, the final contest proved to be a hard-hitting affair. The Giants took a six-to-three lead in the first, and then fell behind, ten to seven, after six innings. After scoring one run in the seventh, a three-run rally in the eighth led to an eleven-to-ten X Giants win. The Cuban X Giants defeated the Chicago Unions for the Colored Championship of the West for the second straight year. But the Unions did receive some vindication in the remaining games of the barnstorming tour. In late September, the Unions played four games with the Giants in Elkhorn, Wisconsin; Michigan City, Michigan; and Sheldon, Illinois. The Unions won three out of the four games.[31]

Upon their return to the East, J. M. Bright relented, once again, to a three-game series with the Cuban X Giants. However, this series was not billed as the Colored Championship of the East. Regardless of how the series was promoted, the Cuban X Giants continued their dominance over the Cuban Giants by winning the series in two games. For the second straight year, the Cuban X Giants had a spectacular season. They played 136 games, winning 101, losing 31, and tying 4.[32]

Forming this cooperative enterprise with E. B. Lamar was a wise business decision. Of the several members who formed the Cuban X Giants, both Lamar and the players had successfully created a demand for their club within the ranks of white semipros clubs, as well as with several black teams in the West and South. Their extended barnstorming tour exemplified a type of emancipation from the shackles of J. M. Bright's conservative and underhanded operation. The Cuban X Giants' poor performance against the Page Fence Giants in 1896 served as a wake-up call in terms of sustaining their reputation as the late-nineteenth-century elite Afro-American club. Moreover, the Cuban X Giants' performance in 1897 and 1898 illustrated that they could meet the challenge sparked by competition, which generated a significant degree of publicity for the black game.

In contrast, the Chicago Unions' 1898 season proved to be a bizarre one. The Unions maintained their barnstorming pattern of touring the states of Wisconsin, Illinois, Michigan, and Indiana during the week, and returning to Chicago for Sunday games. Peters scheduled several games with Western League clubs throughout the season, playing several close games with the Detroits and Charles Comiskey's St. Paul club. Scheduling games with Ban Johnson's Western League during the season attested to both Peters's business acumen and his Unions' competitiveness on the field.[33]

By mid-August, the seeds of decline were sown. Several factors contributed to the Unions' decline from the elite black clubs. The rise of the Columbia Giants constituted the first factor. Sol White stated that in 1899 the Page Fence Giants were stationed in Chicago. However, according to the *Chicago Inter Ocean*, the Page club had relocated a year earlier. It is unclear why the Page club relocated to Chicago. Thomas Powers contends that the nation's economic downturn resulted in a decline in attendance at Giants games.[34] What is often overlooked is the fact that the Page Fence Giants' home base, Adrian, Michigan, was a small city. Although Adrian was only sixty miles from Detroit, this Western League city did not have a semipro baseball infrastructure comparable to Chicago's. Racial prejudice was, no doubt, another reason the Giants played virtually no games in Detroit, but the thought of playing a club the caliber of the Page Fence Giants could have intimidated Detroit's fledgling semipro teams. Thus, the Windy City became the logical place to relocate.

A group known as the Columbia Club financially supported the Giants. Although the evidence is limited, Columbia Club members appear to have come from the ranks of Chicago's Afro-American elite. From the outset, the Afro-American leadership mounted a campaign against a biracial system, in an effort to reach the ultimate goal of integration into the mainstream of American society. Their major civic undertakings were designed to secure equal rights for Afro-Americans, and between 1865 and 1900, Afro-American leaders were absorbed in campaigns to secure the ballot, ensure an integrated school system, and pass and then broaden the Civil Rights Act of 1875. Any attempt to organize a separate Afro-American institution was met with stiff opposition from those individuals who regarded it as a form of self-segregation. However, there were some Afro-Americans within Chicago's elite who showed a willingness to work within the framework of a biracial institutional structure. Although the ultimate goal of integration was never abandoned, it was temporarily relegated to the background. These leaders emphasized self-reliance and racial cooperation, instead of protesting against mounting injustices.[35]

Julius Avendorph represents the Afro-American elite who sought to operate a segregated enterprise within the framework of the white baseball world. Historian Allan Spear points out that Avendorph was the "Ward McAlister of the South Side," limiting his activities to social affairs. It also appears that Avendorph was active in entrepreneurial endeavors. While he was Chicago's "undisputed social leader from 1886 to about 1910," Avendorph, along with Alvin Garrett, formed the Columbia Club, which sponsored the Page Fence Giants in the Windy City. The Columbia Club facilitated the business strategy of economic cooperation that was prevalent among black clubs in the late nineteenth century.[36]

From the outset, the Columbia Club attempted to operate the Giants as a full-time operation. John W. Patterson was the team's field manager. In 1893, Patterson joined the Cuban Giants as a substitute second baseman, and eventually became the starting left fielder. Patterson was also a member of the Page Fence Giants when they defeated the Cuban X Giants for the Colored Championship. According to Sol White, the Columbia Giants were the "best equipped colored team that was ever in the business." The players possessed two sets of uniforms—whites for home games and grays for on the road. The Giants leased a playing ground on Thirty-ninth Street and Wentworth Avenue, an area located on Chicago's South Side. The Giants, however, were no threat to the Unions in their inaugural season. White stated that the Giants drew well on Sunday games in Chicago, but were less financially successful on the road.[37]

To William Peters and Frank Leland, the Columbia Giants were an unwanted competitor. The Unions had benefited from being the only black game in town. Since the Page Fence Giants' inception in 1896, the Unions had rarely played them. Instead of acknowledging the Columbia Giants as a potential rival, the Unions chose to avoid these unwanted competitors.

The Columbia Giants arrived in Chicago at a time when it appeared that the Unions' business relationship with the top white semipros had begun to disintegrate. On August 23, the *Chicago Inter Ocean* reported that Peters had deposited fifty dollars with sports editor and CABA secretary Louis Houseman for a game between the Unions and the Mandel Brothers. Evidently, this deposit represented the Unions' half of a one hundred-dollar purse agreed upon by both clubs. Peters added that if the Mandel Brothers did not post their half of the purse by six o'clock, his Unions would play some other team.[38]

The following day, Mandel Brothers owner R. M. Foltz responded to the imposed deadline. Foltz was obviously irritated by this mandate. He complained that Peters was attempting to gain an advantage by declaring the game would be canceled if he did not post his half of the purse. Foltz added, "I will be a much surprised man if Mr. Peters does not . . . try to break his contract."[39] Peters did not break the contract, and the Unions defeated the Mandel Brothers and won the one hundred-dollar purse.

On September 1, Peters attempted to arrange a three-game series with the Marquettes. He reportedly enclosed a ten-dollar deposit with Houseman, and proposed that each game be played for fifty dollars. Peters's rationale was somewhat odd. The Unions' owner indicated that "[J. P.] Keary [was] going to get the best players that can be found in this city." Peters declared his Unions could possibly win two out of three games, but because the club would play in Freeport, Illinois, on Saturday, his players would "not get home until late and will not get their proper rest." Moreover, according to the *Chicago Inter Ocean*, Peters failed to enclose the ten-dollar deposit to Houseman. On the following day, Peters rectified this oversight. Marquettes manager J. P. Keary was puzzled by Peters's uncharacteristic behavior. Keary asked why Peters would expect him to field a poor ball club just because the Unions traveled all night. Keary accused Peters of making excuses for his Unions, should they lose the series. The Marquettes' manager concluded, "Let him get his men and I will get mine."[40]

Apparently, the three-game series never occurred. On September 9, the *Chicago Inter Ocean* reported that the Unions had played the Cuban X Giants in what turned out to be the first game of the Colored Championship. This obvious breach irritated Keary, who declared that Peters could make money by playing his Marquettes for fifty dollars a game.[41] Peters did not respond to the challenge.

William Peters's search for the "true" Colored Champion resulted in a conflict of interest. The Unions financially benefited by playing the Cuban X Giants. The Giants' reputation alone made them a premier gate attraction, but the Unions' involvement in the Colored Championship series came at the expense of rupturing the symbiotic business relationship with Chicago's white semipros. Moreover, the substantial side bets stimulated fierce rivalries and increased spectatorship. The thought of losing a side bet, particularly a substantial one, was obviously causing insurmountable pressure on both players and owners.

The end of the 1898 season marked the start of black baseball entering another transitory period. New York's and Chicago's black clubs continued their rivalries on the diamond. The Cuban X Giants mapped out a new market to exploit on the Cuban islands. The competition for players and a decline in business relations with white clubs, however, resulted in the Chicago Unions and the Columbia Giants undergoing a significant change.

9

Rivalries, a New Frontier, and Reorganization

*R*ivalries permeated the 1899 season. The Chicago Unions and Cuban X Giants continued to promote black baseball in the Midwest with their combination barnstorming tour and Colored Championship series. Simultaneously, for the first time an all-star squad made up of Cuban ballplayers from Havana, Cuba, toured throughout New York and New Jersey, and also challenged the Cuban X Giants to a championship series. At the same time, the Columbia Giants challenged the Unions for supremacy in the Windy City. The Columbias' victorious effort over the Unions culminated with a Colored Championship series with the Cuban X Giants.

By 1900, black baseball entered another transitional period. The Cuban X Giants barnstormed the Cuban islands in an effort to expand into an international market with the potential for commercial and economic gain. Also, Chicago's semiprofessional infrastructure underwent a significant transformation, which adversely affected the way the Chicago Unions conducted business. The Columbia Giants' rise to prominence resulted in a conflict, primarily over players, among the club owners, William Peters, Frank Leland, and Julius Avendorph. By August 1900, Leland broke with Peters, signed several players from the Unions and the Columbias, and formed the Chicago Union Giants.

◇ ◇ ◇

The Chicago Unions began the 1899 season with a two-game series with Northwestern University. The *Chicago Inter Ocean* reported that Northwestern's ball club "induced" the Unions "to give [their] ball team practice." The Unions outplayed Northwestern in every facet of the game, engaging in their own brand of vaudevillian baseball and comical coaching. According to the *Inter Ocean*, the Unions' coaching antics and pitcher Bert Jones's "capers in the box" resulted in the "royal purple men" nearly losing their dignity. The paper added that the trees overlooking the baseball grounds were "thickly peopled with colored men and boys" who had come to see the game. Obviously, the Afro-American populous was delighted to see the Unions defeat Northwestern, eleven to five. The Unions were also victorious in the second contest.[1]

The Unions and the Cuban X Giants constructed a barnstorming tour along the same lines that William Peters had used to operate his club for the past seven years. In the month of June, both clubs played a series of games with each other throughout Illinois, Indiana, and Wisconsin; they returned to Chicago for Sunday games. Contests in the Windy City were billed as the Colored Championship series, and Fred Pfeffer umpired the games. Although the Cuban X Giants maintained their dominance over the Unions, the Chicago club provided them with some fierce competition.[2]

The Chicago Unions-Cuban X Giants barnstorming tours did more to promote the black game in the Midwest, and also illustrated that the baseball business could be a profitable venture. For three consecutive years, their barnstorming tours created a demand for their clubs in several locales. Even though the Cuban X Giants dominated the series, this imbalance was offset by the high caliber of play between the two clubs. The lack of evidence makes it problematic to determine accurately how profitable this way of doing business was, but because the Unions and Cuban X Giants operated this way for three straight years, it is evident that both clubs were turning a profit. Why would the Cuban X Giants travel west if profits could not be realized? More important, given these two clubs' success, it was no coincidence that many Afro-American entrepreneurs in the opening decades of the twentieth century attempted to operate black baseball clubs for commercial and economic gain.

As the Cuban X Giants returned east, the *Sporting News* printed the following article: "The picked team of Cubans will begin their tour of the United States in August and will remain in [the] country until the latter part of September. Abel Linares, the Cuban's [*sic*] manager . . . is anxious to complete his team's schedule before they leave Cuba. W. W. Laidlaw, THE SPORTING NEWS Havana representative, who is connected with the United States Quartermaster's Department in that city, is associated with Mr. Linares." This all-star team was made up of Cuban players from the Almendarista, Cuba, and Habanist clubs. The club was promoted around their unique style of coaching in Spanish, and the players were characterized by their "excitable temperament" and enthusiasm. Two benefit games were played in Havana to finance the All Cubans' trip to the United States. Laidlaw assisted Linares in his efforts to schedule games with minor league and independent clubs throughout Connecticut, New York, Ohio, Michigan, Indiana, Illinois, Wisconsin, Kentucky, Pennsylvania, West Virginia, Maryland, and New Jersey—an ambitious undertaking.[3]

The All Cubans' arrival in the United States marked the start of what Roberto Gonzalez Echevarria refers to as "the Golden Age of sport in Cuba." Their visit also marked the beginning of black baseball and the Cuban League becoming important chapters in each other's histories. Echevarria points out that baseball had languished in Cuba during the War of Independence (1895–1898), but had been reinvigorated with the U.S. intervention and the subsequent economic recovery. The war had brought many whites and blacks together in a common cause of liberating Cuba from Spain. At the same time, the increasing professionalism of Cuban baseball in the 1870s and 1890s transformed the sport into a potentially lucrative spectacle. As Lisa Brock and Bijan Bayne point out, more than two hundred baseball clubs organized across the islands.[4] In addition, as nationalist revolutionary clubs were established in Tampa, New Orleans, New York, and Philadelphia, they too organized ball clubs. In some ways, the arrival of the All Cubans to the United States served as a symbolic gesture of their liberation from Spain, enabling entrepreneurs to seize the opportunity to transform baseball into a paying proposition.

Abel Linares was the entrepreneur responsible for bringing the All Cubans to the United States. Little is known about Linares's early background. Echevarria states that Linares was one of three promoters who shaped the early history of professional Cuban baseball. Agustin "Tinti" Molina and Alejandro Pompez were the other influential entrepreneurs. In the mid-1900s, Linares would field a powerful Almendares squad that featured Rafael Almeida and Armando Marsans. Both players had brief stints in the major leagues.[5]

Antonio Garcia and Tinti Molina were among the all-star players who would be influential in the emerging connection between Cuban and black baseball in the early twentieth century. According to James Riley, Garcia was considered the best Cuban player of the nineteenth century. His career spanned twenty-four years (1882–1905) in his homeland, and he was an outstanding catcher who also played first base and in the outfield. Molina, on the other hand, was not a star player on the island. A veteran of the Spanish-American War, Molina played several positions, primarily first base, batting a mere .164. As previously stated, Molina would make his mark as a promoter, and he would be Abel Linares's first lieutenant.[6]

The All Cubans were impressive in their head-to-head competition against white semipro teams. On July 28, the All Cubans easily defeated a picked team, twelve to four, in Weehawken, New Jersey. Three days later, a reported crowd of eighteen hundred fans watched the All Cubans lose a close game with the West New York Field Club, eight to five. The All Cubans' "coaching" in Spanish and the players' "thorough knowledge of base ball entertained the fans." According to the *Sporting News*, language was a barrier between the Cuban players and umpire Tim Hurst when the latter called balls and strikes. Hurst explained: "I said for one ball, 'Uno ballo'; for one strike, 'Uno striko'; but after that all bets were off. I couldn't make them understand if I had a Spanish dictionary in one hand and a megaphone in the other." Language did not enter the equation when the All Cubans demolished the Orange Athletics, eighteen to five, in New York. The Mountain A. C. club played the All Cubans tough. The score was tied at three going into the eighth, when the Cubans erupted for four runs in the bottom of the frame and coasted to a nine-to-three win. The Cubans finally met their match in Jersey City, New Jersey, as the Jerseys trounced them, fourteen to four.[7]

By mid-August, the All Cubans challenged the Cuban X Giants. According to the *New York Sun*, the All Cubans protested "against the Cuban X Giants posing as representatives of Cuba." To resolve the alleged dispute, a contest was scheduled on the St. George Cricket grounds in Hoboken, New Jersey. Behind the five-hit pitching of James Robinson, the Giants defeated the All Cubans, seven to three. The game was never in question, as the Giants scored five runs in the first three innings. The All Cubans licked their wounds and challenged the Cuban X Giants to a second game, the winner to receive all the gate receipts. The game was tied at three going into the fourth inning, when the Giants erupted for five runs in the bottom of the frame, coasting to an eleven-to-six victory.[8]

Undoubtedly, the brief two-game series marked the start of the connection between Cuban and black baseball that would significantly shape their historical development in the early twentieth century. As we shall see later, the Cuban X Giants would embark on a barnstorming tour of the Cuban islands prior to the start of the 1900 season. Evidently, it was during this time that Linares and Giants players made the initial arrangements for the Afro-American club to visit the Cuban islands.

While the Cuban X Giants continued their winning ways in the East, the Columbia Giants emerged to challenge the Chicago Unions for black baseball supremacy in the Windy City. Giants owner Julius Avendorph and field manager John W. Patterson managed the club along the same lines that Peters had operated his Unions. The Giants toured Illinois, Indiana, and Michigan during the week, returning to Chicago for Sunday games. Like the Unions, the Giants played two or three games on Sunday at their home grounds, located at Thirty-ninth Street and Wentworth Avenue. The limited press coverage makes it difficult to assess the Giants' revenue potential, but there are indications that Sunday games were well attended. On July 23, the Columbia Giants defeated an Afro-American club from Nashville before a reported crowd of thirty-five hundred. Thirty-eight hundred fans witnessed the Giants defeat the Heaphys, a local white semipro club.[9]

By early September, the Columbia Giants issued a challenge to play the Chicago Unions for the Colored Championship. At first, Peters avoided the Columbia club, primarily because Patterson had signed pitcher Harry Buckner away from the Unions. However, according to Sol White, out of consideration for the public the Unions agreed to a five-game series. No doubt the Giants' attendance at Sunday games also influenced Peters's decision to agree to the series. It was a high-stakes series, as both clubs agreed to a winner-take-all series and a one hundred-dollar side bet on each game. To offset the potential losses, the Giants and Unions scheduled additional Sunday games on the same day they faced each other. The first game set the tone for the whole series. A reported nine thousand fans packed Unions' Park for the opening game. Giants pitcher Harry Buckner shut out his former teammates en route to a one-to-nothing victory. The Unions were never in the series, as they lost the next four games![10]

The Columbia Giants turned their attention toward the Cuban X Giants. Defeating the Cubans would enable the Columbia club to proclaim themselves the world's Colored Champions. The Cuban X Giants were having a phenomenal season, defeating the Unions earlier in the year, and fending off a challenge from the All Cubans. A series of games was scheduled in Chicago and in towns throughout Michigan. In the first game, William Selden held the Columbia club in check, as the Cubans scored five runs in the fourth inning and coasted to a seven-to-four victory. The Cuban X Giants outclassed and outplayed the Columbia club, winning the series, seven games to four. The series victory avenged the 1896 defeat to the then Page Fence Giants.[11]

While the Cuban X Giants, Columbia Giants, and Chicago Unions con-

In 1900, the Cuban X Giants were the first black club to visit Cuba. They played
fifteen games, winning thirteen and losing two. *Courtesy of the National Baseball Hall
of Fame Library, Cooperstown, N.Y.*

tinued to promote the black game in the East and Midwest, J. M. Bright returned to his old conservative ways of operation. Bright's Cubans would make
a tour of the Midwest in 1900.[12] It is evident that Bright lost some degree of
credibility when he failed to stage his "real" Colored Championship series in
1897. He appeared satisfied with operating as a local stay-at-home, capitalizing on the lucrative Sunday games in New York. As the United States entered
the twentieth century, several changes, both internal and external, resulted in
black baseball entering a transitional period.

The Cuban X Giants' barnstorming tour in Cuba constituted the first factor influencing this transitional period. On February 6, 1900, the *Diario de la
Marina* announced: "According to a cablegram sent to this city by Mr. E. B.
Lamar we learn that the latter will sail to Havana from New York next Saturday. The team is coming to play a series of ten matches against the nines of Habana, San Francisco, Almendares, and Cuba." The Giants played a series of
games in Havana against Cuban League clubs and an aggregate of all-star
teams. On February 26, the Cuban X Giants faced Habana, a Cuban League
club, and defeated them, six to five.[13]

The Cuban X Giants rolled up a string of victories against the Cuban League clubs and all-star teams. By March 16, the *New York Sun* reported that the Giants had played seven games on the island, their latest victims the San Franciscos, going down in defeat ten to five. Two days later, the Giants defeated the Liberty club from Regla, despite playing on a field that made it virtually impossible for both clubs to play. The Cuban clubs provided the Giants with some fierce competition. On March 22, the San Franciscos played the Giants tough before bowing to defeat, ten to eight. On March 29, the Havanas lost a four-to-two heartbreaker to the New York nine.[14]

On March 30, 1900, a Cuban club finally defeated the Cuban X Giants. The Criollo club swept the Giants in a two-game series that culminated the New York club's barnstorming tour. Although the Cuban X Giants won thirteen of fifteen games, Criollo's victories reinforced Echevarria's assertion that Cuban baseball had come a long way since a U.S. club, the Athletics, had soundly beaten the Habanas and the Almendares in the 1880s. Moreover, Criollos wins provided Cuban baseball with some vital brand equity that, no doubt, whetted the appetite of Cuban impresarios who saw an opportunity to capitalize upon the sport's potential for commercial and economic gain. After all, a Cuban club had defeated the most dominant "colored baseball" team in the United States.[15]

The Cuban X Giants' barnstorming tour of the Cuban islands illustrated that this club not only was an exceptional team on the diamond, but also possessed an uncanny ability to facilitate entrepreneurship in America's national game. Only Clarence Williams remained from the original club that had started at the Argyle Hotel in 1885. His business acumen, in conjunction with E. B. Lamar's administrative efforts, formed a successful cooperative business enterprise that was rivaled by only the Chicago Unions. Much like his predecessor S. K. Govern, Williams kept a nucleus of quality players together for several years that maintained their dominance on the diamond. Frank Grant, Andy Jackson, Oscar Jackson, James Robinson, and John Nelson formed a club that exemplified the modern-day New York Yankees.

The Cuban X Giants' most significant contribution was establishing the benchmark for both the business and the marketing practices for independent ball clubs, black or white. The fundamental business philosophy of going where the money was and creating a demand for their club in several locales served as the fundamental way black baseball teams operated successfully. Managing a segregated ball club within the framework of the white baseball world exemplified the Afro-American entrepreneurs' willingness to work within the confines of a biracial institutional structure. Engaging in vaudevillian baseball and comical coaching served to sustain fan interest when games became too one-sided. The Giants' trip to Cuba served as a means of expanding into an international market with promising economic potential. Moreover, the Cuban X Giants were able to maintain their cooperative enterprise in the face of several racial, economic, and structural barriers that impeded their progress.

The transformation of Chicago's semiprofessional scene represented the second factor influencing black baseball's transitional phase. The leading white semipro clubs in Chicago—the Dalys, Edgars, and Schroeder Brothers—disbanded. Press coverage of these clubs began to decline in 1899, and by 1901 was virtually nonexistent. The limited evidence makes it difficult to assess why these clubs folded, but their disappearance marked the end of the rivalries they had with the Unions. Only the Mandel Brothers remained from this group of clubs that made up the elite of semipro teams in Chicago.

The collapse of the Chicago Amateur Baseball Association constituted the third factor affecting black baseball's transition. As early as 1897, internal division existed within the association, leading to the creation of a new one, the Associated Baseball Clubs (ABC). Evidently, with the CABA's collapse in 1898, the ABC became the official governing body for the Windy City's semipro clubs. Its primary function was to schedule games for semipro clubs at the various parks throughout Chicago. Thus, the ABC served essentially as a booking agent.[16]

On May 26, 1900, the *Chicago Inter Ocean* reported that a dispute over the division of gate receipts had occurred between the Sycamore Baseball Club and the Chicago Unions. According to the *Inter Ocean*, Peters had agreed to pay the Sycamore Club 40 percent of the gate receipts, but the Unions' owner was twenty-five dollars short. The Sycamore Club appealed to the ABC in an effort to collect their money. The ABC directors ruled in favor of the Sycamore club and gave Peters three days to pay the balance or be suspended from the association. Peters declared the case to be a "holdup" and stated he would not pay another cent to the Sycamore team.[17]

The Sycamore incident highlighted the fourth factor affecting black baseball's transition, which was the declining business relationship between the Chicago Unions and white semipro clubs. When Peters began to book more black clubs into Unions' Park for Sunday games, particularly the Cuban X Giants and Cuban Giants, it led to some bitter feelings among white operators looking for a big payday. Previously, Peters bypassing the Marquette club to play the Cuban Giants in a Colored Championship series had outraged manager J. P. Keary.[18] In addition, the winner-take-all series and the substantial side bets on some series further exacerbated this antagonism. The Unions' dominance over white semipro clubs could have possibly made the latter reluctant to play them, in spite of the economic reward. As their record indicates, the Unions played to win, despite the possible racial hostility it could generate. A black club consistently beating a white one was a hard pill to swallow in nineteenth-century America.

The increased animosity between the Chicago Unions and the Columbia Giants represented the final factor affecting black baseball's transitional phase. From the outset, Sol White stated that both clubs were at "loggerheads" with each other. The Columbia club's defeat of the Unions in 1899 ranked them among the elite in Chicago's semipro circles. In 1900, the Columbia Giants defeated J. M. Bright's Cuban Giants in a series that was not billed as a Colored Championship series. Concurrently, the Unions defeated the Cuban X Giants, marking the first time the Windy City club beat the New York nine in a series. But a disputed championship for local supremacy between the Columbia club and the Unions intensified the resentment.[19]

In spite of this dispute, the Columbia Giants further elevated their status with a season-ending series with Charles Comiskey's White Stockings. Comiskey had moved his club from St. Paul, Minnesota, to Chicago as part of Ban Johnson's effort to make his Western League a second major league. It was renamed the American League (AL) in 1900 to denote its growing ambition, with franchises in Buffalo, Chicago, Cleveland, Detroit, Indianapolis, Kansas City, Milwaukee, and Minneapolis. Comiskey moved his club to the Windy City after receiving the local NL club's permission. He agreed to relocate to the South Side and allow the Chicago Colts to draft two players after the season. Comiskey confiscated the familiar old nickname "White Stockings," shortened it to White Sox two years later, but was not allowed to include the word *Chicago* in front of *White Sox*. In any event, a two-game series was scheduled between the two clubs at the Giants' home grounds at Thirty-ninth and Wentworth. The Columbias scored four runs in the first three innings, Harry Buckner held the White Stockings' hitters in check, and the Giants won, five to three. The second game lasted only four innings, as inclement weather shortened the contest with the White Stockings ahead, eight to four.[20]

The Columbia Giants' rise in status resulted in a war over players and the eventual dismantling of the Giants and Chicago Unions. On April 5, 1901, the *Chicago Inter Ocean* reported that the Unions had signed John Patterson and

Harry Buckner away from the Columbia Giants. One month later, the Unions signed Bert Jones and Harry Moore from the Columbia club.[21] The Unions' signing of these players left the Columbia Giants in a crippled condition, but they managed to finish the season. Although the evidence is limited, it appears that Frank Leland was behind the efforts to sign these players away from the Columbia Giants. Evidently, Leland grew weary of being Peters's lieutenant. He had also recognized that the Unions' business relationship with white semipros was deteriorating. In addition, the rivalries the Unions had over the years with the Edgars, Dalys, and Schroeder Brothers no longer existed. By August 1901, Leland broke with Peters and formed the Chicago Union Giants. As the name illustrates, several players from the Unions and Giants formed this new club. There were now three black clubs operating in the Windy City.

The dismantling of the Chicago Unions and Columbia Giants resulted in a gnawing dilemma. Players benefited from these club owners' willingness to bid for their services. The presence of three black baseball clubs provided the players options previously unavailable to them. However, as the Cubans-Gorhams war over players illustrated, black baseball magnates' increased payroll diminished their profits. Both the management and the player force lost out if the club did not generate substantial gate receipts on a consistent basis to offset expenses. This dilemma could be more problematic if the owner and players agreed to a co-op plan. In any event, Leland's break with Peters resulted in the Unions losing their lease on Unions' Park at Thirty-seventh Street and Butler Avenue. For the remainder of the season, the Unions were relegated to a traveling team, and they no longer maintained the barnstorming patterns that had sustained their operations throughout the 1890s. The dismantling of both the Unions and the Giants brought to an end the East-West connection with the Cuban X Giants.[22]

The 1901 season did end, somewhat, on a positive note. The Chicago Union Giants and Columbia Giants agreed to a season-ending series for the "colored championship of the world." A best-two-out-of-three series was scheduled on consecutive Sundays at Charles Comiskey's American League Park. The Columbia club was victorious in the first game. In the second game, four hundred fans braved the cold, and, according to the *Chicago Inter Ocean*, both clubs played on a field that "was fit for mud horses." The game was tied at two, when the Columbias scored one run in the seventh inning and won three to two, proclaiming themselves the "colored champions of the world."[23] Of course, this proclamation was premature, even under the informal parameters that determined the world's Colored Champion. However, the season-ending series marked the end of one era and the beginning of a new one in black baseball history.

Epilogue: Toward the Rise of the Negro Leagues

As the Columbia Giants and Chicago Union Giants completed the 1901 season, the components that formed black baseball's institutional structure were fully developed. From the beginning, black baseball's institutional development occurred within the framework of community building in the 1840s, and was grounded in the need for nineteenth-century Afro-Americans to address health concerns that resulted in a high mortality rate. Baseball also served as a vehicle in the Afro-American pursuit for self-determination, self-improvement, self-help, and freedom. Theoretically, the Philadelphia Pythians' membership in the Pennsylvania Association of Amateur Base Ball Players would symbolically achieve this goal.

Despite the Pythians' failure to gain entry into the PAABBP, black baseball continued to flourish among Afro-Americans. The sport was transformed into a commercial enterprise by Afro-Americans who were willing to operate within the parameters of a biracial institutional structure. Much like other black businesses of the era, Afro-American baseball entrepreneurs recognized that in order to do business in capitalist America, they had to negotiate with the white power structure. Therefore, black baseball owners operated their segregated enterprise within the fabric of the developing white baseball world. The mere fact that no large black consumer market existed in the late nineteenth century led these black entrepreneurs to establish business ties with white professional and semiprofessional teams. In essence, black baseball clubs were no longer dependent upon the black community for their institutional and operational existence. Forging business deals with white baseball operators was the only game in town.

The efforts of late-nineteenth-century black baseball entrepreneurs exemplify the overall Afro-American struggle to compete within the framework of the U.S. economy. Their activities were consistent with the ideology commonly attributed to Booker T. Washington, but had its roots in antebellum America.[24] Black businessmen were not to isolate themselves from the larger society, selling only to blacks. Afro-Americans were to advance themselves by free competition on the open market. Nineteenth-century black baseball entrepreneurs' economic philosophy was essentially a laissez-faire formula for black advancement through individual commitment by individual blacks through the gospel of work and wealth. The purpose of self-help and racial solidarity was to encourage black unity and self-assertion on a political level, while encouraging cultural and economic assimilation. Doing so would, theoretically, result in the integration of blacks into mainstream American society. In the case of black baseball, it meant integrating into the white professional and semiprofessional baseball infrastructure.

The ownership-managerial structure also developed along biracial lines. Black baseball clubs exemplified the cooperative enterprise philosophy so prevalent among Afro-American businessmen of the nineteenth and early twentieth centuries. Individuals from outside the baseball world—like headwaiters, barbers, and petty entrepreneurs—as well as from the player force emerged as club owners. Clubs were either black-owned exclusively or partnerships developed with whites that had some significant influence. The team manager, who performed like a modern-day general manager, and the team captain completed the ownership-managerial structure.

There were several reasons that whites became involved with the early black clubs. Albert Reach's involvement with the Philadelphia Pythians of the National Colored League served as a means of tapping into a potentially lucrative market for his sporting goods industry. Walter Cook attempted to operate a successful cooperative enterprise with S. K. Govern. Cook used his influence in Trenton, New Jersey, to provide the Cuban Giants with a suitable playing facility, while Govern managed the day-to-day operations. Gus Parsons's ties with the Page Fence Wire Company provided the needed capital for the creation of the Page Fence Giants, and the club served as a source of market promotion for its sponsors. E. B. Lamar's willingness to operate within the confines of a cooperative enterprise, formed by the players themselves, allowed the Cuban X Giants to become the premier black club of the 1890s.

John M. Bright represented the stingy, and often unethical, white owner who also became involved with black baseball clubs. His constant meddling in the Cuban Giants' day-to-day operations resulted in S. K. Govern leaving the club. Bright devised promotional strategies that failed to materialize. He had a habit of antagonizing a ball club's most important asset—the player force. Because it was more convenient to negotiate with white semipro clubs and park managers in the greater New York area with a white face at the helm, black players tolerated Bright's unsavory ways. Bright also recognized the need for a black player in a position of authority if he wanted to continue operating a successful ball club. This fact, more than anything else, was the primary reason J. M. Bright survived as one of the leading black baseball owners.

Barnstorming became, and would remain, the fundamental mode of operation for black baseball clubs. Attempting to develop a local-to-regional, and ideally a national-to-international, format became the most successful way black baseball clubs functioned. Operating in this fashion required the presence of home grounds within the boundaries of a large urban area that could sustain a commercialized amusement. Clubs that could not consistently navigate this format were less successful.

Without question, S. K. Govern and William Peters were the most successful black baseball entrepreneurs in the late nineteenth century, particularly in the construction of local-to-regional barnstorming tours. Although the Cuban Giants never reached Govern's and Cook's expectations in terms of economic potential, utilizing Trenton as a home base during the week and playing Sunday games in the greater New York area proved to be an efficient way to manage an independent club. Moving to a better location in Trenton did result in Govern scheduling more games with major and minor league clubs and college and semipro teams. By 1887, efforts were made to expand the Cubans' barnstorming tour to a national level, by scheduling games in the Midwest and upper South. By 1897, the Cuban X Giants emulated Govern's earlier efforts by embarking on the longest-known barnstorming tour by a black club in the late nineteenth century. By the turn of the century, the Giants made their initial efforts to tap into an international market by touring the Cuban islands.

On the other hand, William Peters constructed his barnstorming tours in a different manner. The Chicago Unions were the most successful black club that was exclusively owned and operated by blacks in the late nineteenth century. Much of this success was, in part, owing to the willingness of white club owners and park managers to do business with an all-black club, particularly if it meant filling their coffers. Success was also influenced by the development of a white semiprofessional infrastructure that had no rival in the Midwest. From 1893 to 1900, Peters's Unions consistently toured Illinois, Indiana, Michigan, and Wisconsin during the week and returned to Chicago for Sunday games. Rivalries were the lifeblood of semipro clubs in Chicago. Construction of local semipro championships, with a significant degree of gambling, served to stimulate fan interest. Furthermore, Peters scheduled two, sometimes three, games on a single Sunday to cover side bets and generate additional revenue.

Whereas scheduling games remained a primary obstacle for magnates to overcome, Govern and Peters did manage to systematically construct their barnstorming tours to maximize profits. This obstacle was owing to the unstable existence of white semipro teams, and at times minor league clubs, and a reluctance of National League clubs to schedule games with black clubs in the 1890s. In any event, both men utilized the press early in the season to develop their schedules for the upcoming season. Weekend games were crucial to an independent club's economic survival, and Govern and Peters kept their clubs active on the weekends. Both men also recognized the need to schedule a substantial number of games to ensure a season was economically rewarding. Based upon press reports, it appears that scheduling roughly 120 to 144 games was the target. While their clubs were on the road, it also appears that both men had to schedule games spontaneously throughout the season.[25] This fact was probably owing to inclement weather, clubs failing to appear, a need to generate revenue to cover expenses, or the possibility of earning some extra money. Moreover, S. K. Govern and William Peters established the barnstorming patterns that early-twentieth-century black baseball entrepreneurs attempted to emulate.

Because the successful black club operated essentially on an independent basis, Afro-American entrepreneurs had to be more innovative than their white counterparts in terms of market promotion. It began with the development of vaudevillian baseball and comical coaching. Early black baseball clubs were both competitors and entertainers. The tenor of the game and the level of competition provided by their opponents determined the kind of contest that would ensue. The primary purpose of vaudevillian baseball and comical coaching was to keep the fans entertained in the midst of a one-sided game.

Because they were competitors and entertainers does not adequately explain why white clubs played black clubs in the first place. The answer is grounded in the fact that the elite black baseball clubs benefited from the major and minor leagues and semiprofessional teams struggling to place their product on a sound economic footing. The revenue the Cuban Giants and Chicago Unions generated from Sunday games alone made it problematic for white clubs to avoid playing these black teams. For example, in 1887, the Newark club of the International League had to make long road trips into Canada and play clubs in smaller cities, such as Utica and Oswego in upstate

New York. Travel and overhead expenses diminished whatever profits Newark might realize, and this situation was further exacerbated if those games did not draw a good gate.[26] Playing exhibition games with the Cuban Giants at the Polo Grounds or the Elysian Field served to alleviate these expenses or could result in a club breaking even or landing in the black. In some cases, one game with the Cuban Giants could meet the payroll for a white club for an entire week. For some struggling minor league and semipro clubs, this economic reality was too hard to ignore.

However, racial prejudice still overrode this economic imperative. The deep-seated prejudice that defined race relations between blacks and whites in the nineteenth century overrode good business sense. Nothing illustrates this predicament more than Cap Anson's refusal to play the Chicago Unions in the 1890s. After the second war over players between the National League and American Association, Anson's White Stockings declined, finishing no higher than fourth place in a twelve-team league from 1892 to 1900.[27] Despite the Unions' fan following and their business relationship with the top white semipros, no evidence was uncovered to show that these clubs ever played each other. Anson was not alone in his refusal to play black clubs, particularly in a decade when the National League was floundering. Undoubtedly, racial prejudice prevailed over any attempt to make good business decisions from which both parties could have benefited.

The Colored Championship series served to stimulate fan interest in the black game and created a demand for black baseball clubs, particularly in large metropolitan areas. Despite its unstructured format, the Colored Championship generated valuable publicity for black baseball in the late nineteenth century. William Peters used variations of this championship format to create rivalries with white semipro clubs in Chicago. He established a triangular series among his Unions, the Cuban Giants, and the Edgars. In conjunction with the Cuban X Giants, Peters developed the combination barnstorming tour and Colored Championship that began in 1897 and ended in 1900 with the dismantling of his club.

Why would white fans patronize a game between two black clubs? Melvin Adelman asserts that the introduction of business into baseball did not rest upon the distinction between private clubs or private ownership. Rather, it was the willingness of the public to pay the price that contributed to this phenomenon.[28] From the beginning, black baseball entrepreneurs marketed their clubs to a white middle-class clientele. Targeting the white middle class was more out of necessity, as blacks did not constitute a majority in metropolitan cities such as New York, Chicago, and Philadelphia. Faced with this predicament, black baseball entrepreneurs sought to project an image that emulated white middle-class values. Simultaneously, these black operators were willing to make compromises by accommodating racial prejudice and downplaying any situation that may have had racial implications.

Black baseball entrepreneurs were ahead of their time in terms of recognizing sports as entertainment. This fact was, in part, owing to their inability to schedule games with major and minor league clubs on a consistent basis. Playing clubs that were no match for these talented black clubs led to the creation of vaudevillian baseball. Simultaneously, black operators devised promotional schemes to stimulate fan interest, such as sponsoring footraces, constructing local championships, and developing rivalries. In this way, black baseball entrepreneurs created a demand for their product that whites were willing to patronize. Moreover, black baseball entrepreneurs developed a fan base by maintaining this mode of operation over several years.

Maintaining continuity in the player force was crucial to any black baseball club's success. It became extremely important when a black club had some unwanted competition within its territorial region. Black baseball owners such as William Peters benefited from being the only game in town. It served to restrict player movement somewhat, as player contracts were negotiated on a yearly basis. With the rise of competition in the presence of another club, however, players had more options available to them. This demand led to club owners bidding for players' services, resulting in the former paying higher salaries and increasing their overhead expenses.

As the 1902 season approached, both professional and semiprofessional baseball entered a new era. Ban Johnson's effort to make his American League a second major league resulted in another baseball war. The conflict culminated in the formulation of a new national agreement in 1903 and the NL and AL becoming the major leagues of organized baseball. Semiprofessional clubs in New York and Chicago would once again form leagues and associations and seek to establish a governance structure to sustain them. Cuban and black baseball became more inextricably linked in the opening decades of the twentieth century. Black baseball would also enter a brief period of cutthroat competition, as Afro-American entrepreneurs attempted to capitalize upon the baseball craze. Like their white counterparts, black baseball entrepreneurs would make several efforts to form black leagues and associations.

The transformation of northern black communities would also influence black baseball's growth and development. The rise of large black urban centers, such as Chicago and New York, occurred because increased racial hostility coincided with a dramatic change in the patterns of urban life. Migration from other states was the primary source of most of this growth, as the declining or unstable economic conditions, particularly in the South, influenced many to move. A fundamental shift in the character of both black business and the Afro-American class structure resulted in black baseball entrepreneurs relying less upon the support of white customers, and catering to a growing black market. Simultaneously, these magnates maintained their symbiotic business relationship with white semiprofessional teams.

The exploits of the late-nineteenth-century Afro-American entrepreneurs created the blueprint for the successful operation of an independent club. These men operated by any means necessary to transform baseball into a commercialized amusement that was uniquely Afro-American. S. K. Govern, Ambrose Davis, William Peters, and to a lesser degree Bud Fowler, Benjamin Butler, Frank Leland, Julius Avendorph, and Clarence Williams created an enterprise that a new generation of black baseball entrepreneurs would inherit. This new generation would transform black baseball into the modern sport industry that became the Negro Leagues.

Notes

Bibliography

Index

Notes

Introduction

1. I am drawing primarily from Stephen Hardy's work to establish my framework of analysis. See "Entrepreneurs, Organizations, and the Sport Marketplace: The Search for Historians."

2. See Harold Seymour, *Baseball: The Early Years*, *Baseball: The Golden Years*, and *Baseball: The People's Game*; and David Q. Voigt, *American Baseball: From Gentleman's Sport to the Commissioner System*, *American Baseball: From Postwar Expansion to the Electronic Age*, and *American Baseball: From the Commissioner to Continental Expansion*.

3. The *Baseball Research Journal* and the *National Pastime* have several articles on black baseball players in the late nineteenth and early twentieth centuries that exemplify the oral history genre. See, for example, Dick Clark and John B. Holway, "Willie Powell: An American Giant." Several articles written by Holway include "The Black Bomber Named Beckwith," "The Cannonball," "Charlie 'Chino' Smith," "Cuba's Black Diamond," "Louis Santop, the Big Bertha," "Sam Streeter: Smartest Pitcher in Negro Leagues," and "Spotswood Poles." See also Jorge S. Figueredo, "November 4, 1920: The Day Torriente Outclassed Ruth"; Lou Hunsinger, "George W. Stovey"; Merl F. Kleinknecht, "Blacks in 19th Century Organized Baseball"; Bob Tholkes, "Bud Fowler, Black Pioneer and the 1884 Stillwaters"; and William J. Weiss, "The First Negro in 20th Century O. B."

4. See Robert Peterson, *Only the Ball Was White*; and John Holway, *Voices from the Great Negro Baseball Leagues*. Other works by Holway utilizing the oral history genre include *Blackball Stars: Negro League Pioneers*, *Black Diamonds: Life in the Negro Leagues from the Men Who Lived It*, and *Josh and Satch: The Life of Josh Gibson and Satchel Paige*. Ocana Chalk also provides a glimpse of preintegration black baseball in *Pioneers of Black Sport*. Other works that exemplify the oral history genre include Effa Manley and Leon Hardwick, *Negro Baseball . . . Before Integration*; Art Rust, *"Get That Nigger Off the Field": A Sparkling Informal History*; and Quincy Troppe, *20 Years Too Soon*.

5. Camden House in South Carolina reissued Sol White's classic work, *History of Colored Baseball*, in 1984. It was again rereleased, with additional documents, by the University of Nebraska Press in 1995. *The Beadle Dime Base-Ball Player*, one of the early baseball guidebooks, was instrumental in making the style of play developed in New York the national pastime. A few years later, guidebooks for all sports comprised a substantial segment of entrepreneurs, such as Albert Spalding, establishing a sports empire, netting them vast profits, and supporting the influence of governing bodies whose rules they published. For a detailed discussion on guidebooks, see Seymour, *Baseball: The Early Years*, 44; and Voigt, *American Baseball: Gentleman's Sport*, 91. For Spald-

ing's connections to guidebooks, see Peter Levine, *A. G. Spalding and the Rise of Baseball,* 71–96; and Hardy, "Entrepreneurs," 17–18. In the 1930s, popular works by James Weldon Johnson *(Black Manhattan)* and writers of the Works Project Administration (Roi Ottley and William J. Weatherby, eds., *The Negro in New York: An Informal Social History)* reinforced S. White's assessment of black baseball. They chronicle the career of John "Bud" Fowler, the first black player to play in white organized leagues; outline the exploits of the Cuban Giants; and briefly discuss early-twentieth-century teams, such as the Bacharach Giants. These works merely serve to preserve the exploits of these early black teams and players, and provide little or no analysis.

6. See John Bodnar, *Remaking America: Public Memory, Commemoration, and Patriotism in the Twentieth Century;* and Jules Tygiel, "The Negro Leagues Revisited."

7. Secondary accounts that combine oral history with newspaper accounts include Larry Bowman, "Moses Fleetwood Walker: The First Black Major League Baseball Player"; Phil Dixon and Patrick J. Hannigan, *The Negro Baseball Leagues, 1867–1955;* Donald Lankiewicz, "Fleet Walker in the Twilight Zone"; Jerry Malloy, "The Birth of the Cuban Giants: The Origins of Black Professional Baseball"; Malloy, "Out at Home: Baseball Draws the Color Line"; G. B. McKinney, "Negro Professional Baseball Players in the Upper South and the Gilded Age"; Thomas E. Powers, "The Page Fence Giants Play Ball"; Mark Ribowsky, *A Complete History of the Negro League, 1884 to 1955;* James A. Riley, *The Biographical Encyclopedia of the Negro Baseball Leagues;* Mark Savoie, "Drawing the Line: The Trials of African American Baseball Players in the International League (1886–1889)"; Richard White, "Baseball's John Fowler: The 1887 Season in Binghamton, New York"; and Jerry Jaye Wright, "From Giants to Monarchs: The 1890 Season of the Colored Monarchs of York, Pennsylvania."

8. See Donn Rogosin, *Invisible Men: Life in Baseball's Negro Leagues,* 32; Janet Bruce, *The Kansas City Monarchs: Champions of Black Baseball;* Rob Ruck, *Sandlot Seasons: Sport in Black Pittsburgh;* Neil Lanctot, *Fair Dealing and Clean Playing: The Hilldale Club and the Development of Black Professional Baseball, 1910–1932;* and James Overmyer, *Queen of the Negro Leagues: Effa Manley and the Newark Eagles.* Other scholarly works include Michael E. Lomax, "Black Baseball's First Rivalry: The Cuban Giants Versus the Gorhams of New York and the Birth of the Colored Championship" and "Black Entrepreneurship in the National Pastime: The Rise of Semiprofessional Baseball in Black Chicago, 1890–1915." David Zang provides an excellent scholarly study of Moses Fleetwood Walker in *Fleet Walker's Divided Heart: The Life of Baseball's First Black Major Leaguer.*

9. See Kenneth L. Kusmer, "The Black Urban Experience in American History," 98; Kusmer, "Urban Black History at the Crossroads"; Gilbert Osofsky, "The Enduring Ghetto"; Joe W. Trotter, "African Americans in the City: The Industrial Era, 1900–1950," who concurs with Kusmer on how problematic it is to draw conclusions from a single community; and Ruck, *Sandlot Seasons.*

10. See Melvin L. Adelman, *A Sporting Time: New York City and the Rise of Modern Athletics, 1820–1870;* Stephen Hardy, *How Boston Played: Sport, Recreation, and Community, 1865–1915;* George B. Kirsch, *The Creation of American Team Sports;* and Steven A. Riess, *City Games: The Evolution of American Urban Society and the Rise of Sports.*

11. See John Silbey Butler, *Entrepreneurship and Self-Help among Black Americans: A Reconsideration of Race and Economics;* Robert Kinzer and Edward Sagarin, "Roots of the Integrationist-

Separatist Dilemma"; Joseph A. Pierce, "The Evolution of Negro Business"; and Juliet E. K. Walker, *The History of Black Business in America: Capitalism, Race, Entrepreneurship.*

12. Scholarly works on the Philadelphia Pythians include Jerold Casway, "Philadelphia's Pythians"; J. Thomas Jable, "Sport in Philadelphia's African-American Community, 1865–1900"; Kirsch, *Creation of Team Sports,* 143–78; Seymour, *Baseball: The People's Game,* 531–46; and Harry Silcox, "Efforts to Desegregate Baseball in Philadelphia: The Pythian Baseball Club, 1866–1872."

13. I am drawing from the analytical framework used in Melvin L. Adelman's forthcoming book, *Before Its Time: The All-America Football Conference in Professional Football in Post World War II America.*

14. For scholars examining intragroup color dynamics in sport, see Lisa Brock and Bijan Bayne, "Not Just Black: African-Americans, Cubans, and Baseball"; and Michael E. Lomax, "'If He Were White': Black and Cuban Players in Organized Baseball, 1880–1920." One study that does attempt to analyze wealth among African Americans is Theodore Hershberg and Henry Williams, "Mulattoes and Blacks: Intra-group Color Differences and Social Stratification in Nineteenth-Century Philadelphia." See also James Horton, *Free People of Color: Inside the African American Community;* Bart Landry, *The New Black Middle Class;* and John G. Mencke, *Mulattoes and Race Mixture: American Attitudes and Images, 1865–1918.*

1. Entrepreneurship and the Rise of Black Baseball

1. "Letter from Jamaica, L.I.," *Anglo-African Weekly,* Jan. 21, 1860, 3.

2. For population figures, see Vincent Harding, *There Is a River: The Black Struggle for Freedom in America,* 117. See also Ira Berlin, *Slaves Without Masters: The Free Negro in the Antebellum South;* Leon F. Litwack, *North of Slavery: The Free Negro in the Free States, 1790–1860;* and C. Vann Woodward, *The Strange Career of Jim Crow.* For a legal historical perspective, see Lawrence M. Friedman, *A History of American Law.*

3. Harding, *There Is a River,* 143–44.

4. See James L. Huston, "Economic Change and Political Realignment in Antebellum Pennsylvania"; Theodore Hershberg et al., "Free Blacks in Antebellum Philadelphia: A Study of Ex-Slaves, Freeborn, and Socioeconomic Decline," 375; and Hershberg et al., "A Tale of Three Cities: Blacks, Immigrants, and Opportunity in Philadelphia, 1850–1880, 1930, 1970."

5. Regarding the development of the railroad network, see Sean Dennis Cashman, *America in the Gilded Age: From the Death of Lincoln to the Rise of Theodore Roosevelt,* 23; and Huston, "Economic Change," 352, 362. A number of studies point to the unsettling social and political consequence of market change resulting from improved transportation; see Whitney R. Cross, *The Burned-Over District: The Social and Intellectual History of Enthusiastic Religion in Western New York, 1800–1850;* Leonard P. Curry, *The Free Black in Urban America, 1800–1850: The Shadow of the Dream,* 49–146; Robert A. Gross, "Culture and Cultivation: Agriculture and Society in Thoreau's Concord"; Charles Sellers, *The Market Revolution: Jacksonian America, 1815–1846,* 172–201; and Thomas P. Slaughter, *Bloody Dawn: The Christiana Riot and Racial Violence in the Antebellum North.*

6. For a discussion of economic reshuffling, see Stanley Lebergott, *The Americans: An Economic Record,* 100, 281–82. Gerrit Smith, a leading abolitionist of the time, was the exception regarding giving free blacks employment opportunities. See Arnett G. Lindsey, "The Economic

Condition of the Negroes of New York prior to 1861," 195; and John R. McKlivigan and Madeleine McKlivigan, "'He Stands Like Jupiter': The Autobiography of Gerrit Smith." The letter from "P. O." and the census data are in Hershberg et al., "Free Blacks," 375–76.

7. *New York Daily Tribune*, Mar. 20, 1851, quoting report of the Committee on the Social Condition of the Negro Race, in Leo H. Hirsch, "The Negro and New York, 1783 to 1865," 437.

8. For census figures, see John Hope Franklin, *From Slavery to Freedom: A History of Negro Americans*, 158; E. Franklin Frazier, *Black Bourgeoisie*, 13–15; and Landry, *New Black Middle Class*, 24–27.

9. See Landry, *New Black Middle Class*, 26–27; and Hershberg and Williams, "Mulattos and Blacks," 426–27.

10. Litwack, *North of Slavery*, 182. See also Mencke, *Mulattoes and Race Mixture*, 2–3; and Horton, *Free People of Color*, 122–45.

11. See Robert Ernst, "The Economic Status of New York City Negroes, 1850–1863," 139–40; and J. H. Harmon Jr., Arnett G. Lindsey, and Carter G. Woodson, *The Negro as Business Man*, 2–6. For an account of blacks making large sums of money as boat stewards, see Carter G. Woodson, "The Negroes of Cincinnati prior to the Civil War," 10–11.

12. For accounts of the ways in which blacks facilitated entrepreneurship prior to the Civil War, see Butler, *Entrepreneurship and Self-Help*; Abram L. Harris, *The Negro as Capitalist: A Study of Banking and Business among American Negroes*; and Walker, *History of Black Business*. 13. Litwack, *North of Slavery*, 180–81.

14. See Walker, *History of Black Business*, 83–126.

15. See Harris, *Negro as Capitalist*, 20–21. David Perlman highlights the obstacles that free blacks confronted in organizing mutual aid societies in New York in "Organization of the Free Negro in New York City, 1800–1860." See also Curry, *Free Black*, 196–215.

16. See Floyd J. Miller, *The Search for a Black Nationality: Black Emigration and Colonization, 1787–1863*, 8–14; and Julian Rammelkamp, "The Providence Negro Community, 1820–1840," 20.

17. Ibid. For a detailed account of the rise of mutual aid societies in Philadelphia, see Roger Lane, *William Dorsey's Philadelphia and Ours: On the Past and Future of the Black City in America*, 279–308; and Dorothy Porter, "The Organized Educational Activities of Negro Literary Societies, 1828–1846," 557–58. For Amos G. Beman's efforts in New Haven, see Robert Warner, *New Haven Negroes*, 93.

18. Undoubtedly, the high death rate among Afro-Americans in the nineteenth century led to the insurance business becoming one of the most successful businesses among blacks. See Harmon, Lindsey, and Woodson, *Negro as Business Man*, 88. For the population figures, see Gilbert Osofsky, *Harlem: The Making of a Ghetto, Negro New York, 1890–1930*, 7–8.

19. Walker, *History of Black Business*, 86.

20. Vincent Harding, *The Other American Revolution*, 30.

21. See Eugene D. Genovese, *Roll, Jordan, Roll: The World the Slaves Made*, 566–67. For a detailed discussion of emancipation celebrations, see William Wiggins, *O Freedom! Afro-American Emancipation Celebration*, 25–48. The majority of scholarly works on the black sporting culture in antebellum America focus on slavery. For an examination of sport and leisure among slaves, see David K. Wiggins, "The Play of Slave Children in the Plantation Communities of the Old South, 1820–1860," "Sport and Popular Pastimes: Shadows of the Slave Quarter," and "Leisure Time on

the Southern Plantation: The Slaves' Respite from Constant Toil, 1810–1860"; John W. Blasingame, *The Slave Community: Plantation Life in the Antebellum South;* and Thomas L. Webber, *Deep Like the Rivers: Education in the Slave Quarter Community, 1831–1865,* 180–90. To date, the Philadelphia Pythians have received the most scholarly attention in terms of examining the black sporting culture among free blacks. See Casway, "Philadelphia's Pythians"; Lane, *Dorsey's Philadelphia;* Michael E. Lomax, "Black Baseball, Black Community, Black Entrepreneurs: The History of Negro National and Eastern Colored Leagues, 1880–1930"; Seymour, *Baseball: The People's Game;* and Silcox, "Efforts to Desegregate Baseball."

22. See Frederick Douglass, "Narrative of the Life of Frederick Douglass, an American Slave"; Genovese, *Roll, Jordan, Roll,* 577; and D. K. Wiggins, "Play of Slave Children," 27.

23. *Brooklyn Eagle,* Oct. 17, 1863; *Newark Daily Advertiser,* Oct. 23, 1866. For black clubs emerging throughout the United States, see *Newark Daily Advertiser,* Oct. 2, 4, 1867; *New York Clipper,* 14 (Oct. 13, 1866): 210; 15 (July 6, 1867): 99; (July 13, 1867): 107; (July 27, 1867): 123; (Oct. 19, 1867): 220; 17 (Oct. 2, 1869): 203, 205; *Wilkes Spirit of the Times* 17 (Oct. 5, 1867): 133; 20 (Aug. 14, 1869): 407; 21 (Sept. 4, 1869): 39; and 21 (Sept. 11, 1869): 55. For information about black clubs in Chicago, see *Chicago Tribune,* Aug. 24, 1870.

24. Franklin, *From Slavery to Freedom,* 159–60. For accounts regarding the baseball explosion among whites in the 1850s, see Adelman, *Sporting Time,* 121–44; Seymour, *Baseball: The Early Years,* 23–34; and Voigt, *American Baseball: Gentleman's Sport,* 3–13.

25. Joseph R. Gusfield, *Symbolic Crusade: Status, Politics, and the American Temperance Movement,* 5. For an account regarding black leaders promoting the need for self-improvement and moral reform, see Frederick Cooper, "Elevating the Race: The Social Thought of Black Leaders, 1827–50"; and Wilson Jeremiah Moses, *The Golden Age of Black Nationalism, 1850–1925,* 15–31. For a contemporary account regarding race elevation, see Martin Robison Delany, *The Elevation, Emigration, and Destiny of the Colored People of the United States,* 41–47.

26. For an account of the sports creed, see John R. Betts, "Mind and Body in Early American Thought"; Riess, *City Games,* 26–32; and Riess, "Sport and the Redefinition of American Middle-Class Masculinity."

27. See Riess, *City Games,* 28. Philadelphia coroner's report in Litwack, *North of Slavery,* 169; New York City inspector's report in Robert Ernst, *Immigrant Life in New York City, 1825–1863,* 53, 238.

28. See Seymour, *Baseball: The Early Years,* 23, 31.

2. From Social Organization to Commercial Enterprise

1. See Roger Lane, *Roots of Violence in Black Philadelphia, 1860–1900,* 16–21.

2. See W. E. B. DuBois, *The Philadelphia Negro: A Social Study,* 296.

3. Silcox, "Efforts to Desegregate Baseball," 1–2.

4. For a detailed account of the background of Octavius Catto, see Harry C. Silcox, "Nineteenth Century Philadelphia Black Militant: Octavius V. Catto (1839–1871)."

5. For an account of Jacob White, see Lane, *Dorsey's Philadelphia,* 106–7; and Harry C. Silcox, "Philadelphia Negro Educator: Jacob C. White, Jr., 1837–1902."

6. See Casway, "Philadelphia's Pythians," 122; and Lane, *Roots of Violence,* 52. Unless otherwise stated, the statistics cited in this study of Philadelphia's black population were compiled from

data gathered by the Philadelphia Social History Project, Center for Philadelphia Studies, University of Pennsylvania.

7. For an account of the white amateur clubs' organizational structure and social customs, see Warren Goldstein, *Playing for Keeps: A History of Early Baseball*, 17–20; and Seymour, *Baseball: The Early Years*, 13–22. The Mutuals issued a challenge to play the Pythians in 1867. See George Johnson to Jacob White, June 15, 1867, and White to Johnson, June 22, 1867, Papers of the Pythians Base Ball Club, American Historical Society of Pennsylvania. The Pythians advertised their match with the Alert club from Washington, D.C. See *New York Clipper* 15 (July 6, 1867): 99; and 15 (July 13, 1867): 107.

8. On the Alerts visiting Philadelphia, see Charles R. Douglass to Jacob White, Aug. 3, 1867, and White to Douglass, Aug. 8, 1867, Papers of the Pythians Base Ball Club, American Historical Society of Pennsylvania; and Silcox, "Efforts to Desegregate Baseball," 2–3. Carl W. Bolivar was a local historian in Philadelphia's black community in the late nineteenth and early twentieth centuries. Bolivar wrote a weekly historical editorial titled "Pencil Pusher Points." He frequently wrote about the Pythians during the Civil War era. Bolivar's editorials were accurate with the records the Pythians organization left behind. See, for example, *Philadelphia Tribune*, Aug. 21, 1912.

9. Report to the Pythians Base Ball Club, June 3, 1868, Papers of the Pythians Base Ball Club, American Historical Society of Pennsylvania.

10. William Still to the Pythians Base Ball Club, Jan. 30, 1869, and Jacob White to Still, Mar. 1, 1869, ibid. The Still-White debate goes beyond the scope of this study. To Still, the race was weakened because too few blacks were going into business. Failing to win respect from whites and spending money in white stores served as the root causes for moral failure among young blacks. In contrast, Still's own "hard labor, strict temperance, rigid economy, and . . . impeachable character" would win whites' respect (Lane, *Dorsey's Philadelphia*, 106). Seeking to play in a "true championship" with a white baseball club would be, in Still's view, as he said in his letter to White, wasting their time in an "idle and frivolous society." For a detailed account of the struggle to end streetcar segregation, see Philip S. Foner, "The Battle to End Discrimination vs. Negroes on Philadelphia Streetcars," pt. 2.

11. J. C. White to Philadore S. Bell, Esq., Sept. 7, 1868, Papers of the Pythians Base Ball Club, American Historical Society of Pennsylvania. See also *Philadelphia Tribune*, Aug. 12, 1912, May 3, 1913.

12. Adelman, *Sporting Time*, 146–47.

13. *Newark Daily Advertiser*, Oct. 2, 1867; *New York Clipper* 14 (Oct. 13, 1866): 210. See also Adelman, *Sporting Time*, 157–58.

14. *Philadelphia Sunday Mercury*, July 21, 1867.

15. See August Meier and Elliott Rudwick, *From Plantation to Ghetto*, 118.

16. NABBP quoted in Seymour, *Baseball: The Early Years*, 37. See also Adelman, *Sporting Time*; Robert F. Burk, *Never Just a Game: Players, Owners, and American Baseball to 1920*; Goldstein, *Playing for Keeps*; Kirsch, *Creation of Team Sports*; Albert G. Spalding, *America's National Game: Historic Facts Concerning the Beginning Evolution, Development, and Popularity of Base Ball*, 68–70; and Voigt, *American Baseball: Gentleman's Sport*.

17. See Seymour, *Baseball: The Early Years*, 36–37.

18. See *New York Clipper* 14 (Dec. 1, 1866): 266; 14 (Dec. 22, 1866): 290; 15 (Dec. 21, 1867): 291; and Kirsch, *Creation of Team Sports*, 210–11.

19. *New York Clipper* 14 (Dec. 1, 1866): 266.

20. On formation of the PAABBP, see *Beadle Dime*, 49.

21. See "Report of a Delegate of the Pythians to the Pennsylvania State Convention," Oct. 16, 1867, Leon Gardiner Collection, American Negro Historical Society Papers, Historical Society of Pennsylvania; and *Philadelphia Sunday Mercury*, Oct. 20, 1867.

22. "Report of a Delegate," Oct. 16, 1867, Leon Gardiner Collection, American Negro Historical Society Papers.

23. Ibid.

24. Ibid.

25. *Beadle Dime*, 55.

26. *Wilkes Spirit of the Times* quoted in Adelman, *Sporting Time*, 176; *New York Daily Tribune*, Dec. 12, 1867.

27. Seymour, *Baseball: The Early Years*, 42; Adelman, *Sporting Time*, 176; Goldstein, *Playing for Keeps*, 88; Burk, *Never Just a Game*, 34.

28. For a view of northern racism toward free blacks before 1860, see Eugene Berwanger, *The Frontier Against Slavery: Western Anti-Negro Prejudice and the Slavery Extension Controversy*; and Litwack, *North of Slavery*.

29. See Hershberg and Williams, "Mulattoes and Blacks," 415–21.

30. For an account of the repeal of the Black Laws in Illinois, see Roger D. Bridges, "Equality Deferred: Civil Rights for Illinois Blacks, 1865–1885"; and Charles A. Gliozzo, "John Jones: A Study of a Black Chicagoan," 184–88. For an account of the efforts to desegregate schools in Rhode Island, see Meier and Rudwick, *From Plantation to Ghetto*, 182. For an account of the efforts to desegregate streetcars in Washington, D.C., see Harding, *There Is a River*, 281–83.

31. See Silcox, "Nineteenth Century," 69.

32. See Goldstein, *Playing for Keeps*, 67–84; Seymour, *Baseball: The Early Years*, 47–72; and Voigt, *American Baseball: Gentleman's Sport*, 14–34.

33. *Wilkes Spirit of the Times* 21 (Sept. 4, 1869): 39; *New York Clipper* 17 (Oct. 2, 1869): 203. Another Colored Championship took place in 1870 between the Wide Awake of Johnstown, New York, and the Fearless of Utica. See *New York Clipper* 18 (July 30, 1870): 131.

34. *New York Clipper* 18 (Oct. 15, 1870): 220.

35. *New York Clipper* 18 (Sept. 3, 1870): 173.

36. *Philadelphia Tribune*, Aug. 24, Nov. 16, 1912. On Daniel Adger's resignation, see Lane, *Dorsey's Philadelphia*, 323.

37. *Philadelphia Sunday Dispatch*, Sept. 5, 1869; *Wilkes Spirit of the Times*, 21 (Sept. 11, 1869): 55. On the Pythians-City Items contest, see Casway, "Philadelphia's Pythians," 122.

38. *New York Clipper* 17 (Oct. 2, 1869): 205.

39. See *New York Clipper* 18 (Oct. 8, 1870): 213.

40. For an account of the symbiotic relationship between black and white clubs, see Lomax, "Black Baseball, Community, Entrepreneurs."

41. Charles R. Douglass to Jacob C. White, Esq., Sept. 10, 1869, Papers of the Pythians Base Ball Club, American Historical Society of Pennsylvania; *Philadelphia Tribune*, Aug. 24, 1912.

42. See Silcox, "Nineteenth Century," 72–74.

43. Eric Foner, *Reconstruction: America's Unfinished Revolution, 1863–1877*, 101.

44. See Roger L. Ransom, *Conflict and Compromise: The Political Economy of Slavery, Emancipation, and the American Civil War*, 127–34.

45. Ibid.; Joel H. Sibley, ed., *The Partisan Imperative: The Dynamics of American Politics Before the Civil War*, 100.

46. Kirsch, *Creation of Team Sports*, 9. See also Benjamin G. Rader, "The Quest for Subcommunities and the Rise of American Sport"; and Riess, *City Games*, 21–23.

47. See Adelman, *Sporting Time*, 148–50.

48. See Litwack, *North of Slavery*, 247–79; and Ransom, *Conflict and Compromise*, 123–70.

49. *Negro Population in the United States, 1790–1915*, 44.

50. Juliet E. K. Walker, "Racism, Slavery, and Free Enterprise: Black Entrepreneurship in the United States Before the Civil War," 377–79; Milton Friedman, *Capitalism and Freedom*, 109. For an account of free blacks and property ownership in colonial America, see Walker, *History of Black Business*, 32–51.

51. Adelman, *Sporting Time*, 150. On park ownership among black entrepreneurs, see Lomax, "Black Baseball, Community, Entrepreneurs," 207–86.

52. For accounts of the notion of operating a segregated enterprise within the fabric of a national economy, see Vishnu V. Oak, *The Negro's Adventure in General Business*. For an account of how this concept applied to black baseball, see Lomax, "Black Entrepreneurship."

53. Arthur H. Cole, *Business Enterprise in Its Social Setting*, 156.

3. The Birth of a Commercial Enterprise

1. See Charles C. Alexander, *Our Game: An American Baseball History*; Burk, *Never Just a Game*; Goldstein, *Playing for Keeps*; Seymour, *Baseball: The Early Years*; and Voigt, *American Baseball: Gentleman's Sport*.

2. Seymour, *Baseball: The Early Years*, 75.

3. For an account of the need for competitive balance in professional sports, see Walter C. Neale, "The Peculiar Economics of Professional Sports: A Contribution to the Theory of the Firm in Sporting Competition and in Market Competition."

4. Hulbert quoted in Albert G. Spalding, *America's National Game*, 209. See also Seymour, *Baseball: The Early Years*, 80; and Voigt, *American Baseball: Gentleman's Sport*, 64.

5. See Seymour, *Baseball: The Early Years*, 80–81; U.S. Congress, House, *Organized Baseball: Report of the Subcommittee on Study of Monopoly Power of the Committee on the Judiciary*, 19–20; and Voigt, *American Baseball: Gentleman's Sport*, 63–65.

6. See Alexander, *Our Game*, 26–27; and Voigt, *American Baseball: Gentleman's Sport*, 64–65.

7. See Seymour, *Baseball: The Early Years*, 80–81; U.S. Congress, House, *Organized Baseball*, 19–20; and Voigt, *American Baseball: Gentleman's Sport*, 63–65.

8. See Seymour, *Baseball: The Early Years*, 85.

9. Paul M. Gregory, *The Baseball Player: An Economic Study*, 150. See also James B. Dworkin, *Owners Versus Players: Baseball and Collective Bargaining*, 44–47; and U.S. Congress, House, *Organized Baseball*, 22–26.

10. See Voigt, *American Baseball: Gentleman's Sport*, 69–70.

11. Ibid., 76–79.

12. Ibid.

13. See Burk, *Never Just a Game*, 72–73; and Seymour, *Baseball: The Early Years*, 143–144.

14. For accounts of the life of Moses Fleetwood Walker, see Bowman, "Moses Fleetwood Walker"; Lankiewicz, "Fleet Walker"; and Zang, *Walker's Divided Heart*.

15. See Robert Obojski, *Bush League: A History of Minor League Baseball*, 7.

16. *Columbus Dispatch*, Apr. 24, 1883. Throughout the 1883 season, the *Toledo Blade* constantly praised Walker for his gentlemanly character. Evidently, the *Blade* editors were impressed with his educational background. His every move was highlighted, even to the point of justifying his shortcomings on the field. See any issue titled "Baseball Notes" or "Diamond Dust."

17. For information regarding Anson's background, see Adrian C. Anson, *A Ball Player's Career: Behind the Personal Experiences and Reminiscences;* and Voigt, *American Baseball: Gentleman's Sport*, 99–120.

18. *Toledo Blade*, Aug. 11, 1883. Zang cites a racial encounter Walker had in 1881. As a member of the White Sewing Machine Company, an independent club, the Louisville Eclipse, an American Association club, objected to Walker's presence. Though Walker was their regular catcher, the Cleveland-based club conceded to the Eclipse's demands and played without him. Ironically, Eclipse second baseman Fritz Pfeffer was also a member of the White Stockings during the Anson incident. See Zang, *Walker's Divided Heart*, 27–28, 38–39.

19. *Toledo Blade*, Aug. 11, 1883. For accounts of Toledo playing American Association clubs in 1883, see *Toledo Blade*, Apr. 26, 27, 30, May 5, July 6, 1883.

20. For an account of organized baseball's war against the Union Association and the origins of the gentlemen's agreement, see Seymour, *Baseball: The Early Years*, 148–61.

21. Jonathon A. Brown to C. H. Morton, Apr. 11, 1884, Files of Moses Fleetwood Walker, Oberlin College Archives.

22. Voigt, *American Baseball: Gentleman's Sport*, 131.

23. See Bowman, "Moses Fleetwood Walker," 65.

24. During this period, Albert Spalding exhibited his uncanny ability to establish a coalition to influence organized baseball policy. He threw his support behind Henry V. Lucas as a means of landing a National League franchise in the St. Louis market, while at the same time placing the American Association in a dilemma regarding the violation of the waiver rule. Although the transaction fell through, Spalding attempted to ship Chicago pitcher Jim McCormick out of the National League to Cincinnati by carefully arranging gentlemen's agreements with other clubs in both leagues. For a detailed account of the internal struggle between the National League and the American Association, see Seymour, *Baseball: The Early Years*, 162–71.

25. *Sporting Life* quoted in Peterson, *Only the Ball*, 23; *Toledo Blade*, May 5, 1884.

26. See Frazier, *Black Bourgeoisie*, 10–22; and Landry, *New Black Middle Class*, 24–36.

27. Ibid.; David Katzman, *Before the Ghetto: Black Detroit in the Nineteenth Century*, 128.

28. I am drawing primarily from Harold Seymour's work in order to make it easier to follow the numerous teams at the local level. His definition uniquely describes the type of black clubs that emerged in the late nineteenth century. See Seymour, *Baseball: The People's Game*, 236–75.

29. For an account of the early business practices of professional baseball, see Gerald W. Scully, *The Business of Major League Baseball*, 1–12.

30. *Metropolitan*, Aug. 12, 1882. See also Steven M. Gelbar, "'Their Hands Are All Out Play-

ing:' Business and Amateur Baseball, 1845–1917," 24–25. Melvin Adelman argues that there are several drawbacks with Gelbar's thesis, including an inadequate explanation regarding the triumph of cricket over baseball. He also cites a problem with the framework, because sociologists of leisure have questioned for more than a decade whether congruent theory does explain the work-leisure relationship. Finally, Adelman accurately points out that baseball's emergence as a popular participatory and spectator sport preceded the rise of the corporate world of business. The drawbacks of the Gelbar thesis go beyond the scope of this study. My purpose is to analyze the forces that led to the professionalization of black baseball. Although the evidence is limited, there is a connection between the rise of the corporate world of business, particularly the hotel industry, and black professional baseball that began in the 1880s. See Adelman, "Baseball, Business, and the Workplace: Gelbar's Thesis Revisited." For businessmen structuring leisure-time activities for their workers in Chicago, see Stephen Freedman, "The Baseball Fad in Chicago, 1865–1870: An Exploration of the Role of Sport in the Nineteenth-Century City," 53–54.

31. *New York Clipper* 29 (Aug. 20, 1881): 346; *Cleveland Leader,* May 7, 1883; *Cincinnati Enquirer* quoted in Peterson, *Only the Ball,* 34; *Sporting Life,* Aug. 27, 1884, Nov. 18, 1885; *New York Sun,* May 11, 15, 19, 1885.

32. For Frank Thompson's background, see *New York Age,* Dec. 21, 1905, Jan. 14, 1906. For S. K. Govern's background, see *Philadelphia Tribune,* Nov. 15, 1924, Nov. 1, 1934. On Govern's acting career, see *People's Advocate,* Apr. 26, May 3, 1879. On Govern managing the Manhattans of Washington, D.C., see *Trenton Times,* June 8, Aug. 19, 1886.

33. *Philadelphia Tribune,* Nov. 1, 1934.

34. *New York Age,* Oct. 15, 1887. See also S. White, *History of Colored Baseball* (1907), 8.

35. On sports as a means of mitigating problems associated with the transforming U.S. society, see Burton J. Bledstein, *The Culture of Professionalism: The Middle Class and the Development of Higher Education in America,* 80–128; Levine, *A. G. Spalding,* 97–122; and Benjamin G. Rader, *American Sports: From the Age of Folk Games to the Age of Spectators,* 145–70. For a secondary account of the evolution of the Cuban Giants, see Malloy, "Birth of Cuban Giants," 233–46.

36. The Cuban Giants were known by many names in their early history (S. White, *History of Colored Baseball* [1907], 8). In order to avoid confusion, I will refer to them primarily as the Cuban Giants.

37. Ibid., 8–9, 150.

38. For the *Babylon South Side Signal*'s account of the Giants' first road trip, see Peterson, *Only the Ball,* 35–36; *Sporting Life,* Oct. 14, 1885.

39. For accounts of the origins of cooperative enterprises, see W. E. B. DuBois, *Dusk of Dawn;* Earl Ofari, *The Myth of Black Capitalism;* Allan H. Spear, *Black Chicago: The Making of a Negro Ghetto, 1890–1920;* Walker, *History of Black Business;* and Booker T. Washington, *The Negro in Business.*

40. See James Kerney, ed., *A History of Trenton, 1679–1929: Two Hundred and Fifty Years of a Notable Town with Links in Four Centuries.*

41. See James M. DiClerico and Barry J. Pavelec, *The Jersey Game: The History of Modern Baseball from Its Birth to the Big Leagues in the Garden State,* 73–75. For a contemporary account of the Eastern League's inaugural season, see *Reach's Base Ball Guide,* 22–24.

42. *Trenton True American,* Apr. 16, 30, May 3, 4, 1886.

43. See Francis Bazley Lee, ed., *Genealogical and Personal Memoirs of Mercer County, New Jersey*, 107–8; and DeClerico and Pavelec, *The Jersey Game*, 137–38. The *Trenton True American* reported that the Cuban Giants were under new management and named Cook as the club's new manager on May 13, 1886. See also Malloy, "Birth of Cuban Giants," 239. The evidence is limited regarding the partnership of Walter Cook and John Bright. The *True American* reported on June 16, 1887, that their partnership had been dissolved and Cook had become sole proprietor.

44. For an example of Govern signing players and making schedule inquiries, see *Sporting Life*, Dec. 8, 1886; and *Trenton Times*, Aug. 19, 1886. For player salaries, see S. White, *History of Colored Baseball* (1907), 10.

45. *Trenton Times*, May 10, 1886. Interestingly enough, the *Trenton True American* reported on the same day that the Giants were a club of Cuban players.

46. See Alexander, *Our Game*, 27; and Voigt, *American Baseball: Gentleman's Sport*, 64–65.

47. *Trenton True American*, May 21, 1886; *Trenton Times*, May 10, 1886.

48. The Giants' sporadic attendance was based on the press reports of both the *Trenton Times* and the *Trenton True American* from May to October 1886. Both dailies emphasized that the Cuban Giants were a first-class club and deserved to be patronized.

49. *Trenton True American*, May 28, 1886.

50. See Hunsinger, "George W. Stovey." Powers eventually became president of the International League in 1893, a post he held until 1911. Under his leadership, the International League "became an institution—an accomplishment recognized by his election into the league's Hall of Fame in 1961." See DiClerico and Pavelec, *Jersey Game*, 74–75; *Trenton Times*, June 24, 26, 1886; and *Trenton True American*, June 27, 1886.

51. See *Trenton True American*, July 12, 16, 21, 1886.

52. *Newark News* quoted in *Trenton True American*, July 19, 1886; *Meriden Journal* quoted in *Trenton Times*, July 23, 1886.

53. *Spalding's Official Base Ball Guide* (1887), 79.

54. *Trenton True American*, Sept. 13, 1886. The average attendance figures are based on the newspaper accounts of both the *Trenton Times* and the *True American*. However, this average is somewhat skewed. When the newspapers did indicate that the Cubans drew a good crowd, no estimate was given. The highest reported home attendance was 2,100 fans on Independence Day. See *Trenton True American*, July 7, 1886. For the reported attendance figures of the Cubans' games on Long Island, see *Trenton Times*, May 10, 1886; and *Trenton True American*, July 12, Aug. 2, 1886.

55. Walker, *History of Black Business*.

4. Windows of Opportunity and Mounting Obstacles, 1887

1. *Sporting Life*, Nov. 17, 24, Dec. 1, 8, 1886. In 1885, a black professional league was also organized in the South. However, because of its geographic location, the Southern League did not seek protection under the terms of the National Agreement and was not a part of organized baseball's structure. For a secondary account of the Southern League, see Bill Plott, "The Southern League of Colored Base Ballists."

2. See *Baltimore Morning Herald*, Dec. 10, 1886; *Philadelphia Evening Item*, Dec. 10, 1886; *Pittsburgh Daily Post*, Dec. 10, 1886; and *Sporting Life*, Dec. 8, 15, 1886. Bud Fowler's background

was derived from the following sources: Dixon and Hannigan, *Negro Baseball Leagues*, 43–44; *New York Age*, Feb. 25, 1909; Peterson, *Only the Ball*, 18–20; Riley, *Biographical Encyclopedia*, 294–95; and Tholkes, "Bud Fowler."

3. On election of officers, see *Sporting Life*, Dec. 8, 1886. For Gilbert Ball's background, see Lane, *Roots of Violence*, 57–58; and Lane, *Dorsey's Philadelphia*, 126–27.

4. Ibid. For Still's background, see Lane, *Dorsey's Philadelphia*, 105, 218.

5. For a discussion of Albert Reach's sporting goods empire, see Stephen A. Hardy, "'Adopted by All the Leading Clubs': Sporting Goods and the Shaping of Leisure, 1800–1900," 79–81.

6. *Sporting Life*, Jan. 5, Feb. 9, 1887; *New York Age*, Apr. 15, 1915. For accounts of the early evolution of the Gorhams, see *New York Age*, June 9, Aug. 11, 1888; and S. White, *History of Colored Baseball*, 3d ed., 14–16. In a retirement announcement, Sims V. Emery, catcher of the Gorhams, reinforced White's oral history regarding the formation of the Gorhams and their brief history.

7. *Sporting Life*, Apr. 13, 1887.

8. Voigt, *American Baseball: Gentleman's Sport*, 215–18. For an account of Spalding gaining hegemony in the sporting goods industry, see Levine, *A. G. Spalding*, 71–96.

9. *Binghamton Daily Leader*, Dec. 7, 1886. On Fowler's ability to locate talent, organizational skills, and reputation as an itinerant, see Powers, "Page Fence Giants."

10. See S. White, *History of Colored Baseball*, 3d ed., 14. On the plight of the Northwestern League, see chapter 3.

11. See *Sporting Life*, Dec. 15, 1886, Jan. 5, 1887.

12. See *Baltimore American*, Mar. 15, 1887; *Baltimore Morning Herald*, Mar. 15, 16, 1887; *Pittsburgh Daily Post*, Mar. 16, 1887; and *Sporting Life*, Mar. 23, 1887.

13. See *Philadelphia Sunday Item*, Apr. 24, 1887; *Pittsburgh Daily Post*, Apr. 21, 22, 1887; *Sporting Life*, May 11, 1887; and *Trenton Times*, Apr. 23, 27, 1887.

14. *Baltimore Morning Herald*, Apr. 27, 1887. On Baltimore's black population, see U.S. Bureau of the Census, *Abstract of the Eleventh Census: 1890*, 34. For newspaper accounts citing Colored League attendance, see *Philadelphia Evening Item*, May 10, 1887; and *Pittsburgh Daily Post*, May 18, 1887.

15. *Chicago Inter Ocean*, Apr. 27, 1887. For a secondary account of the Interstate Commerce Act, see Cashman, *America in the Gilded Age*, 359–60; and Carl N. Degler, *The Age of the Economic Revolution, 1876–1900*, 24–27.

16. *Baltimore Morning Herald*, May 6, 7, 1887; *Pittsburgh Daily Post*, May 7, 1887.

17. See *Baltimore Morning Herald*, May 11, 1887; *Chicago Inter Ocean*, May 11, 1887; *Philadelphia Evening Item*, May 11, 1887; and *Pittsburgh Daily Post*, May 11, 1887.

18. See *New York Daily Tribune*, May 26, 1887; *Philadelphia Evening Item*, May 26, 1887; and *Sporting Life*, June 1, 1887.

19. For a newspaper account covering the Colored League in Canada, see *Toronto World*, May 27, 1887.

20. See *Sporting Life*, Dec. 8, 1886, Jan. 19, 1887.

21. *Trenton Times*, Apr. 12, May 7, 1887. It should be noted that the press reports from both the *Trenton Times* and the *Trenton True American* were identical.

22. *Trenton Times*, May 11, 13, 14, 1887. The increasing showmanship at Cuban Giants games will be discussed in detail later in the chapter.

23. *Trenton True American*, May 16, 1887. No evidence was found in regards to Newark accepting the *True American*'s challenge.

24. Voigt, *American Baseball: Gentleman's Sport*, 110–14; *Trenton Times*, May 26, 1887.

25. Voigt, *American Baseball: Gentleman's Sport*, 115. On Mutrie devising the name "Giants," see June Rankin, *The New York and Brooklyn Base Ball Clubs with Portraits of the Managers and Individual Players* (New York: Richard Fox, 1888), cited in Glenn Moore, "The Great Baseball Tour of 1888–89: A Tale of Image-Making, Intrigue, and Labor Relations in the Gilded Age," 439, 454. Moore quote on 439.

26. See *Trenton True American*, June 21, 1887. For an account of Mike Tiernan's background, see DiClerico and Pavelec, *Jersey Game*, 52, 60.

27. For other games against both major and minor league clubs, see *Trenton Times*, Apr. 16, June 15, July 15, 1887. On June 7, 1887, the *Trenton True American* provided a list of games the Giants had played against major and minor league clubs up to June 1. For an account regarding the press encouraging Trenton fans to patronize the Cuban Giants, see *Trenton True American*, May 14, 1887. For accounts of games played in both New York and Hoboken, see *New York Daily Tribune*, July 28, 30, 1887; and *New York Sun*, June 5, 7, 19, 26, July 30, 31, 1887.

28. *Trenton True American*, July 28, 29 (Cook quote), Aug. 5, 1887. The Gorhams of New York had also declined to join the Eastern League. See *Newark Evening News*, Aug. 4, 1887. For the Eastern League's chaotic season, see *Spalding's Official Base Ball Guide* (1888), 77–78.

29. *Sporting Life*, Oct. 19, 1887. On the Keystones defeating the Cubans, see Dixon and Hannigan, *Negro Baseball Leagues*, 66.

30. S. White, *History of Colored Baseball*, 3d ed., 10.

31. *Trenton True American*, Aug. 15, 1886.

32. *Sporting Life*, Aug. 10, 1887, Nov. 18, 1885.

33. S. White, *History of Colored Baseball*, 3d ed., 35.

34. See Ottley and Weatherby, *Negro in New York*, 145–49; and Seth Scheiner, *Negro Mecca: A History of the Negro in New York City, 1865–1920*, 96–97.

35. See Johnson, *Black Manhattan*, 74–78, 104–8, 118–20. On the notion of the Cuban Giants attempting to "pass" as Cubans, see Alvin Harrow, "Unrecognized Stars." Scholars that advocate this notion include Bruce, *Kansas City Monarchs*, 6; Peterson, *Only the Ball*, 36; and Seymour, *Baseball: The People's Game*, 539. Bud Fowler's plight with the Binghamton Bingos will be discussed in detail later in the chapter.

36. For an account of the dance known as the cakewalk, see Lane, *Dorsey's Philadelphia*, 329. For the Giants dropping to their knees and clapping their hands, see *New York Sun*, Aug. 23, 1886.

37. *Trenton True American*, May 14, 1887; *New York Age*, Aug. 25, 1888.

38. On game one of the Colored Championship series, see S. White, *History of Colored Baseball*, 3d ed., 36. For accounts of games two and three, see *New York Daily Tribune*, Sept. 9, 1887; and *New York Sun*, Sept. 22, 1887.

39. See *Sporting Life*, Dec. 10, 17, 1884, Mar. 18, 25, Apr. 8, Oct. 21, 1885. For secondary accounts of the early evolution of the International League, see DiClerico and Pavelec, *Jersey Game*; Obojski, *Bush League*; Bill O'Neal, *The International League: A Baseball History, 1884–1991*; Neil J.

Sullivan, *The Minors: The Struggles and the Triumph of Baseball's Poor Relation from 1876 to the Present;* and Marshall D. Wright, *The International League: Year-by-Year Statistics, 1884–1953.* For secondary accounts of the plight of Afro-American players in the International League, see Burk, *Never Just a Game;* Chalk, *Pioneers of Black Sport;* Dixon and Hannigan, *Negro Baseball Leagues;* Malloy, "Out at Home"; Peterson, *Only the Ball;* Ribowsky, *Complete History;* Savoie, "Drawing the Line"; R. White, "Baseball's John Fowler"; S. White, *History of Colored Baseball;* and Zang, *Walker's Divided Heart.*

40. See *Sporting Life,* Nov. 4, Dec. 9, 23, 1885, Jan. 6, Mar. 24, 1886.

41. See O'Neal, *International League,* 6–7.

42. See *Sporting Life,* Mar. 14, 1888.

43. See Malloy, "Out at Home," 16.

44. See *Oswego Palladium,* June 1, 1887; *Sporting Life,* June 8, 1887; and *Toronto World,* June 2, 1887.

45. See *Sporting Life,* Apr. 13, May 4, 18, 1887; and Malloy, "Out at Home," 21–23.

46. See ibid.

47. *Toronto World,* May 26, 1887.

48. See Malloy, "Out at Home," 22–23; *Sporting News,* June 11, 1887; and *Toronto World,* May 27, June 6, 1887.

49. *Toronto World,* June 6, 1887.

50. *Binghamton Daily Republican,* June 28, 1887; *Binghamton Daily Leader,* June 28, 1887.

51. *Binghamton Daily Leader,* July 2, 1887.

52. *Binghamton Daily Leader,* Aug. 8, 1887. See also *Binghamton Daily Republican,* Aug. 9, 1887; and R. White, "John Fowler," 12–14.

53. See Savoie, "Drawing the Line," 48.

54. *Sporting Life,* July 20, 1887.

55. See *Sporting Life,* Nov. 23, 30, 1887, Feb. 8, 1888; and *Toronto World,* Nov. 17, 18, 1887.

56. *New York Sun,* Sept. 12, 1887.

57. Voigt, *American Baseball: Gentleman's Sport,* 138; Seymour, *Baseball: The Early Years,* 187. For an account of the "World Championship Series," see Larry G. Bowman, "Christian Von der Ahe, the St. Louis Browns, and the World's Championship Playoffs, 1885–1888."

58. *Sporting Life* account in Voigt, *American Baseball: Gentleman's Sport,* 140.

59. Ibid., 140–41.

60. *Sporting Life,* Sept. 21, 1887. See also *New York Sun,* Sept. 12, 1887.

61. *New York Daily Tribune,* Sept. 13, 1887.

62. Ibid.; *New York Clipper* 35 (Sept. 24, 1887): 442.

63. For an account of the dissension among American Association owners, see Seymour, *Baseball: The Early Years,* 207–20.

64. *New York Clipper* 35 (Sept. 17, 1887): 428.

5. A New Frontier and New Challenges, 1888–1889

1. *Trenton True American,* June 26, 1888.

2. *Amsterdam News* account and S. White quote in S. White, *History of Colored Baseball,* 3d ed., 149–51.

3. *New York Sun,* Apr. 20, 1888.

4. *Trenton Sunday Advertiser,* May 27, 1888; *Trenton True American,* June 14, 15, 1888.

5. *New York Age,* June 19, Aug. 11, 25, 1888.

6. See *New York Age,* Sept. 1, 8, 15, 1888.

7. *New York Age,* Aug. 11, 1888.

8. Cleveland Amory, *The Last Resorts,* 19.

9. See Edward N. Akin, *Flagler: Rockefeller Partner and Florida Robber Baron,* 116–17; John Temple Graves, *The Winter Resorts of Florida, South Georgia, Louisiana, Texas, California, Mexico, and Cuba: Containing a Brief Description of Points of Interest to the Tourist, Invalid, Immigrant, or Sportsman, and How to Reach Them,* 33; and Sidney Walter Martin, *Flagler's Florida,* 90–91.

10. See Akin, *Flagler,* 117; and Joseph W. Howe, *Winter Homes for Invalids: An Account of the Various Localities in Europe and America, Suitable for Consumptives and Other Invalids During the Winter Months, with Special Reference to the Climatic Variations at Each Place, and Their Influence on Disease,* 50–51.

11. See Akin, *Flagler,* 117–18.

12. See Martin, *Flagler's Florida,* 117–18.

13. See Thomas Graham, "Flagler's Magnificent Hotel Ponce de Leon," 5–9.

14. *St. Augustine Weekly News* account in Malloy, "Birth of Cuban Giants," 236–38; *New York Age,* Sept. 15, 1888.

15. *New York Age,* Feb. 23, 1889.

16. For an account of Negro thought and ideology, see August Meier, *Negro Thought in America, 1880–1915.* For a Black Nationalist perspective on racial solidarity and self-help, see Moses, *Golden Age.* For a business perspective on racial solidarity and self-help, see Harris, *Negro as Capitalist;* and Walker, *History of Black Business.* Manning Marable provides a Marxist perspective in *How Capitalism Underdeveloped Black America: Problems in Race, Political Economy, and Society.*

17. Leslie Fishel Jr., "Repercussions of Reconstruction: The Northern Negro, 1870–1883," 328.

18. *Trenton True American,* May 10, 1886. For a detailed account of the history of baseball in Cuba, see Roberto Gonzalez Echevarria, *The Pride of Havana: A History of Cuban Baseball;* Louis A. Perez Jr., "Between Baseball and Bullfighting: The Quest for Nationality in Cuba, 1868–1898"; Perez, *On Becoming Cuban: Identity, Nationality, and Culture;* Rob Ruck, *The Tropic of Baseball: Baseball in the Dominican Republic;* Seymour, *Baseball: The People's Game;* and Eric A. Wagner, "Baseball in Cuba." On Dec. 28, 1916, the *New York Age* printed an article that highlighted the year-round format that the top black baseball club followed.

19. See *New York Clipper* (Apr. 13, 1889): 79; *Philadelphia Inquirer,* Nov. 12, 1888; and *Sporting Life,* Nov. 21, 1888.

20. See *New York Sun,* May 13, 1889; *Philadelphia Inquirer,* May 13, 1889; and *Trenton True American,* May 14, 1889.

21. See *New York Sun,* May 17, 1889; and *Philadelphia Inquirer,* May 16, 1889.

22. For the *Philadelphia Press* report, see *York Gazette,* June 17, 1889. For additional press reports on Lancaster disbanding, see *New York Sun,* June 16, 18, 1889; and *Philadelphia Inquirer,* June 18, 1889. For an account of Reading disbanding, see *New York Clipper* (June 29, 1889): 261; and *Philadelphia Inquirer,* June 19, 1889. For the plight of the Philadelphia Giants, see *Philadelphia Inquirer,* Apr. 6, June 26, 1889. There is evidence of player raiding and player desertion in the MSL.

See *Harrisburg Patriot,* June 28, 1889; *New York Sun,* June 29, July 2, 1889; and *York Gazette,* June 19, 25, July 2, 1889.

23. *Norwalk Hour,* May 4, 1889. For the Gorhams' admission into the MSL, see *New York Sun,* June 27, 1889; and *York Gazette,* June 29, 1889.

24. *New York Sun,* June 9, 1889.

25. *Philadelphia Inquirer,* June 13, 1889.

26. *Harrisburg Patriot,* June 29, July 19, 1889.

27. *York Gazette,* July 18, 1889; *Philadelphia Inquirer,* July 8, 1889.

28. *New York Sun,* July 22, 1889.

29. See *New York Sun,* July 22, Aug. 12, 1889.

30. See *Harrisburg Patriot,* Aug. 9, 1889.

31. *Trenton Sunday Advertiser,* Aug. 25, 1889.

32. For rumors on Davis pulling the Gorhams out of the MSL, see *Harrisburg Patriot,* Aug. 22, 1889; *New York Sun,* Aug. 22, 1889; and *York Gazette,* Aug. 23, 1889. For an account of Easton disbanding and dropping out of the Atlantic Association, see *Philadelphia Inquirer,* June 27, 1889.

33. *York Gazette,* Aug. 23, 1889.

34. *New York Sun,* Sept. 16, 17, 23, 24, Oct. 3, 1889. For the Gorhams' record, see *New York Sun,* Oct. 15, 1889.

35. For Hazleton joining the MSL, see *Philadelphia Inquirer,* July 2, 1889. For Shenandoah joining the MSL, see *New York Clipper* 36 (June 22, 1889): 245. For Shenandoah's and Norwalk's expulsions, see *New York Sun,* Aug. 7, 1889; *Norwalk Hour,* Aug. 10, 1889; and *Philadelphia Inquirer,* Aug. 8, 1889. For the MSL's reorganization, see *Harrisburg Patriot,* Aug. 10, 1889; and *Philadelphia Inquirer,* Aug. 10, 1889. By the end of August, Norristown also disbanded. See *Philadelphia Inquirer,* Aug. 20, 21, 27, 1889. For York's disbandment, see *York Gazette,* Sept. 5, 1889.

36. *York Gazette,* Sept. 14, 16, 1889; *New York Sun,* Sept. 13, 1889.

37. *Harrisburg Patriot,* Sept. 21, 1889; *New York Sun,* Sept. 23, 1889; *Harrisburg Patriot,* Sept. 24, 1889.

38. *New York Sun,* Oct. 9, 1889; *Philadelphia Inquirer,* Oct. 9, 1889.

39. Ibid.

40. *New York Sun,* Oct. 12, 1889.

41. Ibid.

42. See *Harrisburg Patriot,* Aug. 26, Sept. 25, 1889; and *Philadelphia Inquirer,* Sept. 19, 1889.

43. *Trenton Sunday Advertiser,* July 22, 1888; *Harrisburg Patriot,* May 15, 1889; *York Gazette,* Aug. 7, 1889; S. White, *History of Colored Baseball,* 3d ed., 10.

6. The War over Players, 1890–1891

1. *Trenton True American,* Jan. 2, 1890; *New York Sun,* Aug. 26, 1890.

2. *Trenton True American,* Jan. 2, 1890.

3. See *Sporting Life,* Feb. 19, 1890; and *Trenton True American,* Jan. 6, 1890.

4. See *Harrisburg Patriot,* Nov. 22, 1889; and *Sporting Life,* Oct. 30, Nov. 13, 27, 1889.

5. See *Harrisburg Patriot,* Dec. 3, 1889; and *Sporting Life,* Dec. 11, 1889.

6. There is evidence that suggests that the old Harrisburg club was instrumental in the East-

ern Interstate League not receiving protection. On Jan. 2, 1890, Fred Ebel told the *Harrisburg Patriot* that the EIL was not under agreement protection. If part of the old club's strategy was to block the league from obtaining agreement protection, it was successful. The EIL did not receive protection under the terms of the National Agreement. See *Harrisburg Patriot*, Dec. 4, 1889, Jan. 3, 1890.

7. See *Harrisburg Patriot*, Jan. 21, 1890.

8. Delegates from the York club had problems paying the five hundred-dollar guarantee, so William Voltz waived it. See *York Gazette*, Feb. 13, 25, 1890; and *Sporting Life*, Mar. 5, 19, 1890.

9. See *Sporting Life*, Apr. 2, 1890.

10. J. J. Wright, *From Giants to Monarchs*, 252–53; *York Gazette*, Mar. 29, Apr. 4, 8, 22, 1890; S. White, *History of Colored Baseball*, 3d ed., 21.

11. See *York Gazette*, Apr. 23, 29, 1890.

12. *York Gazette*, May 8, 1890.

13. See *Harrisburg Patriot*, May 9, 13, 15, 16, 20, June 9, 1890; *Philadelphia Inquirer*, Apr. 20, May 7, 8, 9, 13, 17, 18, 20, June 8, 1890; and *York Gazette*, Apr. 21, May 20, 1890. According to the *Philadelphia Inquirer* on May 6, 1890, Frank Grant received "vociferous applause" in his debut with the Harrisburg Ponies.

14. *York Gazette*, June 16, 1890. For the division of gate receipts, ticket prices, and the guarantee, see *Harrisburg Patriot*, Dec. 3, 1889; and *Sporting Life*, Dec. 11, 1889.

15. For EIL clubs disbanding, see *Harrisburg Patriot*, July 11, 1890; *Philadelphia Inquirer*, May 12, 27, July 6, 8, 1890; and *York Gazette*, May 27, 1890. For the league's administrative problems, see *Philadelphia Inquirer*, June 9, July 15, 21, 1890.

16. See *Harrisburg Patriot*, June 4, July 16, 19, 21, 1890.

17. See *Cleveland Gazette*, Oct. 11, 1890; *Harrisburg Patriot*, July 21, 1890; and *York Gazette*, July 24, 1890. For efforts on scheduling games in the New York area, see *New York Sun*, July 26, 1890.

18. See *Cleveland Gazette*, May 3, 10, Sept. 6, 1890; *Harrisburg Patriot*, Apr. 19, 1890; and *New York Sun*, Apr. 7, 13, 23, 29, May 6, June 21, 1890.

19. *New York Sun*, Sept. 15, 17, 22, 1890.

20. *Sporting Life*, Jan. 10, 1891.

21. See *Sporting Life*, Apr. 11, 1891.

22. *New York Clipper* 38 (Mar. 7, 1891): 825, (Apr. 11, 1891): 83, (May 2, 1891): 141. See also *New York Sun*, Apr. 3, 21, 1891.

23. See *New York Clipper* 39 (Mar. 21, 1891): 29; *New Haven Journal and Courier*, Mar. 2, 5, 1891; and *Sporting Life*, Mar. 7, 21, Apr. 4, 1891.

24. See *New Haven Journal and Courier*, Mar. 22, 23, 1891.

25. *Sporting Life*, May 2, 1891. See also *New Haven Journal and Courier*, Mar. 20, 23, Apr. 6, 20, 22, 28, 1891; *New York Clipper* 39 (May 9, 1891): 157; and *New York Sun*, Apr. 27, 1891.

26. *New York Sun*, May 2, 1891.

27. *New York Sun*, May 20, 21, 1891.

28. S. White, *History of Colored Baseball*, 3d ed., 20.

29. *New York Sun*, June 17, 1891.

30. See *New Haven Journal and Courier*, June 1, 1891; *New York Clipper* 39 (June 13, 1891): 237; *New York Sun*, June 9, 1891; and *Sporting Life*, June 6, 20, 1891.

31. See *New York Clipper* 39 (June 27, 1891): 271, (July 4, 1891): 287, (July 11, 1891): 303; *New York Sun*, June 26, July 20, 1891; and *Sporting Life*, Aug. 1, 1891.

32. *New York Sun*, Aug. 22, 1891.

33. See *Harrisburg Patriot*, June 1, 12, 13, 1891.

34. S. White, *History of Colored Baseball*, 3d ed., 77.

35. For the Gorhams being classified as a second-class ball club, see *Trenton True American* Jan. 2, 1890.

36. For a detailed account of the players' revolt and second association war, see Burk, *Never Just a Game*; Seymour, *Baseball: The Early Years*; and Voigt, *American Baseball: Gentleman's Sport*.

37. Riess, *City Games*, 214.

7. The Lean Years, 1892–1895

1. S. White, *History of Colored Baseball*, 3d ed., 26.

2. Seymour, *Baseball: The People's Game*, 213–17. See also Gelbar, "'Their Hands Are All Out Playing,'" 22–23. For an account of the rise of baseball in Chicago prior to the 1880s, see Freedman, "Baseball Fad in Chicago." Robert Pruter analyzes the rise of youth baseball in the Windy City in "Youth Baseball in Chicago, 1868–1890: Not Always Sandlot Ball." See any issue of the *Chicago Inter Ocean* from May to late September. Mondays provided the most coverage for amateur leagues.

3. *Chicago Inter Ocean*, May 6, 1887. For an excellent account of the rise of semiprofessional baseball in Chicago, see Ray Schmidt, "The Golden Age of Chicago Baseball."

4. See *Chicago Inter Ocean*, Mar. 23, Apr. 27, 1890; and Schmidt, "Golden Age," 40.

5. *Chicago Inter Ocean*, Apr. 27, 1890. See also Schmidt, "Golden Age," 40.

6. For secondary accounts on Henry Teenan Jones, see Harold F. Gosnell, *Negro Politicians: The Rise of Negro Politics in Chicago*; and Spear, *Black Chicago*. For a secondary account regarding these entrepreneurs' efforts in black baseball, see Lomax, "Black Entrepreneurship"; and *Chicago Inter Ocean*, Sept. 2, 27, 1897.

7. For an example of a side bet, see *Chicago Inter Ocean*, May 26, 1889. On the Unions sponsoring a footrace, see *Chicago Inter Ocean*, June 30, 1889. On the Unions' contest with the Models, see *Chicago Inter Ocean*, Aug. 1, 1889.

8. See *Chicago Inter Ocean*, Aug. 21, 22, 23, 24, 1888. For secondary accounts on the Pinchbacks, see Peterson, *Only the Ball*, 38.

9. See *Chicago Inter Ocean*, Aug. 22, 28, 29, Sept. 1, 1889.

10. *Chicago Inter Ocean*, Apr. 2, 1890.

11. For an account of Cusack as the CABA president, see *Chicago Inter Ocean*, June 24, 1895. For the reorganized CABA's objectives, see *Chicago Inter Ocean*, Aug. 1, 1891.

12. See *Chicago Inter Ocean*, Aug. 12, 19, 30, Sept. 1, 2, 1891.

13. See, for example, *Chicago Inter Ocean*, May 8, 1894.

14. For accounts of the Unions playing Michigan-Wisconsin League clubs, see *Chicago Inter Ocean*, June 25, July 2, 3, 4, 5, 6, 8, 10, 11, Aug. 3, 4, 6, 10, 1892.

15. *Chicago Inter Ocean*, Apr. 29, 1894. On Leland serving as secretary and traveling manager, see *Chicago Inter Ocean*, Sept. 23, 1897. For the 1893 series, see *Chicago Inter Ocean*, Sept. 24, 1893. For the proposed 1894 five-game series, see *Chicago Inter Ocean*, May 13, 20, 27, July 13, 1894.

16. S. White, *History of Colored Base Ball*, 3d ed., 26; *Chicago Inter Ocean*, Sept. 23, 1897. For accounts of Unions players, see Riley, *Biographical Encyclopedia*, 286, 345, 392, 405, 454, 563.

17. *Chicago Inter Ocean*, July 20, 1894. For the series of scheduled games between Ward's Unions and the Edgars, see *Chicago Inter Ocean*, Aug. 4, 1894. For the two defeats suffered by Ward's Unions, see *Chicago Inter Ocean*, Aug. 12, 21, 1894.

18. See *New York Sun*, May 16, July 5, 1892.

19. *New York Sun*, Apr. 7, 1892.

20. See *New York Sun*, June 17, July 25, 1892.

21. For accounts of Cuban players John Patterson, Dan Penno, and James Robinson, see Riley, *Biographical Encyclopedia*, 609–10, 617–18, 673.

22. *New York Sun*, Apr. 20, 1893.

23. See chapter six for the Altoona deal.

24. *New York Sun*, May 8, 15, 16, 1893. For an account of Sunday ball in New York and the way in which baseball magnates circumvented blue laws, see Steven A. Riess, *Touching Base: Professional Baseball and American Culture in the Progressive Era*, 121–50.

25. See *New York Sun*, July 31, 1893. For the Cubans' won-lost record, see *New York Sun*, Aug. 30, 1893.

26. *New York Sun*, Apr. 24, 1894.

27. S. White, *History of Colored Base Ball*, 3d ed., 24. For Grant Johnson's background, see Riley, *Biographical Encyclopedia*, 434–36.

28. *Adrian Daily Times and Expositor*, Sept. 21, 1894. See any issue of the *Detroit Free Press* for the Overman bicycle advertisement in 1895.

29. See Andrew Ritchie, *Major Taylor: The Extraordinary Career of a Champion Bicycle Racer*, 29–31. For an account of the history of the Overman Wheel Company, see Robert A. Smith, *A Social History of the Bicycle: Its Early Life and Times in America*, 17–40. Peter Levine points out that Albert Spalding traveled to Chicopee Falls, Massachusetts, and negotiated an agreement to market bicycles produced by Overman. However, by 1894, court proceedings terminated the Overman connection after both companies sued each other for breach of contract. See Levine, *A. G. Spalding*, 90–91.

30. On brand equity, see George R. Milne and Mark A. McDonald, *Sport Marketing: Managing the Exchange Process*, 44–50. For an account of integrated marketing, see Ralph V. Bellamy, Jr., "The Evolving Television Sports Marketplace."

31. See Dixon and Hannigan, *Negro Baseball Leagues*, 23; and "Gus Parsons Pioneered Public Relations for Industry," Files of Walker, Page Fence Giants file, Oberlin College Archives.

32. *Cincinnati Enquirer*, Apr. 9, 10, 12, 13, 1895. On Parsons distributing souvenirs, see "Parsons Pioneered," Files of Walker, Page Fence Giants file, Oberlin College Archives.

33. Powers, "Page Fence Giants," 16.

34. For the Grand Rapids series, see *Detroit Free Press*, Apr. 14, 15, 17, 1895.

35. *Detroit Free Press*, July 13, 1895; *Adrian Daily Times and Expositor*, Aug. 3, 1895.

36. See *Detroit Free Press*, Oct. 8, 9, 10, 1895.

37. See Riley, *Biographical Encyclopedia*, 294.

38. *Sporting News* Apr. 8, 1899.

39. See *Chicago Inter Ocean*, Apr. 11, 17, May 9, 1895. On Unions-Edgars games, see *Chicago Inter Ocean*, June 30, Aug. 18, 1895.

40. *Chicago Inter Ocean,* May 20, Sept. 2, 16, 1895.

41. *Chicago Inter Ocean,* June 15, Aug. 7, 1895.

42. Seymour, *Baseball: The Early Years,* 32–33.

43. *Chicago Inter Ocean,* Aug. 20, 27, 30, 1895.

44. *Chicago Inter Ocean,* Sept. 25, 1895.

45. Ibid. For an account of the National League relaxing its policy regarding Sunday ball, see Seymour, *Baseball: The Early Years,* 294–95. For an account of Sunday ball in Chicago, see Riess, *Touching Base,* 135–38.

46. From 1890 to 1895, the Chicago White Stockings finished second, second, seventh, ninth, eighth, and fourth, respectively. See Hy Turkin and S. C. Thompson, eds., *The Official Encyclopedia of Baseball.* Richter's comment in Seymour, *Baseball: The Early Years,* 306.

8. The Search for a Colored Champion

1. *New York Sun,* Mar. 15, 1896. On Malloy, see S. White, *History of Colored Baseball,* 3d ed., xxxvi. See also Dixon and Hannigan, *Negro Baseball Leagues;* Peterson, *Only the Ball;* and Ribowsky, *Complete History.*

2. *Pittsburgh Courier,* Mar. 12, 1927.

3. *New York Sun,* Mar. 17, 1896. On Bright releasing players, see *Sporting Life,* Apr. 11, 1896. On Lamar challenging Bright, see *New York Sun,* Mar. 19, 1896.

4. For games against these minor league clubs, see *New York Sun,* Mar. 15, Apr. 3, 15, 16, 17, 28, May 2, 1896.

5. *New York Sun,* Aug. 13, 15, 1896.

6. *Adrian Daily Times and Expositor,* Apr. 17, 1896.

7. *Detroit Free Press,* Apr. 12, 13, 15, 1896.

8. *Detroit Free Press,* June 11, 1896. For the contests between Grand Rapids and the Page Fence Giants at Adrian, Michigan, see *Detroit Free Press,* July 1, Aug. 21, 1896.

9. *Detroit Free Press,* July 30, Sept. 3, 1896.

10. For Miller allegedly throwing a game, see *Adrian Daily Times and Expositor,* July 2, 1896. For complete details of the Miller-Parsons conflict, see "Pending Complication," *Adrian Daily Times and Expositor,* Sept. 11, 1896. For background information on Joseph Miller and Frank Miller, see Riley, *Biographical Encyclopedia,* 550–51.

11. See *New York Sun,* Sept. 18, 21, 22, 23, 24, 25, 28, Oct. 3, 1896; *Detroit Free Press,* Sept. 17, 18, 20, 21, 22, 24, 25, 26, 27, 29, 1896; *Adrian Daily Times and Expositor,* Sept. 16, 17, 18, 21, 24, 25, 28, Oct. 2, 1896; and *Sporting Life,* Oct. 31, 1896.

12. *Chicago Inter Ocean,* June 10, 12, 18, 30, July 18, Aug. 4, 6, 8, Sept. 16, 1896. See also *Detroit Free Press,* June 25, July 3, 1896. On fans traveling to Whiting, Indiana, see *Chicago Inter Ocean,* Sept. 17, 1896.

13. *Chicago Inter Ocean,* Aug. 9, 10, 1896.

14. *Chicago Inter Ocean,* Aug. 15, 16, 17, 31, Sept. 6, 7, 21, 24, 1896.

15. *Chicago Inter Ocean,* Sept. 26, Oct. 1, 1896.

16. *Chicago Inter Ocean,* Sept. 28, 1896.

17. See *Chicago Inter Ocean,* Oct. 4, 5, 17, 26, 1896; and *New York Sun,* Oct. 4, 1896.

18. *Chicago Inter Ocean,* Nov. 2, 1896.

19. *Sporting Life*, Feb. 13, 1897.

20. *Sporting Life*, Feb. 27, 1897.

21. For games booked against the top black clubs of the South and East, see *Chicago Inter Ocean*, May 6, 1897. For Peters organizing a junior semiprofessional club, see *Chicago Inter Ocean*, May 10, 31, 1897.

22. *Chicago Inter Ocean*, June 9, 18, 19, 1897.

23. *Cincinnati Enquirer*, June 26, 1897. See also *DeGraff Journal*, July 2, 1897; *Marion Daily Star*, July 2, 5, 1897; and *New York Sun*, June 14, 17, 20, 21, 22, 23, 25, 26, 27, 28, 29, 30, July 1, 3, 4, 7, 10, 1897.

24. *Chicago Inter Ocean*, July 4, 5, 1897.

25. *Chicago Inter Ocean*, Aug. 28, 29, 30, 1897.

26. On Fred Pfeffer Day and the festivities, see *Chicago Inter Ocean*, Sept. 19, 1897. For Fred Pfeffer's background, see Levine, *A. G. Spalding*; Seymour, *Baseball: The Early Years*; and Voigt, *American Baseball: Gentleman's Sport*. For Pfeffer leaving the field while Fleet Walker warmed up in Louisville, see Zang, *Walker's Divided Heart*. According to Seymour, Buckenberger and Barnie appeared before the league board to get back in good standing if the new league failed to materialize. Buckenberger signed an affidavit stating that he had no further interest in the proposed association while employed by the league. He was hired to manage St. Louis in 1895. The league committee handed Barnie a loyalty oath to sign, which included a promise of future allegiance. Although Barnie refused to sign, the board reluctantly reinstated him for lack of positive evidence. Barnie served as manager of Scranton of the Eastern League for 1895, and by 1897 he was back in the big league as manager of Brooklyn.

27. See *New York Sun*, Sept. 18, Oct. 4, 5, 9, 11, 1897. For R. L. White's challenge, see *New York Sun*, Sept. 21, 1897.

28. *Sporting Life*, Mar. 26, 1898.

29. Ibid.

30. *Sporting Life*, Apr. 16, 1898.

31. See *Chicago Inter Ocean*, Sept. 7, 11, 12, 17, 18, 19, 1898; and *New York Sun*, Sept. 12, 15, 17, 20, 21, 1898.

32. See *New York Sun*, Oct. 3, 10, 1898. For the Cuban X Giants' won-lost record, see *Sporting Life*, Nov. 5, 1898.

33. For the Unions' games against Western League clubs, see *Chicago Inter Ocean*, May 30, July 9, 11, 15, 17, Sept. 25, 26, Oct. 1, 2, 17, 1898.

34. S. White, *History of Colored Baseball*, 3d ed., 28. Throughout the 1898 season, the Columbia Giants were referred to only as the Giants. For accounts placing the Columbia Giants in Chicago in 1898, see *Chicago Inter Ocean*, Apr. 15, 22, June 20, Aug. 8, 14, 1898. Powers, "Page Fence Giants," 17–18.

35. For accounts dealing with Afro-American thought in the nineteenth century, see Meier, *Negro Thought*; and Moses, *Golden Age*.

36. Spear, *Black Chicago*, 65–66. For accounts of Avendorph serving as one of the Giants' financiers, see *Chicago Inter Ocean*, May 18, 1900; and *Chicago Defender*, May 12, 1922.

37. S. White, *History of Colored Baseball*, 3d ed., 28. See also *Chicago Inter Ocean*, Apr. 15, 22, June 20, Aug. 8, 15, 1898.

38. *Chicago Inter Ocean*, Aug. 23, 1898.

39. *Chicago Inter Ocean*, Aug. 24, 1898.

40. *Chicago Inter Ocean*, Sept. 1, 2, 3, 1898.

41. *Chicago Inter Ocean*, Sept. 9, 1898.

9. Rivalries, a New Frontier, and Reorganization

1. *Chicago Inter Ocean*, Apr. 16, 19, 1899.

2. See *Chicago Inter Ocean*, June 10, 11, 12, 16, 18, 21, 26, 1899; and *New York Sun*, June 15, 16, 17, 19, 21, 23, 26, 28, July 1, 1899.

3. *Sporting News*, June 24, 1899. An announcement of the All Cubans' arrival in the United States also placed in the *New York Sun*, July 25, 1899. For an account of the two benefit games played in Havana, see *Sporting News*, July 29, 1899. For Laidlaw assisting Linares, see *Sporting Life*, July 15, 29, 1899.

4. Echevarria, *Pride of Havana*; Brock and Bayne, "Not Just Black," 174.

5. Echevarria, *Pride of Havana*, 113, 123. For an account of Rafael Almeida's and Armando Marsans's brief stints in the major leagues, see Lomax, "'If He Were White.' "

6. See *New York Sun*, July 26, 1899; and Riley, *Biographical Encyclopedia*, 303, 558.

7. *Sporting Life*, Aug. 5, 1899. For Tim Hurst's account, see *Sporting News*, Aug. 5, 1899. See also *New York Sun*, July 29, Aug. 2, 24, Sept. 4, 1899.

8. *New York Sun*, Aug. 12, 14, 18, 21, 1899.

9. For press reports regarding Columbia Giants games, see *Chicago Inter Ocean*, May 12, 13, July 10, 24, 30, Aug. 21, 28, 1899.

10. S. White, *History of Colored Baseball*, 3d ed., 28–31, 38–40. For an account regarding the terms of the series, see *Chicago Inter Ocean*, Sept. 3, 1899. For attendance figure, see *Chicago Inter Ocean*, Sept. 4, 1899. See also *Chicago Inter Ocean*, Sept. 18, 1899.

11. See *Chicago Inter Ocean*, Sept. 11, 1899; and S. White, *History of Colored Baseball*, 3d ed., 38.

12. See *Chicago Inter Ocean*, June 25, 1900.

13. For quote of *Diario de la Marina* and account of opening game, see Echevarria, *Pride of Havana*, 121. Lamar also published an announcement regarding the Cuban X Giants in the *Sporting Life*, Feb. 17, 1900.

14. Mar. 16 report cited in *New York Sun*, Mar. 22, 1900. See also Mar. 28, 30, Apr. 4, 1900.

15. *New York Sun*, Apr. 7, 1900. Evidently, the Cuban X Giants took issue with this series defeat. They soundly beat their next two opponents, the Independents and Cubas, by scores of twelve to six and twenty-six to fourteen. See also Echevarria, *Pride of Havana*, 122; and *New York Sun*, Apr. 8, 10, 1900.

16. See *Chicago Inter Ocean*, Apr. 20, May 4, 1897.

17. *Chicago Inter Ocean*, May 26, 1900.

18. See chapter eight regarding the Keary incident.

19. S. White, *History of Colored Baseball*, 3d ed., 38. On Unions defeating the Cuban X Giants, see *Chicago Inter Ocean*, June 25, July 2, 1900.

20. For an account of Comiskey's part in elevating the Western League to a second major league, see Eugene Murdock, *Ban Johnson: Czar of Baseball*; Riess, *Touching Base*; and Seymour, *Baseball: The Early Years*. See also *Chicago Inter Ocean*, Oct. 1, 8, 1900.

21. *Chicago Inter Ocean*, Apr. 5, May 17, 1901.

22. See chapter six regarding the war over players between the Cuban Giants and the Gorhams. My argument regarding the Chicago Unions is based upon the press reports provided by the *Chicago Inter Ocean*. A clear indication of the Unions no longer maintaining their barnstorming pattern is the absence of Peters's advertisements of Sunday games at Unions' Park during the week. See *Chicago Inter Ocean*, Apr. 8, May 6, June 10, 1901. For accounts of the Chicago Union Giants playing during the 1901 season, see *Chicago Inter Ocean*, Aug. 5, 11, Sept. 7, 15, 16, 1901.

23. *Chicago Inter Ocean*, Sept. 25, Oct. 13, 14, 1901.

24. For an account of the origins of the self-help philosophy in antebellum America, see Hershberg et al., "Free Blacks," 368–91; Moses, *Golden Age*, 83–102; and Oak, *Negro's Adventure*, 9–25.

25. Voigt analyzes the problems scheduling created in the National Association of Professional Base Ball Players in *American Baseball: Gentleman's Sport*, 35–59.

26. See chapter four regarding the Cuban Giants playing Newark of the International League.

27. For the White Stockings' yearly finishes in the 1890s, see Turkin and Thompson, *Official Encyclopedia of Baseball*.

28. Adelman, *Sporting Time*, 148–50.

Bibliography

Manuscript Collections

American Negro Historical Society Papers. Leon Gardiner Collection. American Historical Society of Pennsylvania, Philadelphia.

Philadelphia Social History Project. Center for Philadelphia Studies, University of Pennsylvania, Philadelphia.

Pythians Base Ball Club. Papers. American Historical Society of Pennsylvania, Philadelphia.

Walker, Moses Fleetwood. Files. Oberlin College Archives. Oberlin, Ohio.

Newspapers

Adrian (Mich.) Daily Times and Expositor, 1894–1896.
Anglo-African Weekly, 1860.
Babylon (N.Y.) South Side Signal, 1885.
Baltimore American, 1887.
Baltimore Morning Herald, 1886.
Binghamton (N.Y.) Daily Leader, 1887.
Binghamton (N.Y.) Daily Republican, 1887.
Brooklyn Eagle, 1862.
Chicago Defender, 1922.
Chicago Inter Ocean, 1887–1901.
Chicago Tribune, 1870.
Cincinnati Enquirer, 1895–1897.
Cleveland Gazette, 1890.
Cleveland Leader, 1883.
Columbus Dispatch, 1883.
DeGraff Journal, 1897.
Detroit Free Press, 1895–1896.
Harrisburg (Pa.) Patriot, 1889–1891.
Marion (Ohio) Daily Star, 1897.

Newark Daily Advertiser, 1866–1867.

Newark Evening News, 1887.

New Haven Journal and Courier, 1891.

New York Age, 1887–1916.

New York Clipper, 1866–1891.

New York Daily Tribune, 1867–1887.

New York Metropolitan, 1882.

New York Sun, 1885–1901.

Norwalk (Conn.) Hour, 1889.

Oswego (N.Y.) Palladium, 1887.

People's Advocate, 1879.

Philadelphia Evening Item, 1886.

Philadelphia Inquirer, 1888–1890.

Philadelphia Sunday Dispatch, 1869.

Philadelphia Sunday Item, 1887.

Philadelphia Sunday Mercury, 1867.

Philadelphia Tribune, 1912–1934.

Pittsburgh Courier, 1927.

Pittsburgh Daily Post, 1886.

Sporting Life, 1884–1900.

Sporting News, 1899.

Toledo (Ohio) Blade, 1883.

Toronto World, 1887.

Trenton (N.J.) Sunday Advertiser, 1888.

Trenton (N.J.) Times, 1886–1887.

Trenton (N.J.) True American, 1886–1890.

Wilkes (Pa.) Spirit of the Times, 1867–1869.

York (Pa.) Gazette, 1889–1890.

Other Sources

Adelman, Melvin L. "Baseball, Business, and the Workplace: Gelbar's Thesis Revisited." *Journal of Social History* 23 (1989): 285–304.

———. *Before Its Time: The All-America Football Conference in Professional Football in Post World War II America.* Forthcoming.

———. *A Sporting Time: New York City and the Rise of Modern Athletics, 1820–1870.* Urbana: Univ. of Illinois Press, 1986.

Akin, Edward N. *Flagler: Rockefeller Partner and Florida Robber Baron.* Kent: Kent State Univ. Press, 1988.

Alexander, Charles C. *Our Game: An American Baseball History.* New York: Henry Holt, 1991.

Amory, Cleveland. *The Last Resorts.* New York: Harper, 1952.

Anson, Adrian C. *A Ball Player's Career: Behind the Personal Experiences and Reminiscences.* Chicago: Era Publishing, 1900.

Beadle Dime Base-Ball Player. New York: Beadle, 1868.

Bellamy, Ralph V., Jr. "The Evolving Television Sports Marketplace." In *MediaSport,* ed. Lawrence A. Wenner, 73–87. London: Routledge, 1998.

Berlin, Ira. *Slaves Without Masters: The Free Negro in the Antebellum South.* Rev. ed. New York: New Press, 1992.

Berwanger, Eugene. *The Frontier Against Slavery: Western Anti-Negro Prejudice and the Slavery Extension Controversy.* Urbana: Univ. of Illinois Press, 1967.

Betts, John R. "Mind and Body in Early American Thought." *Journal of American History* 54 (Mar. 1968): 787–805.

Blasingame, John W. *The Slave Community: Plantation Life in the Antebellum South.* New York: Oxford Univ. Press, 1979.

Bledstein, Burton J. *The Culture of Professionalism: The Middle Class and the Development of Higher Education in America.* New York: W. W. Norton, 1976.

Bodnar, John. *Remaking America: Public Memory, Commemoration, and Patriotism in the Twentieth Century.* Princeton: Princeton Univ. Press, 1992.

Bowman, Larry. "Christian Von der Ahe, the St. Louis Browns, and the World's Championship Playoffs, 1885–1888." *Missouri Historical Review* 91 (July 1997): 385–405.

———. "Moses Fleetwood Walker: The First Black Major League Baseball Player." In *Baseball History: An Annual of Original Baseball Research,* ed. Peter Levine, 61–74. Westport, Conn.: Meckler, 1989.

Bridges, Roger D. "Equality Deferred: Civil Rights for Illinois Blacks, 1865–1885." *Journal of the State of Illinois State Historical Society* 74 (summer 1981): 83–108.

Brock, Lisa, and Bijan Bayne. "Not Just Black: African-Americans, Cubans, and Baseball." In *Between Race and Empire: African-Americans and Cubans Before the Cuban Revolution,* ed. Lisa Brock and Digna Castaneda Fuertes, 168–204. Philadelphia: Temple Univ. Press, 1998.

Bruce, Janet. *The Kansas City Monarchs: Champions of Black Baseball.* Lawrence: Univ. Press of Kansas, 1985.

Burk, Robert F. *Never Just a Game: Players, Owners, and American Baseball to 1920.* Chapel Hill: Univ. of North Carolina Press, 1994.

Butler, John Silbey. *Entrepreneurship and Self-Help among Black Americans: A Reconsideration of Race and Economics.* New York: State Univ. of New York Press, 1991.

Cashman, Sean Dennis. *America in the Gilded Age: From the Death of Lincoln to the Rise of Theodore Roosevelt.* 3d ed. New York: New York Univ. Press, 1993.

Casway, Jerold. "Philadelphia's Pythians." *National Pastime* 15 (1995): 120–23.

Chalk, Ocana. *Pioneers of Black Sport.* New York: Dodd, Mead, 1975.

Clark, Dick, and John B. Holway. "Willie Powell: An American Giant." *National Pastime* 2 (winter 1985): 28–34.

Cole, Arthur H. *Business Enterprise in Its Social Setting.* Cambridge: Harvard Univ. Press, 1959.

Cooper, Frederick. "Elevating the Race: The Social Thought of Black Leaders, 1827–50." *American Quarterly* 24 (Dec. 1972): 604–25.

Cross, Whitney R. *The Burned-Over District: The Social and Intellectual History of Enthusiastic Religion in Western New York, 1800–1850.* Ithaca: Cornell Univ. Press, 1950.

Curry, Leonard P. *The Free Black in Urban America, 1800–1850: The Shadow of the Dream.* Chicago: Univ. of Chicago Press, 1981.

Degler, Carl N. *The Age of the Economic Revolution, 1876–1900.* 2d ed. Dallas: Scott, Foresman, 1977.

Delany, Martin Robison. *The Elevation, Emigration, and Destiny of the Colored People of the United States.* New York: Arno Press, 1968.

DiClerico, James M., and Barry J. Pavelec. *The Jersey Game: The History of Modern Baseball from Its Birth to the Big Leagues in the Garden State.* New Brunswick: Rutgers Univ. Press, 1991.

Dixon, Phil, and Patrick J. Hannigan. *The Negro Baseball Leagues, 1867–1955.* Mattituck, N.Y.: Ameron House, 1992.

Douglass, Frederick. "Narrative of the Life of Frederick Douglass, an American Slave." In *Black Voices: An Anthology of Afro-American Literature,* ed. Abraham Chapman, 254. New York: New American Library, 1968.

DuBois, W. E. B. *Dusk of Dawn.* New York: Harcourt, Brace, 1940.

———. *The Philadelphia Negro: A Social Study.* 1899. Reprint, Millwood, N.Y.: Kraus-Thompson, 1973.

Dworkin, James B. *Owners Versus Players: Baseball and Collective Bargaining.* Boston: Auburn House Publishing, 1981.

Echevarria, Roberto Gonzalez. *The Pride of Havana: A History of Cuban Baseball.* New York: Oxford Univ. Press, 1999.

Ernst, Robert. "The Economic Status of New York City Negroes, 1850–1863." *Negro History Bulletin* 12 (Mar. 1949): 131–43.

———. *Immigrant Life in New York City, 1825–1863.* New York: King's Crown Press, 1949.

Figueredo, Jorge S. "November 4, 1920: The Day Torriente Outclassed Ruth." *Baseball Research Journal* (Dec. 1982): 130–31.

Fishel, Leslie, Jr. "Repercussions of Reconstruction: The Northern Negro, 1870–1883." *Civil War History* 14 (1968): 325–45.

Foner, Eric. *Reconstruction: America's Unfinished Revolution, 1863–1877.* New York: Harper and Row, 1988.

Foner, Philip S. "The Battle to End Discrimination vs. Negroes on Philadelphia Streetcars." Part 1, "The Beginning of the Battle." *Pennsylvania History* 40 (July 1973): 261–90. Part 2, "The Victory." *Pennsylvania History* 40 (Oct. 1973): 353–80.

Franklin, John Hope. *From Slavery to Freedom: A History of Negro Americans.* 5th ed. New York: Alfred A. Knopf, 1980.

Frazier, E. Franklin. *Black Bourgeoisie.* Glencoe, Ill.: Free Press, 1957.

Freedman, Stephen. "The Baseball Fad in Chicago, 1865–1870: An Exploration of the Role of Sport in the Nineteenth-Century City." *Journal of Sport History* 5 (summer 1978): 42–64.

Friedman, Lawrence M. *A History of American Law.* Rev. ed. New York: Simon and Schuster, 1985.

Friedman, Milton. *Capitalism and Freedom.* Chicago: Univ. of Chicago Press, 1962.

Gelbar, Steven M. "'Their Hands Are All Out Playing': Business and Amateur Baseball, 1845–1917." *Journal of Sport History* 11 (1984): 5–25.

Genovese, Eugene D. *Roll, Jordan, Roll: The World the Slaves Made.* New York: Pantheon Books, 1974.

Gliozzo, Charles A. "John Jones: A Study of a Black Chicagoan." *Illinois Historical Journal* 80 (autumn 1987): 177–88.

Goldstein, Warren. *Playing for Keeps: A History of Early Baseball.* Ithaca: Cornell Univ. Press, 1989.

Gosnell, Harold F. *Negro Politicians: The Rise of Negro Politics in Chicago.* Chicago: Univ. of Chicago Press, 1935.

Graham, Thomas. "Flagler's Magnificent Hotel Ponce de Leon." *Florida Historical Quarterly* 54 (July 1975): 1–17.

Graves, John Temple. *The Winter Resorts of Florida, South Georgia, Louisiana, Texas, California, Mexico, and Cuba: Containing a Brief Description of Points of Interest to the Tourist, Invalid, Immigrant, or Sportsman, and How to Reach Them.* New York: C. G. Crawford, 1883.

Gregory, Paul M. *The Baseball Player: An Economic Study.* Washington, D.C.: Public Affairs Press, 1956.

Gross, Robert A. "Culture and Cultivation: Agriculture and Society in Thoreau's Concord." *Journal of American History* 69 (1982): 42–61.

Gusfield, Joseph R. *Symbolic Crusade: Status, Politics, and the American Temperance Movement.* Urbana: Univ. of Illinois Press, 1963.

Harding, Vincent. *The Other American Revolution.* Los Angeles: Center for Afro-American Studies, 1980.

———. *There Is a River: The Black Struggle for Freedom in America.* San Diego: Harcourt, Brace, 1981.

Hardy, Stephen. "'Adopted by All the Leading Clubs': Sporting Goods and the Shaping of Leisure, 1800–1900." In *For Fun and Profit: The Transformation of Leisure and Consumption,* ed. Richard Butsch, 71–101. Philadelphia: Temple Univ. Press, 1990.

———. "Entrepreneurs, Organizations, and the Sport Marketplace: The Search for Historians." *Journal of Sport History* 13 (spring 1986): 14–33.

———. *How Boston Played: Sport, Recreation, and Community, 1865–1915*. Boston: Northeastern Univ. Press, 1982.

Harmon, J. H., Jr., Arnett Lindsey, and Carter G. Woodson. *The Negro as Business Man*. College Park, Md.: McGrath Publishing, 1929.

Harris, Abram L. *The Negro as Capitalist: A Study of Banking and Business among American Negroes*. Philadelphia: American Academy of Political and Social Science, 1936.

Harrow, Alvin. "Unrecognized Stars." *Esquire* (Sept. 1938): 75, 119–20.

Hershberg, Theodore, Stephanie W. Greenberg, Alan N. Burstein, William L. Yancy, and Eugene P. Erickson. "Free Blacks in Antebellum Philadelphia: A Study of Ex-Slaves, Freeborn, and Socioeconomic Decline." In *Philadelphia: Work, Space, and Group Experience in the Nineteenth Century*, ed. Theodore Hershberg, 368–91. New York: Oxford Univ. Press, 1981.

———. "A Tale of Three Cities: Blacks, Immigrants, and Opportunity in Philadelphia, 1850–1880, 1930, 1970." In *Philadelphia: Work, Space, and Group Experience in the Nineteenth Century*, ed. Theodore Hershberg, 461–91. New York: Oxford Univ. Press, 1981.

Hershberg, Theodore, and Henry Williams. "Mulattoes and Blacks: Intra-group Color Differences and Social Stratification in Nineteenth-Century Philadelphia." In *Philadelphia: Work, Space, and Group Experience in the Nineteenth Century*, ed. Theodore Hershberg, 392–434. New York: Oxford Univ. Press, 1981.

Hirsch, Leo H. "The Negro and New York, 1783 to 1865." *Journal of Negro History* 16 (1931): 382–473.

Holway, John B. *Blackball Stars: Negro League Pioneers*. New York: Carroll and Graff, 1988.

———. "The Black Bomber Named Beckwith." *Baseball Research Journal* (Apr. 1976): 100–103.

———. *Black Diamonds: Life in the Negro Leagues from the Men Who Lived It*. Westport, Conn.: Meckler, 1989.

———. "The Cannonball." Ninth Annual Historical and Statistical Review of the Society for American Baseball Research. *Baseball Research Journal* (1980): 99–103.

———. "Charlie 'Chino' Smith." Seventh Annual Historical and Statistical Review of the Society for American Baseball Research. *Baseball Research Journal* (1978): 63–67.

———. "Cuba's Black Diamond." *Baseball Research Journal* (Nov. 1981): 139–45.

———. *Josh and Satch: The Life of Josh Gibson and Satchel Paige*. Westport, Conn.: Meckler, 1991.

———. "Louis Santop, the Big Bertha." *Baseball Research Journal* (Aug. 1979): 93–97.

———. "Sam Streeter: Smartest Pitcher in Negro Leagues." *Baseball Research Journal* (1984): 71–72.

———. "Spotswood Poles." Fourth Annual Historical and Statistical Review of the Society for American Baseball Research. *Baseball Research Journal* (1975): 66–68.

———. *Voices from the Great Negro Baseball Leagues.* New York: Dodd, Mead, 1975.

Horton, James. *Free People of Color: Inside the African American Community.* Washington, D.C.: Smithsonian Institution Press, 1993.

Howe, Joseph W. *Winter Homes for Invalids: An Account of the Various Localities in Europe and America, Suitable for Consumptives and Other Invalids During the Winter Months, with Special Reference to the Climatic Variations at Each Place, and Their Influence on Disease.* New York: G. P. Putnam's Sons, 1875.

Hunsinger, Lou. "George W. Stovey." *National Pastime* 14 (1994): 80–82.

Huston, James L. "Economic Change and Political Realignment in Antebellum Pennsylvania." *Pennsylvania Magazine of History and Biography* 113 (1989): 347–95.

Jable, J. Thomas. "Sport in Philadelphia's African-American Community, 1865–1900." In *Ethnicity and Sport in North American History and Culture*, ed. George Eisen and David K. Wiggins, 157–76. Westport, Conn.: Praeger, 1995.

Johnson, James Weldon. *Black Manhattan.* New York: Viking Press, 1930.

Katzman, David. *Before the Ghetto: Black Detroit in the Nineteenth Century.* Urbana: Univ. of Illinois Press, 1973.

Kerney, James, ed. *A History of Trenton, 1679–1929: Two Hundred and Fifty Years of a Notable Town with Links in Four Centuries.* Princeton: Princeton Univ. Press, 1929.

Kinzer, Robert, and Edward Sagarin. "Roots of the Integrationist-Separatist Dilemma." In *Black Business Enterprise: Historical and Contemporary Perspectives*, ed. Ronald W. Bailey, 47–60. New York: Basic Books, 1971.

Kirsch, George B. *The Creation of American Team Sports.* Urbana: Univ. of Illinois Press, 1989.

Kleinknecht, Merl F. "Blacks in 19th Century Organized Baseball." *Baseball Research Journal* (May 1977): 118–27.

Kusmer, Kenneth L. "The Black Urban Experience in American History." In *The State of Afro-American History: Past, Present, and Future*, ed. Darlene Clark Hine, 91–122. Baton Rouge: Louisiana State Univ. Press, 1986.

———. "Urban Black History at the Crossroads." *Journal of Urban History* 13 (Aug. 1987): 460–70.

Landry, Bart. *The New Black Middle Class.* Berkeley and Los Angeles: Univ. of California Press, 1987.

Lanctot, Neil. *Fair Dealing and Clean Playing: The Hilldale Club and the Development of Black Professional Baseball, 1910–1932.* Jefferson, N.C.: McFarland, 1994.

Lane, Roger. *Roots of Violence in Black Philadelphia, 1860–1900.* Cambridge: Harvard Univ. Press, 1986.

———. *William Dorsey's Philadelphia and Ours: On the Past and Future of the Black City in America.* New York: Oxford Univ. Press, 1991.

Lankiewicz, Donald. "Fleet Walker in the Twilight Zone." *Queen City Heritage* 2 (summer 1992): 3–11.

Lebergott, Stanley. *The Americans: An Economic Record.* New York: W. W. Norton, 1984.

Lee, Francis Bazley, ed. *Genealogical and Personal Memoirs of Mercer County, New Jersey.* Vol. 1. Chicago: Lewis Publishing, 1908.

Levine, Peter. *A. G. Spalding and the Rise of Baseball.* New York: Oxford Univ. Press, 1985.

Lindsey, Arnett G. "The Economic Condition of the Negroes of New York prior to 1861." *Journal of Negro History* 6 (Apr. 1921): 190–99.

Litwack, Leon F. *North of Slavery: The Free Negro in the Free States, 1790–1860.* Chicago: Univ. of Chicago Press, 1961.

Lomax, Michael E. "Black Baseball, Black Community, Black Entrepreneurs: The History of the Negro National and Eastern Colored Leagues, 1880–1930." Ph.D. diss., Ohio State Univ., 1996.

———. "Black Baseball's First Rivalry: The Cuban Giants Versus the Gorhams of New York and the Birth of the Colored Championship." *Sport History Review* 28 (Nov. 1997): 134–45.

———. "Black Entrepreneurship in the National Pastime: The Rise of Semiprofessional Baseball in Black Chicago, 1890–1915." *Journal of Sport History* 25 (spring 1998): 43–64.

———. "'If He Were White': Black and Cuban Players in Organized Baseball, 1880–1920." *Journal of African American Men* 3 (winter 1998): 31–44.

Malloy, Jerry. "The Birth of the Cuban Giants: The Origins of Black Professional Baseball." *Nine: Journal of Baseball History and Social Perspectives* 2 (1994): 233–47.

———. "Out at Home: Baseball Draws the Color Line." *National Pastime* 2 (fall 1982): 14–33.

Manley, Effa, and Leon Hardwick. *Negro Baseball . . . Before Integration.* Chicago: Adams Press, 1976.

Marable, Manning. *How Capitalism Underdeveloped Black America: Problems in Race, Political Economy, and Society.* Boston: South End Press, 1983.

Martin, Sidney Walter. *Flagler's Florida.* Athens: Univ. of Georgia Press, 1949.

McKinney, G. B. "Negro Professional Baseball Players in the Upper South and the Gilded Age." *Journal of Sport History* 3 (winter 1976): 273–80.

McKlivigan, John R., and Madeleine McKlivigan. "'He Stands Like Jupiter': The Autobiography of Gerit Smith." *New York History* 65 (1984): 189–200.

Meier, August. *Negro Thought in America, 1880–1915.* Ann Arbor: Univ. of Michigan Press, 1963.

Meier, August, and Elliott Rudwick. *From Plantation to Ghetto.* 3d ed. New York: Hill and Wang, 1976.

Mencke, John G. *Mulattoes and Race Mixture: American Attitudes and Images, 1865–1918.* [Ann Arbor, Mich.]: UMI Research Press, 1979.

Miller, Floyd J. *The Search for a Black Nationality: Black Emigration and Colonization, 1787–1863.* Urbana: Univ. of Illinois Press, 1975.

Milne, George R., and Mark A. McDonald. *Sport Marketing: Managing the Exchange Process.* Boston: Jones and Bartlett, 1999.

Moore, Glenn. "The Great Baseball Tour of 1888–89: A Tale of Image-Making, Intrigue, and Labor Relations in the Gilded Age." *International Journal of the History of Sport* 11 (Dec. 1994): 431–56.

Moses, Wilson Jeremiah. *The Golden Age of Black Nationalism, 1850–1925.* New York: Oxford Univ. Press, 1978.

Murdock, Eugene. *Ban Johnson: Czar of Baseball.* Westport, Conn.: Greenwood Press, 1982.

Neale, Walter C. "The Peculiar Economics of Professional Sports: A Contribution to the Theory of the Firm in Sporting Competition and in Market Competition." *Quarterly Journal of Economics* 1 (1964): 1–14.

Negro Population in the United States, 1790–1915. New York: Arno Press, 1968.

Oak, Vishnu V. *The Negro's Adventure in General Business.* Yellow Springs, Ohio: Antioch Press, 1949.

Obojski, Robert. *Bush League: A History of Minor League Baseball.* New York: Macmillan, 1975.

Ofari, Earl. *The Myth of Black Capitalism.* New York: Monthly Review Press, 1970.

O'Neal, Bill. *The International League: A Baseball History, 1884–1991.* Austin: Eakin Press, 1992.

Osofsky, Gilbert. "The Enduring Ghetto." *Journal of American History* 55 (1968): 243–55.

———. *Harlem: The Making of a Ghetto, Negro New York, 1890–1930.* New York: Harper and Row, 1966.

Ottley, Roi, and William J. Weatherby, eds. *The Negro in New York: An Informal Social History.* New York: Oceana Publications, 1967.

Overmyer, James. *Queen of the Negro Leagues: Effa Manley and the Newark Eagles.* Lanham, Md.: Scarecrow Press, 1998.

Perez, Louis A., Jr. "Between Baseball and Bullfighting: The Quest for Nationality in Cuba, 1868–1898." *Journal of American History* 81 (Sept. 1994): 493–517.

———. *On Becoming Cuban: Identity, Nationality, and Culture.* Chapel Hill: Univ. of North Carolina Press, 1999.

Perlman, David. "Organization of the Free Negro in New York City, 1800–1860." *Journal of Negro History* 56 (1971): 181–97.

Peterson, Robert. *Only the Ball Was White.* Englewood Cliffs, N.J.: Prentice-Hall, 1970.

Pierce, Joseph A. "The Evolution of Negro Business." In *Black Business Enterprise: Historical and Contemporary Perspectives*, ed. Ronald W. Bailey, 25–46. New York: Basic Books, 1971.

Plott, Bill. "The Southern League of Colored Base Ballists." Third Annual Historical and Statistical Review of the Society for American Baseball Research. *Baseball Research Journal* 4 (1974): 91–95.

Porter, Dorothy. "The Organized Educational Activities of Negro Literary Societies, 1828–1846." *Journal of Negro Education* 5 (1936): 555–76.

Powers, Thomas E. "The Page Fence Giants Play Ball." *Chronicle: The Quarterly Magazine of the Historical Society of Michigan* 19 (spring 1983): 14–18.

Pruter, Robert. "Youth Baseball in Chicago, 1868–1890: Not Always Sandlot Ball." *Journal of Sport History* 26 (spring 1999): 1–28.

Rader, Benjamin G. *American Sports: From the Age of Folk Games to the Age of Spectators.* Englewood Cliffs, N.J.: Prentice-Hall, 1983.

———. "The Quest for Subcommunities and the Rise of American Sport." *American Quarterly* 29 (fall 1977): 355–69.

Rammelkamp, Julian. "The Providence Negro Community, 1820–1840." *Rhode Island History* 7 (Jan. 1948): 20–33.

Ransom, Roger L. *Conflict and Compromise: The Political Economy of Slavery, Emancipation, and the American Civil War.* New York: Cambridge Univ. Press, 1989.

Reach's Base Ball Guide. Philadelphia: A. J. Reach, 1884.

Ribowsky, Mark. *A Complete History of the Negro League, 1884 to 1955.* Toronto: Citadel Press, 1995.

Riess, Steven A. *City Games: The Evolution of American Urban Society and the Rise of Sports.* Urbana: Univ. of Illinois Press, 1989.

———. "Sport and the Redefinition of American Middle-Class Masculinity." *International Journal of the History of Sport* 8 (1991): 5–27.

———. *Touching Base: Professional Baseball and American Culture in the Progressive Era.* Rev. ed. Urbana: Univ. of Illinois Press, 1999.

Riley, James A. *The Biographical Encyclopedia of the Negro Baseball Leagues.* New York: Carroll and Graff, 1994.

Ritchie, Andrew. *Major Taylor: The Extraordinary Career of a Champion Bicycle Racer.* Baltimore: Johns Hopkins Univ. Press, 1988.

Rogosin, Donn. *Invisible Men: Life in Baseball's Negro Leagues.* New York: Antheneum, 1985.

Ruck, Rob. *Sandlot Seasons: Sport in Black Pittsburgh.* Urbana: Univ. of Illinois Press, 1987.

———. *The Tropic of Baseball: Baseball in the Dominican Republic.* Westport, Conn.: Meckler, 1991.

Rust, Art. *"Get That Nigger Off the Field": A Sparkling Informal History.* New York: Delacorte Press, 1976.

Savoie, Mark. "Drawing the Line: The Trials of African American Baseball Players in the International League (1886–1889)." *Nine: Journal of Baseball History and Social Perspectives* 1 (1992): 42–60.

Scheiner, Seth. *Negro Mecca: A History of the Negro in New York City, 1865–1920.* New York: New York Univ. Press, 1965.

Schmidt, Ray. "The Golden Age of Chicago Baseball." *Chicago History* 29 (winter 2000): 38–59.

Scully, Gerald W. *The Business of Major League Baseball.* Chicago: Univ. of Chicago Press, 1989.

Sellers, Charles. *The Market Revolution: Jacksonian America, 1815–1846.* New York: Oxford Univ. Press, 1991.

Seymour, Harold. *Baseball: The Early Years.* New York: Oxford Univ. Press, 1960.

———. *Baseball: The Golden Years.* New York: Oxford Univ. Press, 1970.

———. *Baseball: The People's Game.* New York: Oxford Univ. Press, 1990.

Sibley, Joel H., ed. *The Partisan Imperative: The Dynamics of American Politics Before the Civil War.* New York: Oxford Univ. Press, 1985.

Silcox, Harry C. "Efforts to Desegregate Baseball in Philadelphia: The Pythian Baseball Club, 1866–1872." *Baseball Research Journal* (Jan. 1973): 1–10.

———. "Nineteenth Century Philadelphia Black Militant: Octavius V. Catto (1839–1871)." *Pennsylvania History* 44 (1977): 53–76.

———. "Philadelphia Negro Educator: Jacob C. White, Jr., 1837–1902." *Pennsylvania Magazine of History and Biography* 97 (1973): 75–98.

Slaughter, Thomas P. *Bloody Dawn: The Christiana Riot and Racial Violence in the Antebellum North.* New York: Oxford Univ. Press, 1994.

Smith, Robert A. *A Social History of the Bicycle: Its Early Life and Times in America.* New York: American Heritage Press, 1992.

Spalding, Albert G. *America's National Game.* New York: American Sports Publishing, 1911.

———. *America's National Game: Historic Facts Concerning the Beginning Evolution, Development, and Popularity of Base Ball.* Lincoln: Univ. of Nebraska Press, 1992.

Spalding's Official Base Ball Guide. Chicago: A. G. Spalding, 1887.

Spalding's Official Base Ball Guide. Chicago: A. G. Spalding, 1888.

Spear, Allan H. *Black Chicago: The Making of a Negro Ghetto, 1890–1920.* Chicago: Univ. of Chicago Press, 1967.

Sullivan, Neil J. *The Minors: The Struggles and the Triumph of Baseball's Poor Relation from 1876 to the Present.* New York: St. Martin's Press, 1990.

Tholkes, Bob. "Bud Fowler, Black Pioneer and the 1884 Stillwaters." *Baseball Research Journal* 15 (1986): 11–13.

Troppe, Quincy. *20 Years Too Soon.* Los Angeles: Sands Enterprises, 1977.

Trotter, Joe W. "African Americans in the City: The Industrial Era, 1900–1950." *Journal of Urban History* 21 (May 1995): 438–57.

Turkin, Hy, and S. C. Thompson, eds. *The Official Encyclopedia of Baseball.* 10th ed. Garden City, N.Y.: Doubleday, 1979.

Tygiel, Jules. "The Negro Leagues Revisited." In *The SABR Review of Books,* 5–14. Cooperstown, N.Y.: Society for American Baseball Research, 1986.

U.S. Bureau of the Census. *Abstract of the Eleventh Census, 1890.* Washington, D.C.: Government Printing Office, 1894.

U.S. Congress. House. *Organized Baseball: Report of the Subcommittee on Study of Monopoly Power of the Committee on the Judiciary.* 82d Cong., 2d sess., 1952. H. Rept. 2002.

Voigt, David Q. *American Baseball: From Gentleman's Sport to the Commissioner System.* Norman: Univ. of Oklahoma Press, 1966.

———. *American Baseball: From Postwar Expansion to the Electronic Age.* University Park: Pennsylvania State Univ. Press, 1983.

———. *American Baseball: From the Commissioner to Continental Expansion.* University Park: Pennsylvania State Univ. Press, 1983.

Wagner, Eric A. "Baseball in Cuba." *Journal of Popular Culture* 18 (1984): 113–20.

Walker, Juliet E. K. *The History of Black Business in America: Capitalism, Race, Entrepreneurship.* New York: Macmillan Library Reference USA, 1998.

———. "Racism, Slavery, and Free Enterprise: Black Entrepreneurship in the United States Before the Civil War." *Business History Review* 60 (autumn 1986): 343–82.

Warner, Robert. *New Haven Negroes.* New Haven: Yale Univ. Press, 1940.

Washington, Booker T. *The Negro in Business.* 1907. Reprint, Chicago: Afro-American Press, 1969.

Webber, Thomas L. *Deep Like the Rivers: Education in the Slave Quarter Community, 1831–1865.* New York: W. W. Norton, 1978.

Weiss, William J. "The First Negro in 20th Century O. B." *Baseball Research Journal* (Aug. 1979): 31–35.

White, Richard. "Baseball's John Fowler: The 1887 Season in Binghamton, New York." *Afro-Americans in New York Life and History* 7 (Jan. 1992): 7–17.

White, Sol. *History of Colored Baseball.* Philadelphia: H. Walter Schlicther, 1907.

———. *History of Colored Baseball.* 2d ed. Philadelphia: H. Walter Schlicther, 1984.

———. *History of Colored Baseball.* 3d ed. Lincoln: Univ. of Nebraska Press, 1995.

Wiggins, David K. "Leisure Time on the Southern Plantation: The Slaves' Respite from Constant Toil, 1810–1860." In *Sport in America: New Historical Perspectives,* ed. Donald Spivey, 25–50. Westport, Conn.: Greenwood Press, 1985.

———. "The Play of Slave Children in the Plantation Communities of the Old South, 1820–1860." *Journal of Sport History* 7 (1980): 21–39.

———. "Sport and Popular Pastimes: Shadows of the Slave Quarter." *Canadian Journal of History of Sport* 11 (1980): 61–88.

Wiggins, William. *O Freedom! Afro-American Emancipation Celebration.* Knoxville: Univ. of Tennessee Press, 1987.

Woodson, Carter G. "The Negroes of Cincinnati prior to the Civil War." *Journal of Negro History* 1 (Jan. 1916): 1–22.

Woodward, C. Vann. *The Strange Career of Jim Crow.* 3d rev. ed. New York: Oxford Univ. Press, 1974.

Wright, Jerry Jaye. "From Giants to Monarchs: The 1890 Season of the Colored Monarchs of York, Pennsylvania." *Nine: Journal of Baseball History and Social Perspectives* 3 (1994): 248–59.

Wright, Marshall D. *The International League: Year-by-Year Statistics, 1884–1953.* Jefferson, N.C.: McFarland, 1998.

Zang, David. *Fleet Walker's Divided Heart: The Life of Baseball's First Black Major Leaguer.* Lincoln: Univ. of Nebraska Press, 1995.

Index

Italic page number denotes illustration.